History and development

1

The evolution of social networks in China can roughly be divided into three stages. Network models in the initial stage mainly consisted of instant messaging software such as ICQ, QQ and network communities such as online forums including ChinaRen Alumni, amongst which ChinaRen can be considered as one of the earliest, if not the first, digital social network system in China. Despite the success of these early platforms, the birth of Facebook in 2004 in the western world represented a major influence on how social networking platforms would evolve in China. Even with its growing popularity and permeation across many regions over the world, the Chinese Government banned the use of Facebook in China due to its comparatively ungoverned content, especially from the auspices of the Chinese authorities. This paved the way for Chinese developers to produce a comparable platform that would serve to fill the gap that Facebook had created.

Numerous pioneering platforms were created over this burgeoning period, all of which achieved notable levels of success. These included RenRen Network, Kaixin Network and Sina Blogs. Although each platform was initially developed for different purposes, the competition amongst them proved to be fierce as the respective companies battled to gain dominance in this growing sector of the online space. Chinese users were eventually faced with too much choice when it came to online social networks, and led to repetitive connections between users across the various platforms. Despite the wide variety of platforms, each lacked a key distinctiveness, and there was no clear division within the market occupancy in terms of a leading platform, much less any sort of monopoly, which the companies may have originally hoped. This chapter will attempt to explain the reasons for the subsequent demise of several key players during this developmental period, including Kaixin Network and MSN, and how others evolved in order to cater for the growing needs of users. Under the influence of mobile Internet and smartphone development, Weibo was spawned as a mini version of the original Sina Blog that represents a Chinese equivalent of Twitter.

The third phase of the Chinese social network evolution can be defined from the period when WeChat was created in 2011. Despite the long-lasting success of QQ, Tencent, the current dominant company in the Chinese social network market, launched its sibling product, WeChat. WeChat largely resembles QQ in terms of functionality and achieved miraculous success within a very short period of time. In the current phase of development, the Chinese market has developed clearer signs of division between three major social networks: WeChat—used mainly for close friends and private contacts; QQ—mainly for public correspondence and Weibo—popular

Social Networks in China. https://doi.org/10.1016/B978-0-08-101934-4.00001-7

for celebrity and news distribution. Each platform can be seen to combine certain characteristics from Facebook and Twitter. This chapter will explain how various Chinese social networks have survived or have been eliminated through competition.

1.1 Pre-2004: Exploration in the early stage

The early models of social networks prior to 2004 were comprised of essentially two types of digital social interactions: instant messaging (IM) and network community. The first was mainly dominated by QQ in China, whilst the latter existed in the form of bulletin board systems (BBS), online forums and chat rooms, which were hosted by a variety of Chinese Internet companies. The following sections will provide brief overviews of these two social network types in the initial stage.

1.1.1 Instant messengers

The main IM in China during the pre-2004 period was QQ. It competed with two international rivals at the time: ICQ and MSN Messenger, but QQ retained a dominant advantage in the Chinese market for various reasons as will be discussed next.

1.1.1.1 ICQ

ICQ is one of the earliest examples of IM software in Internet history, which was first developed and popularised by the Israeli company Mirabilis in 1996. The name ICQ was assigned as a mnemonic to denote the phrase *I seek you*. ICQ was released on 15 November 1996, and subsequently revolutionised the way people conversed online. Just 6 months after its release, it claimed the title of the World's largest online communication network, whilst it recorded its millionth user just another month later [1]. Due to its in-built protection from unwanted adverts and viruses, ICQ had the advantage of being a safe and easy piece of software to use, even for relatively new and inexperienced users. The essential identifier required for each user, the ICQ number, was free to obtain, whilst the registration process was designed to be trouble-free, and thus all of these factors contributed towards quickly establishing ICQ as a globally successful IM software. Even cross Asia, where the Internet was comparatively less well developed than in other more developed parts of the world, ICQ had monopolised the Chinese market by 1998 with an 80% penetration ratio [2].

Despite its notable success, ICQ possessed two main implications that led to its eventual downfall: the first being its relative simplicity, which made it comparatively easy for competitors to build similar applications; and second ICQ did not allocate any significant attention to its localisation for countries across the world. Indeed, the company only released an English version during the initial phase of its market development, placing little emphasis on offering specific features that may appeal to different cultures and users in other countries. This latter strategic oversight undoubtedly led to ICQ's eventual declination in later years.

The achievements and the type of communication offered by ICQ quickly inspired other software developers to create similar and competing applications, each with varying levels of success. Take the Chinese market for example. The release of QQ (as it is now known) in 1999 is considered as an imitation product of ICQ [2]. QQ was initially named as OICQ (meaning *Oh I seek you!*) and was largely similar to ICQ across a range of key characteristics such as software design, content and user interface. Despite its clear similarity to ICQ, IOCQ appealed to Chinese users and quickly overtook ICQ as the most popular IM in the country. This was largely a result of ICQ's continued neglect of the requirements from users in different countries, where in the case of the Chinese market, by failing to release a localisation plugin that would allow Chinese users to overcome the difficulty of navigating an English-language interface. By the time ICQ had refocused greater attention to resolving such issues, it was a case of too little, too late as Chinese companies had already cemented their position in the country with respect to IM applications.

1.1.1.2 QQ: Initial development

As mentioned in the previous section, the creation of OICQ was initially inspired by ICQ in 1999. One year later, its name OICQ was shortened and altered to its present form—QQ, whilst its penguin logo has remained the same since 1999. The penguin has also contributed to the appeal of QQ, serving as a visual mascot and potentially delightful to users of any age and gender. The letter *Q* also holds the connotation of being phonetically similar to the word *cute*, and bearing some resemblance to the shape of a penguin, and hence the icon has been considered as an effective and memorable symbol of QQ for its commercial value [3].

In 1998, prior to the existence of QQ, the rapid achievement and success of ICQ led to its acquisition from AOL, thus paving the way for increased financial resources for its development, which helped to consolidate ICQ's status in the Internet communication field. By contrast, QQ was created in 1999 by Tencent (腾讯) company, which comprised of just two employees based in a run-down rental apartment in Shenzhen [2]. The initial design and appearance of QQ's user interface of QQ was simplistic, mirroring several features of ICQ, but as it operates in the Chinese language it was able to immediately appeal to Chinese users in ways ICQ could not. Despite recording a relatively small number of 60,000 users in its year of release, QQ registered 5 million users just 1 year later, with 100,000 simultaneous users recorded at 20:43 on 27 May 2000 [4].

QQ's Chinese user interface may be considered as a crucial element that brought the attention of users, but it is not necessarily sufficient to explain the platform's continued success. Many rivals to QQ emerged in the Chinese market, including PICQ, TICQ, GICQ and Sina Pager, all of which generally followed the trend set by ICQ. However, QQ consistently outperformed its competitors through a series of innovations. Compared to the traditional ICQ infrastructure, QQ offered several notable features since 2000 that drastically increased its popularity and user experience:

(1) ICQ stored user information on the user's terminal computer, which meant all data such as friends and contacts were lost if they logged onto a different computer. By contrast, QQ

stored user profiles on cloud servers, thus allowing users to retain essential information regardless of where they logged-in.

(2) ICQ only permitted users to chat when they were online, whereas QQ was the first IM platform to provide an offline message-pushing service and an invisible-status login. QQ could also choose target users for chats and personalise their avatars with images.

(3) ICQ generated profit via ads banner and customisation for internal use within companies, whilst QQ has been persistently providing consumers free services and seeking unique business opportunities from the tremendous user base. Report [5] shows that only less than 10% of Tencent's profit comes from advertising. Tencent's business model and revenue generation will be discussed in Section 3.4.6.

The success of QQ was therefore far from a coincidence, but the result of consistent innovative practise. Between 1999 and 2004, QQ released a total of 12 successive versions [6], each of which introduced new features or functions towards enhancing user experience and market adaptation. Even though ICQ also released updates (only five versions over 8 years between 1996 and 2004), its core functionalities did not evolve significantly besides changes to the user interface and some elements of usability. Hence, despite the notable similarity between ICQ and OICQ in 1999, the differences between the two platforms became more clearly evident by 2004.

By comparing the user interfaces of the two platforms that were implemented by 2004[1], ICQ remained limited in terms of its functions, which in this case consisted of a chat window, enhanced texting environment (such as formatting and image options), and the ability to link to mobile phones, emails, etc. On the other hand, QQ had, by that same time, introduced a number of cutting-edge functions including video chat, file transfer, invitation of participants, chat mode customisation, the ability to send ring tones and QQ greetings cards and user-to-user gaming. Beyond those essential for the chat process such as inviting and removing users, personal details, preferences, security and help, ICQ did not offer much in the way of additional options. In comparison, QQ offered a broad range of features that extended on the standard set of options. This included a *QQ Show* feature that allowed users to change the theme of the main screen and interface, as well as to customise avatars by altering clothing, appearance and dress. This latter feature enabled users to share their personalised avatars with each other via the chat window, and served to bolster the type of interaction that was impossible via a traditionally text-based platform. QQ also gave users the option to configure a whole host of parameters including network optimisation, software updates, login status (visible, invisible, customised status, etc.) and settings for file transfer. One other key characteristic is that, as consistent with the company's revenue model of the time, ICQ's chat window of 2004 can already be seen to feature a significant portion of commercial adverts (in this case, dating), which represented a major aspect of annoyance quantity of users [7]. Tencent, however, operated on a different financial model and were thus able to keep QQ free of advertisements—this aspect will be discussed in more detail in Section 3.4.6.

[1] ICQ did not release a new version in 2004, and consequently users were still using ICQ Pro 2003b edition for that year.

Table 1.1 **Major events of QQ pre-2004**

1999	60,000 users. IM service open, linking mobile pagers, GSM texts and IP phone
2000	5 million users. Mobile QQ was released
2001	50 million users. Tencent website ranked amongst top-four Internet portals in China
2002	0.1 billion users. Advocated regulation in the sector and signed *Chinese Internet Sector Self-Discipline Convention* [8]. QQ ranked as the *Key Software Enterprise* in Shenzhen city
2003	0.2 billion users. Launched QQ games that dominated Internet entertainment in China. Once again, QQ recognised as the *Key Software Enterprise* in Shenzhen city
2004	0.3 billion users. QQ received three national awards in partnership of China Mobile. QQ Game reached 620,000 simultaneous online users, becoming the top casual game portal in China. Tencent was positioned as the 29th taxpayer of all private business in China, along with being one of the most valuable Internet companies in China. Tencent's website portal was ranked as number 1 in the Chinese commercial survey, surpassing the three other major Chinese Internet portals at the time: Sina, Sohu and NetEase (163).

Consequently, it was not surprising that QQ overtook ICQ as the dominant IM platform in China. QQ experienced exponential growth throughout the initial period of Chinese Internet history, with the number of users reaching 0.3 billion by 2004. The major events in QQ's developmental history prior to 2004 are outlined in Table 1.1. Even when faced with another strong rival in the form of MSN Messenger (discussed in the next section) during this period, QQ was able to preserve its market dominance in the Chinese market.

1.1.1.3 MSN Messenger

The first version of MSN Messenger Service was released on 22 July 1999. Given that its developer—Microsoft—possessed a unique monopoly status over the operating systems market around the globe, MSN Messenger unarguably had a distinctive advantage from the moment of its inception. Microsoft released and promoted the MSN butterfly logo in 2000 in order to highlight the platform's unique vision and desired impact on the Internet. Comprising of a user-friendly design as well as being built on MSN's substantial user base, MSN Messenger attracted 75 million users by 2002 which by 3 December 2003, expanded to 0.11 billion registered and active accounts that logged into MSN Messenger every month [9]. In addition to its core provision of an IM service, MSN Messenger was complimented by an established set of sibling products including MSN Hotmail, MSN web portal and MSN Explorer.

However, despite its success around the world and its potential advantages in nature, MSN Messenger did not establish a notable foothold in the Chinese market. In January 2000, MSN published various editions of Messenger across six key regions in Asia: South Korea, Hong Kong, Taiwan, Singapore, Malaysia and India [10], with China

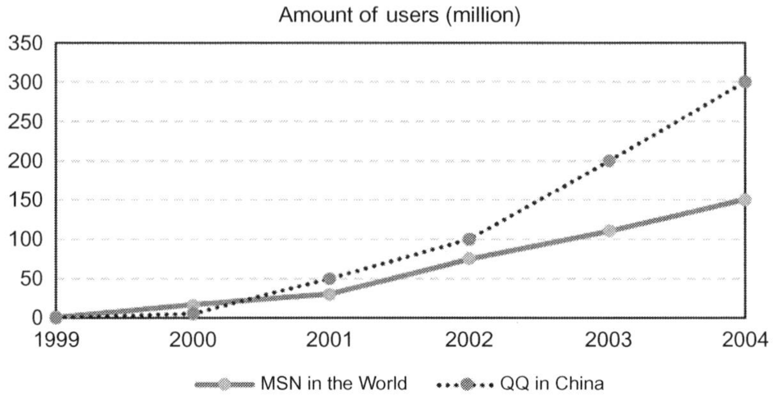

Fig. 1.1 MSN in the World versus QQ in China Prior to 2004.

being omitted from the list. Indeed, it took another 5 years, in 11 May 2005, for Microsoft to launch the MSN platform in China [11]. As shown in Fig. 1.1, QQ surpassed MSN in terms of global user base by 2001, and hence by the time MSN officially entered the Chinese market in 2005, Messenger faced a formidable battle against a highly established platform in the form of QQ. Indeed, certain experts considered such a late entry to the Chinese market by MSN to be a telling strategic mistake [12].

In spite of this, MSN still held certain unique advantages against its rivals. Even before its official launch in China, and thus in absence of any commercial promotion or publicity in China, MSN Messenger still managed to attract around 10–20 million Chinese users, with 1–2 million of those being simultaneously active online by the end of 2004 [12]. The reason for this was that the majority Chinese user base for MSN Messenger consisted of those with access to relatively high-end communication terminals (such as white-collar workers), as well as overseas Chinese users (such as those studying abroad). There has been a surge of young Chinese students studying abroad since 2000 [13], and was therefore considered as the *premium* Chinese user community [12]. These users were much less affected by issues of using software in the English language (an issue that had proved significant for ICQ in China), and were therefore able to utilise platforms (such as MSN Messenger) beyond those intended largely for the Chinese market.

Fig. 1.2 shows the screenshots of MSN Messenger's user interface in 2004. In the year before, MSN Messenger 6.0 was released as a major update of the platform, with improvements to its previously simple text-based interface to include customisable elements such as emoticons, avatars and backgrounds. Version 6.2 was released on 22 April 2004, which served as the last version of the MSN Messenger 6 series. The most notable changes to this final update were a dedicated group for mobile contacts, a network connection troubleshooter and the Launch Site feature (which was later renamed to *Fun & Games*). The functionalities of Messenger in 2004 were quite comparable with QQ at the time. Both had introduced innovative utilities such as file transfer, video conference, group chat and peer-to-peer gaming, as well as customisable

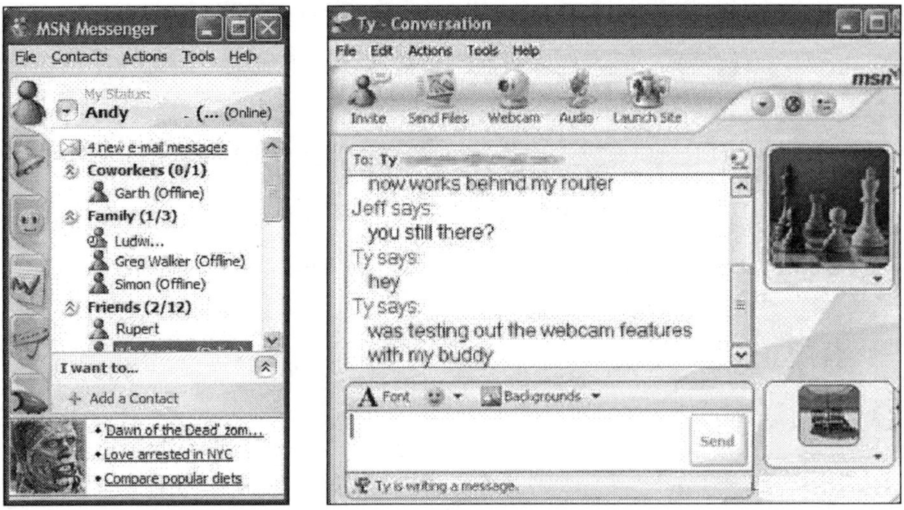

(A) (B)

Fig. 1.2 MSN Messenger in 2004 (Version 6.2). (A) Menu interface. (B) Chat window.

features allowing for a more personal experience—for instance, QQ had *QQ Show* whilst Messenger had customised emoticons; and both offered options for changeable themes. However, one key difference between the two platforms and, as with the case of ICQ outlined earlier, is that of the presence or otherwise of commercial adverts. As can be seen in Fig. 1.2A, a sizeable proportion of Messenger's main screen contains a banner advert, whereas QQ retained its advert-free appearance. This particular nuance and Tencent's strategy for revenue generation will be discussed in Section 3.4.6.

1.1.2 Initial Chinese network community

The early years of Internet development in China comprised of a wide range of network communities hosted by various sources providing services such as BBS (also known as online forums) and chatrooms. The most prominent examples are those hosted by the leading web portals in China including NetEase BBS (网易论坛),[2] Sina BBS (新浪论坛),[3] Sohu Club (搜狐社区),[4] as well as Tianya BBS (天涯社区),[5] Smth BBS (水木清华)[6] and ChinaRen Alumni (ChinaRen 校友录).[7] ChinaRen Alumni will be discussed separately in the next section due to its significance.

[2] URL used to be bbs.163.com.
[3] people.sina.com.cn.
[4] club.sohu.com.
[5] bbs.tianya.cn.
[6] URL used to be smth.edu.cn.
[7] www.chinaren.com.

Table 1.2 **Well-known BBS and forums prior to 2004**

	From	Until	Achievements and comments
NetEase BBS	1997	2012	Its shutdown is commonly considered in China as an end of an era [14]
Sina BBS	1998	Present	It has the longest history amongst all Sina products. On its official page, it claims to be the largest Chinese online community, and the most well-known comprehensive BBS on the Internet
Sohu Club	1999	Present	It claims to be the number 1 Chinese online forum on its official website
Tianya BBS	1999	Present	Rated as the most humanitarian community in China in 1999 and the only Chinese website in the global top-500 websites in 2004 [15]. Considered by many media as the network community with the highest impact in the globe [16]
Smth BBS	1995	2012	The official BBS from Tsinghua University (a top university in China). Used to be one of the most popular BBS in China, representing views and cultures from highly educated user groups

Table 1.2 gives a list of the most well-known BBS and online forums during the developmental period of Internet development in China, of which a large portion are hosted by domestic Chinese web portals (details of web portals are described in Box 1.1). Chinese web portals had from the outset presented their own versions of network communities beyond those offered by IM platforms, providing contents spanning a comprehensive range of topics including culture, life, society, news, sports, technology, education and entertainment. In addition to BBS services, these Internet portals also provided their own chatrooms to allow for more direct interactions between users. Both BBS and online chatrooms are the early shapes of online communities in China. However, the prominence of a number of previously dominant chatrooms could not be sustained along with the Internet evolution, with one example being the NetEase chatroom that was closed in 2008.

Box 1.1 Web portals

Web portal is also known as portal website, portal site or web gateway, which is defined as a comprehensive Internet resource system that provides information services—the initial purpose of web portals was to provide search engine facilities and indexing services, with one example being that of Yahoo that, during the early phases of the Internet, served as an important gateway to information for less experienced users. With the evolution of the Internet, the nature and content of web portals in China has advanced accordingly, progressing from indexing services to news and media services. Modern day web portals in China are considered as a form of *new media* that impacts on traditional media in terms of

Box 1.1 Web portals—cont'd

writing, editing, publishing, commenting and dissemination [17]. Prior to 2001, there were three major web portals in China [18]: Sina (新浪), Sohu (搜狐) and NetEase (网易, also known as 163). These were joined by Tencent and Baidu (百度) from 2001, which eventually formed as the five leading Internet web portals in China [19].

A remarkable feature of these BBS in China is the introduction of opinion leaders (意见领袖), who are core users of a forum and serve as senior network citizens. Normally each user can obtain an ID upon registration in any BBS. Opinion leaders are differentiated from other users by regularly publishing distinctive opinions and tend to exhibit greater levels of analysis in their comments, who can gradually lead the discussions or reviews of certain fields. They are often held in high regard by Chinese Internet users due to the quality and originality of articles they publish. Well-known examples of opinion leaders include Ning Cai Shen (宁财神) and Mu Rong Xue Cun (慕容雪村). Many opinion leaders hold celebrity status in China, whilst some users endeavour to become *celebrities* via BBS. The nature of BBS is that it provides a natural stage for everyone to give his/her voice, therefore some users deliberately exposed themselves in order to obtain a wide level of recognition. One example is Sister Furong (芙蓉姐姐), who leapt from being completely unknown to unexpected national fame via self-hype [known as *Chao Zuo* (炒作) in Chinese] in a matter of days [20]. Overall, opinion leaders had effectively helped to secure and maintain the quantity of customers for the various BBS services, which paved a foundation for the strategy of *celebrity effect* (名人效应) that was later adopted by Sina Blogs and Sina Weibo (will be discussed in Sections 1.2.1 and 4.2.4).

In the above examples, even though the impact of users such as opinion leaders may be generally greater than that of regular users, the latter cannot be neglected as their collective behaviour can also influence the nature of social network communications. One such example is that of the level of user contribution in the BBS platforms. In early versions of BBS, the only notable interaction permitted for users was that of replying to each other's posts, which gave rise to one common behaviour where some users would only view the posts of other users whilst posting no comments of their own. This type of nonresponse was labelled in China as *diving* (潜水), whereby divers would acquire the shared comments, knowledge and information offered by those who posted yet offered no input of their own. The prevalence of this type of behaviour contributed towards the suppression of the contribution from active users, and thus represented a major limiting factor for such forms of online social communities.

There was indeed little or nothing even a proactive publisher could do to change such types of behaviour in a network community. Some BBS offered users a potential solution for this problem via publishing locked posts, which meant that users must first reply to a post before viewing its entire contents. However, this approach had two major implications: first, it would likely reduce the number of potential readers to a significant extent, and second, readers could simply post a worthless reply in order to unlock the post. One other notable technique adopted by many BBS users to encourage participation was that of using intriguing imagery attached to end of a post to stimulate responses.

1.1.3 ChinaRen Alumni: China's earliest social network model

ChinaRen Alumni[8] was created in 1999, as China's first network community that matched the definition of social network model (the earliest recognised social network in the world being SixDegrees.com, launched in 1997). Article [21] defines a social network to be a constitution of three key elements: (1) a public or semipublic profile within a bounded system, (2) a list of other users with whom they share a connection and (3) the ability to view and traverse their list of connections and those made by others within the system, where the nature and nomenclature of such connections may vary from site to site. ChinaRen Alumni possessed all the three elements upon its creation.

As shown in Fig. 1.3, ChinaRen comprised all the essential functionalities required to form a social network. Users can set up a basic profile of themselves, upload pictures and create photo albums, as well as publish posts on a community page. They can locate friends by searching lists of schools or class names towards establishing online relationships. Friends can also be introduced or referred to an existing class so that other friends in the class can associate themselves with the new friend should they wish to. Friends can view each other's profile and status, as well as interact via comments

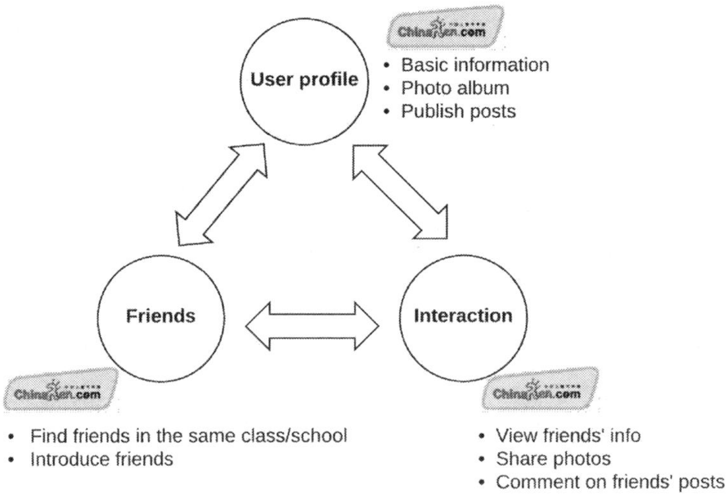

Fig. 1.3 ChinaRen fitting the social network model.

[8]http://www.chinaren.com/.

or photo sharing. Most importantly, ChinaRen puts equal emphasis on the three social network elements: users, friends and interactions.

Being the earliest social network model in China and despite its close adherence to the general definition of the social network model, there is one exception that ChinaRen does not meet in terms of its core function. In highlighting the characteristics of social networks, Ellison [21] points out that the *networking* element of such networks should emphasise relationship initiation, particularly between strangers. Although ChinaRen enables the establishment of online friendships, these entail an inherently preformed foundation in the form of alumni; that is, users are brought together due to their previous acquaintance as classmates in school, and are therefore not strangers. Despite this minor mismatch with the above definition, ChinaRen was still at the cutting-edge of developments during the initial period of social networks in China.

ChinaRen quickly amassed popularity and success within its first year of release. In 2000, having registered three million users, it was acquired by Chinese Internet giant, Sohu. Given that Sohu's own user base at the time (four million) was only slightly higher than that of ChinaRen's, the purchase of ChinaRen was considered as a good investment which subsequently strengthened Sohu's company profile [22].

Despite its remarkable success during the first couple of years of its inception, ChinaRen failed to secure a lasting foothold in the Chinese market due to its inherent nature of being designed for alumni. The system was therefore constrained to groups who received a higher education. Statistics showed 45% of ChinaRen users had a Bachelor degree, whilst 65% of all users were under the age of 30 [23]. To counteract this and to increase its user base, ChinaRen expanded its service to include alumni of primary and secondary schools, but this did little to increase its appeal and relevance to older and more mature age groups. Failure to secure a broad range of users had left opportunities for new forms of social networks to be developed.

1.2 2004–11: The blossoming of social networks

The widespread popularity of Facebook since 2004 proceeded to drastically change the social network landscape in China, not least increasing the awareness of and demand for online social interactions. However, Facebook was soon banned by the Chinese Government, which paved the way for the creation and growth of domestic versions of the burgeoning platform. Between 2004 and 2011, examples such as Kaixin Network (开心网),[9] RenRen Network (人人网),[10] Sina Blog,[11] MSN Space and Qzone, as listed in Table 1.3, all proved successful in offering Chinese users the ability to share content and interact via an online social space, mirroring aspects provided by Facebook and thus serving to fill the void created by its ban.

[9] www.kaixin001.com.
[10] www.renren.com.
[11] blog.sina.com.cn.

Table 1.3 **Well-known social networks in China between 2004 and 2011**

	From	Until	Current status
MSN Space	2004	2010	Closed
Qzone	2005	Present	The QQ product bundle is one of the three social network giants in the current Chinese market
Sina Blog	2005	Present	Has been in decline since around 2011
RenRen Network	2005	Present	Listed in New York Stock Exchange in 2011. Has been in decline since around 2012 in the social network field
Kaixin Network	2008	Present	Received 25 national awards between 2008 and 2011 [24], but social network user base has been in decline since around 2012
Sina Weibo	2009	Present	One of the three social network giants in the current Chinese market

1.2.1 Blogs

Blog services were first invented in 1997 [25], which experienced rapid increases in popularity in the years that followed. Later developments, especially that of Web 2.0 in 2004, contributed significantly to the rise of blogs and its eventual replacement of traditional personal homepages [26]. This second generation of the Internet in the form of Web 2.0 is considered to have two core functions: the ability for users to read and write (and thus, create), which implies a much higher demand for social interactions on the web than was previously possible.

In a strict context of nomenclature, blogs should be considered as more of a form of social media as opposed to social networks [27]. Article [28] proposes a honeycomb model for the definition of social media, consisting of seven functional building blocks:

(1) Identity
(2) Conversations
(3) Sharing
(4) Presence
(5) Relationships
(6) Reputation
(7) Groups

Amongst these, identity stands at the centre for all other functional connections. By contrast, a social network does not emphasise the importance of individuals over others, but is comprised of three equal components: users, friends and interactions. The two models are shown in Fig. 1.4.

According to the earlier distinctions, blogs extend beyond the more simplistic model of social networks as they tend to exhibit the somewhat more expansive elements that characterise social media. Even so, blogs are noteworthy as they contributed to the subsequent growth of social networks in China. Several internationally recognised blogs in the country include Blogger, WordPress and then MSN Space, with the latter

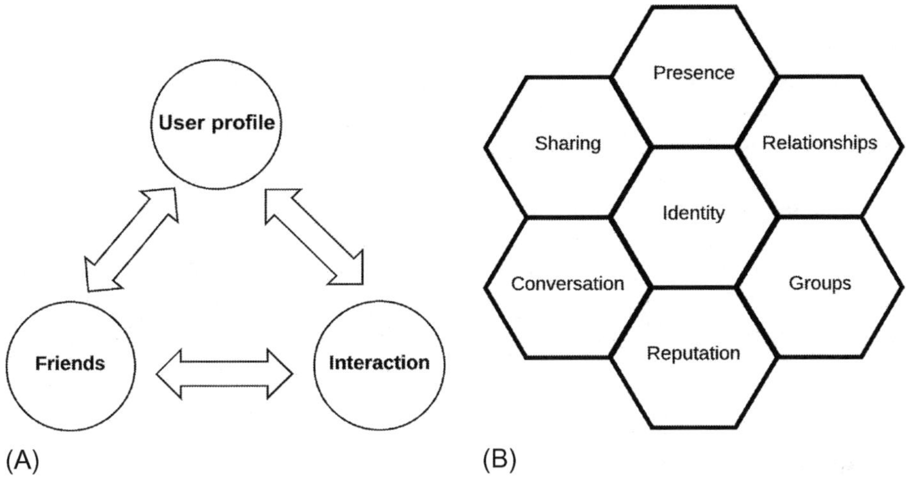

Fig. 1.4 Comparison of social network and social media models. (A) Social network model. (B) Social media model.

being the only western platform that achieved any notable success in China. The domestic market leader, Sina Blog, eclipsed competition from other Chinese rivals including 163 Blogs from NetEase (网易博客),[12] Sohu Blogs (搜狐博客),[13] Tencent Blog (腾讯博客),[14] etc.

Sina Blog was one of the earliest services hosted via a web portal, and established its dominance over a series of key steps, with two being especially noteworthy. The first was the market opportunity created by MSN Space, which, when closed in China in 2010, was capitalised by Sina Blog by its launch of a seamless bridging interface to the Windows platform. This enabled former MSN users to export their blogs, pictures, comments and friends, amongst other content, directly to Sina Blog. To make the process even easier, users could even log into Sina Blog using their Windows Live ID. However, Sina Blog was not the only platform that offered migration services from MSN: others included WordPress, who were once the sole partner to MSN during the transitional period, but the platform encountered telling stability issues in China as some aspects of its site were banned. Sina Blog was eventually chosen as the sole partner to MSN due to its company policing of targeting premium user group [29], and served to form what would become a dominant position of Sina Blog in this online space.

The second critical endeavour by Sina Blog was its promotion of the *celebrity effect*, and is an aspect that continues to play a key role in its sibling product later on, Sina Weibo, a micro blogging service (to be discussed in more detail in Section 1.2.4.1 and

[12] blog.163.com.
[13] blog.sohu.com.
[14] blog.qq.com.

Chapter 4). The celebrity feature helped Sina Blog to quickly grow its user base and stand out amongst its competitors such as 163, Sohu and Tencent during the initial period when blogging was amassing popularity in China. Celebrities in China can include local movie stars, reputable writers, TV presenters, sportsmen and women, established entrepreneurs and leaders of industry, who may each hold a significant fan base. Sina placed efforts on establishing links and attracting celebrities to open blogs on their platform, helping to raise its profile well as further increase subscriber base. The use of celebrity blogs to promote blog services can be considered a unique characteristic of the Chinese online space, which has caused notable disturbance in the Chinese Internet industry. The impact this has placed on the media and broadcast industry, along with the views of academics and industry experts will be discussed in Section 4.2.4.

One example of a celebrity blog (and the notion of *celebrity effect* mentioned earlier) is Jackie's Chan's Blog hosted by Sina. His last blog entry was on 21 January 2011 where Chan commented on his trip to the White House, with the title of the blog being *Obama said he's my fan*. The bottom left corner of the blog page shows official Sina statistics that summarise various popularity measures—Level (an overall evaluation): 23, Points (based on update frequency): 219, Total Visits: 19.8 million, Popularity (indicated by the number of followers): 65,095 and Awarded Pens (a prize from Sina): 80. Blogs have served as a direct portal for celebrities to share their stories and activities with fans, as can be seen in Chan's example. However, blog services gradually declined over the time—a trend that will be considered in more detail in Section 1.2.4.1. Following this decline, the *celebrity effect* strategy has been carried over by Sina to its follow-up social network platform—Weibo.

1.2.2 IM + Blogs bundle

Following the respective success of IM and blog platforms, the next major development of social networks in China during the period between 2004 and 2011 was that of the bundled model, comprising of platforms that combined previously stand-alone services, such as IMs and blogs. Two well-known and successful cases are those of MSN and QQ. Unlike Sina who specialised in blogs, or Kaixin and RenRen who focused solely on social network services (to be discussed in Section 1.2.3), both MSN and QQ sought to provide integrated products consisting of IM, blogs, emails and web portals. The following sections will focus on the nature of these platforms and their development in China.

1.2.2.1 MSN Messenger and MSN space

MSN officially entered Chinese market in 2005. As discussed in Section 1.1.1.3, MSN was introduced to China in a relatively late stage when its instant messaging platform was already facing fierce competition from the domestic leader, QQ. However, given that the owner of MSN, Microsoft is a leader of the operating systems in the world, MSN was positioned with several unique advantages that enabled it to compete in what was becoming an increasingly tough market. Prior to the official launch of MSN in China, without any commercial promotion or publicity, MSN Messenger already managed to attract a total of 10–20 million Chinese users with 1–2 million users being online simultaneously by the end of 2004 [12].

The entry of MSN into the Chinese market in 2004 imposed pressure for others in the market, not least Tencent, whose profit dropped 16.7% in the first quarter of 2005 (although that was not entirely caused by the tension from MSN) [30]. Indeed, MSN's strategy in China was uncompromising, as it sought to become the country's leading web portal. This manifested in the form of MSN Space: the bundling of MSN services with Microsoft's operating system (as similar to the company's integration of Internet Explorer into Windows several years prior), despite the somewhat reluctant admission from their CEO in China at the time, Michael Rawding [12]. The integration of MSN Space and MSN Messenger provided notable convenience for users, enabling rapid growth over a short period after its launch. By the time when MSN Space was closed in 2010, it had secured 30 million users in the world (the total number of Chinese users was unknown).

MSN Space undoubtedly served as a primary stimulant to its equivalent Chinese alternatives such as Sina Blog and Qzone that were released approximately 1 year later in 2005. However, the eventual shutdown of MSN Space in 2010 (despite its rebranding in 2005) represented a major surprise, with experts speculating the core main reason being the platform's disappointing performance in China against rival Chinese products [31, 32]. Such a view is partly qualified by the lack of statistics about the platform during the time of its exit from China, where despite having amassed 30 million users worldwide in 2010, the number of Chinese MSN users remains unknown. One intriguing aspect of analysis, therefore, is what aspects could Chinese social platforms offer that MSN Space could not. This issue can be addressed by examining the biggest rival to MSN at the time, QQ, which similar to MSN Space, also strived to integrate IM with blogs, emails and web portals. Comparisons between these two platforms will be made in the following section.

1.2.2.2 QQ and Qzone

Since its inception in 1999, QQ has been in a state of constant flux in order to address the challenges imposed on it by competitors. It has endured fierce international and national rivalry in numerous forms, initially from ICQ, followed by MSN, and more recently in the shape of Weibo,[15] not to mention other less well-known competitors such as NetEase's IM service—POPO.[16] In response to ever-increasing user requirements and advances in technology, Tencent has consolidated QQ's leading status in the Chinese market by continuously launching novel features and additions to its core platforms. Following the growing popularity of blogs, as discussed earlier, Tencent responded by releasing Qzone in 2005 (the characteristics and features of QQ and Qzone will be outlined discussed in Chapter 3). Since then, the company

[15] Weibo platform will be discussed later sequentially in Sections 1.2.4.1 and 1.3.1.2 and Chapter 4.
[16] http://popo.163.com/.

has embarked on a journey of becoming a multidimensional Internet service provider, focusing on offering broad functionalities in its products towards maintaining and expanding its user base across four fields including online games, social ads, online music and e-commerce. The multidimensional development strategy of Tencent can be traced back to as early as October 2003 [33], and it was officially announced in September 2004 [34].

Table 1.4 briefly compares MSN and QQ in terms of their market orientation and strategy, which is summarised based on the research findings from Refs. [9, 35]. The friend circle, user group and occasions of use can indicate the respective development pathway of the two platforms, whilst factors pertaining to company structure, branding and creativity can serve as important indicators of their eventual success (or otherwise) in China. By 2009, 10 years after both MSN and QQ were created, MSN registered a total of 0.33 billion users across the globe (the total number of Chinese users being unknown), whilst QQ amassed 0.9 billion users in China alone, with 51 million being simultaneously online at 20:00 on 23 February 2009.

1.2.3 SNS models: Kaixin and RenRen

1.2.3.1 Brief history

Whilst the model of IM and blog bundle continued to grow in China, social networks that properly fit the definition of social network services (SNS) [21] started to emerge in China under the influence of Facebook from the west, with two most well-known examples being Kaixin Network and RenRen Network. In addition to ChinaRen which, as discussed earlier in Section 1.1.3, represents the earliest model of social networks in China, Kaixin and RenRen are two pioneering platforms that expanded the awareness and uptake of SNS in China, although no concrete evidence has been found to depict which one is earlier than the other.

Kaixin Network in Chinese can be literally translated as *Happy Network* in English, and RenRen Network can be literally translated as *Everyone's Network*. Prior to 2009, RenRen Network existed in the form of Xiaonei Network (校内网)[17] meaning *In-Campus Network*, which was solely targeted at university students [36]. The historical development of Kaixin and RenRen is briefly outlined in Table 1.5, including statistics on user base that are calculated based on the raw data gathered from Refs. [24, 36–38].

Due to their marked similarity in function and design, Kaixin and RenRen have been involved in intense rivalry over a number of years, not least one involving a bitter legal battle. Upon facing competition from Kaixin in 2009, China InterActive Corp. (the owner of RenRen) registered the domain name of kaixin.com and provided RenRen-compatible SNS to Kaixin users. As may be expected, this rapidly brought RenRen into a law suit with Beijing Happy Person IT Ltd (the owner of Kaixin Network). Following a lengthy legal battle, the Beijing's Second Intermediate People's Court ruled in favour of Kaixin in 2010 on the basis that China InterActive Corp. had clear and sufficient

[17] www.xiaonei.com.

Table 1.4 Comparison of MSN and QQ

	MSN	QQ
Friend circle	Mainly for acquaintance; friends can only be added via known email addresses	Besides the acquaintance, it is also popular amongst strangers. Spam messages can be received unless a setting is made to block them
User groups	Mainly white collar, aged 25–35, who have strong consumption power for high-end products, e.g. designer goods, cars, estates, etc.	Mainly aged 14–20, who posses purchasing ability for day-to-day goods, e.g. food and beverage, clothing
Occasions of use	Although integrating business and entertainment, MSN mainly emphasises the usage in business environments. Many users are happy to use it at work	Mainly focused on entertainment. Users tend to use it for personal matters
Company structure	MSN China was at the bottom of a huge corporate system. Major decisions had to seek approval through MSN Asia-Pacific, MSN Overseas HQ, MSN Business Division and eventually Microsoft HQ. The long decision-making process affected the speed of system upgrade and improvements	QQ, as the pillar product of Tencent, is renowned for its quick reaction to market changes and user needs. For example, QQ was one of the first companies to launch a mobile app and embrace the opportunities of the mobile internet[a]
Branding	In 2006, MSN Messenger was changed to 'Windows Live Messenger' and bundled with a large package of irrelevant software. The three corporate logos (butterfly, buddies and the window) often appeared indiscriminately, thus causing confusion	In 2005 Tencent launched a new logo which inherited the old penguin identity whilst incorporating green, yellow and red colour bands to represent extended services. This was reflective of the platform's past whilst also embracing the future
Creativity	Notable features that were missing from MSN but present in QQ included the screen grab tool, group management and offline file transfers. Research showed that the traditional interface of the Chinese version of MSN was hard for younger Chinese users to have *love-at-first-sight*.	QQ's interface design was made for a relatively easy-to-use experience. QQ was also keen on launching novel functions or modules, such as QQ Show, QQ Pets, QQ Input, VIP, games, etc.

Note: In the second phase of Chinese social network development: 2004–11.

[a]To be discussed in Section 1.2.4.2.

Table 1.5 **Kaixin and RenRen between 2004 and 2011**

		Kaixin	RenRen
History	2008	5 million users. 0.1 billion site visits per month	Formerly known as Xiaonei Network. User base of 11 million since 2005
	2009	15 million users. Released *Stealing Vegetable* game[a]	50 million users
	2010	90 million users	116 million users
	2011	95 million users (40 million active users)	170 million users (95 million active users)
Majority User Group		Aged 20 to 35; white collars	Aged 16 to 25; students
Platform Development		Self-owned	Open source

[a]To be discussed in Section 1.2.3.3.

knowledge of Kaixin's qualification of being a 'well-known service' (this being the significant user base and popularity that Kaixin had already amassed up to that point) before registering the kaixin.com domain. Consequently, this was deemed by the Court to have caused confusion amongst users, and represented unfair practise on the grounds of China's *Anti Unfair-Competition Law* (反不正当竞争法) [39]. China InterActive Corp. was subsequently ordered to revert to renren.com as the platform's sole domain. Interestingly, Kaixin's URL remains to this day not, as one may expect, kaixin.com, but kaixin001.com. The ongoing disputes between Kaixin and RenRen had became one of the reasons for their downfall a couple of years later, which will be fully discussed in Section 1.3.1.1.

1.2.3.2 SNS model comparisons

Both Kaixin and RenRen can be regarded as standard SNS models that have undergone a mature and sustained period of development in China. Kaixin and RenRen are also the two platforms that, by design or otherwise, most closely resemble the general function and appearance of Facebook. The visual composition of Kaixin, RenRen and Facebook in 2009 (and thus targeted principally for use on desktop and laptop machines) was notably similar, with the main tab options situated on the top of the page (such as homepage, friends and news), whilst functional components are listed on the left of the screen (features such as photo album, diary and games). Table 1.6 lists and compares the core functionalities of Kaixin, RenRen and Facebook, as well as ChinaRen, in accordance with the SNS model shown in Fig. 1.3.

Compared with ChinaRen, both Kaixin and RenRen possessed the full characteristics of the social network model. Users were given the freedom of adding any desired person (known or otherwise) to their social circle by perusing the profiles of other users, followed by an activation procedure via a greeting between new friends. However, despite the possibility of interacting with nonacquaintances, no formal evidence exits to prove that such interactions had led to increased activity between

Table 1.6 **SNS models of ChinaRen, Kaixin, RenRen and Facebook as in 2009**

SNS model components		ChinaRen	Kaixin	RenRen	Facebook
User	Profile setup	✓	✓	✓	✓
	Public page	✓	✓	✓	✓
	Photo album	✓	✓	✓	✓
	Diary		✓	✓	✓
	VIP service			✓	
	Network drive		✓		
Friends	Add/delete	✓	✓	✓	✓
	Search	✓	✓	✓	✓
	Allow strangers		✓	✓	✓
	Recommendation		✓	✓	✓
	Group		✓		✓
	Alumni	✓		✓	✓
Interaction	Sharing posts	✓	✓	✓	✓
	Repost		✓	✓	✓
	Comments	✓	✓	✓	✓
	Thumb-up		✓	✓	✓
	Send gifts		✓		✓
	Messaging		✓	✓	✓
	Built-in social games		✓	✓	✓

strangers on these platforms. The veggie-stealing example in the next section will attempt to shed further light on this aspect.

With the elevation of SNS popularity in China, social networks had matured towards a more commercial phase of development. Both Kaixin and RenRen aimed to provide deeper levels of interaction by combining real-life friendships with online activities. Virtual interactions could be made via traditional approaches such as sharing posts, comments and messaging, but also through novel actions such as sending gifts and social games: a list of common features is given in Table 1.6.

1.2.3.3 Veggie-stealing social game

With the development of social networks in China, the increasing emphasis on the provision of e-commerce in social networks was gradually becoming one of the key strategic developments. The ‘veggie-stealing’ game became a prime example of a successful game that Kaixin and RenRen had integrated within their respective platforms. The game essentially consists of an online farm where players can acquire machines to cultivate agricultural produce, with its key feature being the ability to steal vegetables from farms owned by other players—a gameplay mechanic that also exists in games from competing platforms such as Qzone. As opposed to causing conflict between players, the game served as an amusing form of interaction amongst friends

Fig. 1.5 An example of veggie-stealing scene. One user erects a warning sign (*left of screen*) to repel thieves, which reads: *You will pay the price of stealing*.

and strangers, where the act of stealing a vegetable could often be interpreted as a way of saying *hello*. The competition for the plant growth stimulated repeated play, which also encouraged users to dwell on creative methods to prevent stealing in the virtual life (see example in Fig. 1.5). Veggie stealing was later ranked as the number 1 game by Kaixin Network in terms of popularity, and despite some criticisms on using the word 'stealing' from the government and the public [40], the controversial phrase 'veggie stealing' became a widely used term in Chinese social networking environment, attracting older as well as younger players. A popular greeting amongst Internet friends in that period was *Have you stolen veggie today?* [41].

Veggie stealing had became a unique social phenomena in China with the rising of social networks, and the amount of vegetable assets was a hot topic to discuss amongst social network users. A large portion of players (including old age groups) were addicted to the gameplay, devising strategies or keeping an eye on their farm premises. Many users would wake up in the middle of the night to steal vegetables, and some users would even steal vegetables for others as a paid part-time job. The game was officially closed in 2013 due to the falling popularity of its network hosts, Kaixin and RenRen. Unsurprisingly, the game was sorely missed by a large quantity of users [42], and its phenomena attracted the attention of a number of researchers who sought to examine its sociopsychological impact on players, for example, a study by Fan [43] revealed that the veggie-stealing game strengthened existing social links whilst expanding social circle to some extent.

Box 1.2 Strong ties and weak ties

The classification of strong and weak ties was first defined by Granovetter [44].

- *Strong ties* refer to those relationships that are closely bonded and in frequent contact, for example, civil partnership, parents and children, siblings and close friends.
- *Weak ties* refer to acquaintances who have low knowledge of each other but have little communication on everyday basis, for example, colleagues who do not work together frequently, people in the neighbourhood.

Box 1.2 explains the definition of strong ties and weak ties in the society. Perhaps unexpectedly, weak ties are those who are considered to represent the adhesiveness of the society due to its existence in large quantities [44]. China is generally regarded as an *acquaintance society* [45] where individuals are closely bonded with others by blood relations, location proximity and familiarity appearances, and a majority of these relationships can be defined as weak ties. Therefore, weak ties in China are considered to be of great significance. Although the veggie-stealing game did not transform weak ties to strong ties (i.e. by converting general friends to close friends), it had become an amusing and light-hearted method of communication amongst users of weak-tie relationships, therefore maintaining and establishing weak ties on a regular basis [43]. Judged by the interactions in the gameplay, the Veggie stealing possessed four main aspects of social impact, which are listed next.

(1) Communication
  a. The act of stealing represents an alternative form of greeting.
  b. The act of mutual stealing serves as a return greeting.
  c. Acts of stealing and being a victim of theft represent giving attention to others and receiving attention, respectively.

(2) Mutual benefits
  a. Players can gain bonus points by helping friends with cultivating, for example, ploughing and weeding.
  b. Reciprocity of a friend's favour will stimulate further interactions and potentially strengthen their relationship.
  c. Production of the farms can be shared amongst friends.

(3) Cooperation
  a. Players can collude to steal other people's vegetables.
  b. Multiple players can own the same farm and divide responsibilities.
  c. The collaboration can be extended to the reality—friends who are colleagues often talk about work during the farming process [43].

(4) Social expansion
  a. Relationships, whether strong ties or weak ties, can be maintained via a tern active and entertaining way.
  b. Weak ties can be easily established and expanded during the gameplay.
  c. The act and issues associated with veggie stealing became a popular topic of daily discussion in society [43].

1.2.4 Impact of mobile internet and smartphones

The second major phase of Chinese SNS history (2004–11) can be further divided into two major periods: pre- and post-2009, where significant changes to the market were enacted by developments in mobile Internet and the emergence of smartphones. Fig. 1.6 shows the number of Chinese patents regarding various mobile communication technology over the years, which on some level reflects the development trend of mobile Internet evolution. As can be seen from the trend lines, 2009 was the beginning of major peaks for 3G advancement in China. In January 2009, 3G licenses were issued to the three major telecommunication carriers in China: China Mobile, China Telecom and China Unicom [46]. In the same year the iPhone 3G officially entered the Chinese market [47] which, along with its competitors, significantly contributed to the rise of the mobile computing era. Some of the key platforms and features that were developed as a consequence of the rise of mobile devices and Internet connectivity are examined below.

1.2.4.1 Emergence of micro blogs: Weibo

Being built on the foundations already set by traditional blog platforms, the emergence of micro blogs catered for the more immediate needs of those equipped with mobile Internet connectivity. As opposed to being in a fixed location, users could publish and share information on the move via a broad range of mobile devices such as smartphones, tablets and even handheld game machines. Twitter, the world's first micro blog, was launched in 2006, yet it was to suffer the same fate as Facebook of being banned in China by the Chinese authorities. Be that as it may, the tremendous success of Twitter across the globe led to the development of Chinese equivalents, most notably by those who were already firmly established in the web portal arena. In August 2009,

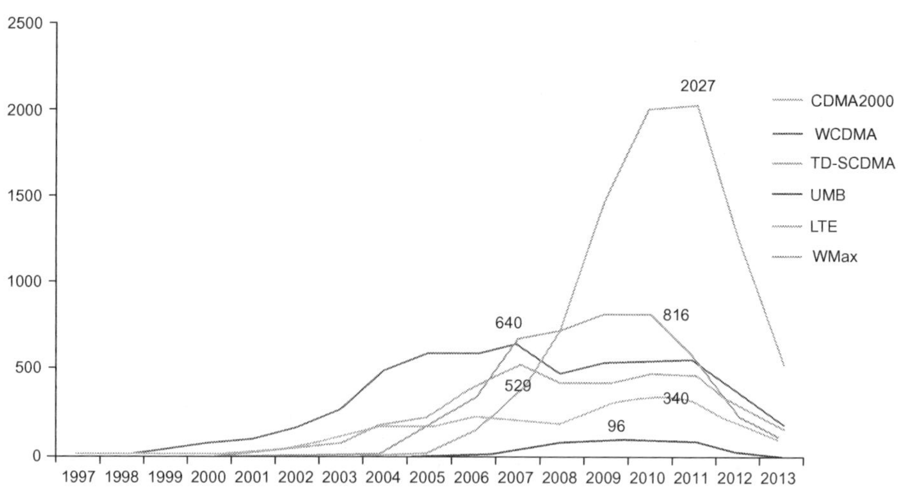

Fig. 1.6 Development trend of Chinese Mobile Telecom Technology (1997–2013) [48].

Sina launched the first official micro blog service in China in the form of *Weibo* (微博), literally translated as 'micro blog'. This was shortly followed by the release of competing services from NetEase, Sohu and Tencent throughout 2010, elevating micro blogs into the mainstream.

Prior to 2011, the term *Weibo* was used merely as a general reference to micro blog services, but in April of that year, Sina took the cunning step of registering the domain name of weibo.com and the trademark of *Weibo*. From that point onwards, the term Weibo became directly synonymous with Sina's platform, where its previously generic application now referred exclusively to Sina's platform and leading to its eventual monopoly of the Chinese micro blog market (the more intricate aspects of competition between the major portals will be discussed in Section 1.3.1.2).

The 2010 transpired as a peak year for Chinese micro blogs. The four major Chinese web portals: Sina, Sohu, NetEase and Tencent, all launched their micro blog services, and a total of over 20 micro blog services had appeared in China by the end of 2010 [49]. The number of users on all platforms skyrockets from 75 million in January 2010 to 195 million by the beginning of 2011, whilst the national penetration ratio was a staggering 40.2% amongst Internet users [50].

As the rapid growth of micro blogs in China continued, the popularity of more traditional blog services started to decline. Earlier SNS networks such as Kaixin and RenRen experienced reductions in their market share under the impact of the growing provision and accessibility of mobile Internet and smartphones (to be discussed in Section 1.3.1.1). The following section will consider the more particular and distinctive features that distinguish micro blogs from their earlier incarnations, which are not necessarily specific to China.

Micro blogs versus blogs

- Terminal platform

One of the most obvious distinctions between micro blogs and traditional blogs is the terminal platform, where the former can be used on a wide variety of computers and mobile devices, and the latter usually requires the use of desktop or laptop computers. Whilst it is beyond the confines of this book to consider the numerous merits and drawbacks of mobile devices as compared to traditional platforms, one important aspect concerns the ease and accessibility of text input via virtual keyboards, which are typically the norm on mobile devices. Generally speaking, the virtual keyboard feature is more constrained in terms of finger movements than those on a traditional computer keyboard [51], which can impose major challenges to users when typing and formatting lengthy articles as they do in blogs. This could represent a main reason why blog providers have so far been reluctant to develop equivalent mobile apps for their established products that are commonly available and successful on traditional platforms. As outlined in Table 1.7, only two mobile apps are available for blog services in China (i.e. NetEase Blogs and Sina Blogs), both of which have noticeably lower ratings (i.e. average 2.5 out of 5) compared to other SNS products. Thus, despite the vast proliferation of mobile devices, there is relative paucity of choice in the blog

Table 1.7 **Mobile apps (iOS) for Chinese social networks**

App	First release	Average rating (by 2016)[a]
QQ	2009	3.0/8973
Tencent Weibo	2010	3.5/781
Sohu Weibo	2010	3.3/41
NetEase Blogs	2010	2.5/521
Kaixin Network	2010	3.0/897
Sina Blogs	2011	2.5/46
Sina Weibo	2011	3.5/7028
Fetion	2011	2.5/185
RenRen Network[b]	2011	3.0/789
WeChat	2011	4.5/33,294
Mobile MSN Messenger[c]	2012	Data unavailable

[a]The first number of the rating stands for a portion out of 5, and the last number represents the total amount of reviewers. For example, 3.0/8973 means there are 8973 users participated the review, and the average rate is 3.0 out of 5.
[b]An iPhone version does not exist. This is an iPad version.
[c]Developed by MSN Shanghai just a few months before MSN Messenger was discontinued and has been removed from the app store. Microsoft never released an app for MSN Space.

market. On the other hand, micro blogs are designed for the mobile computing age, therefore can deliver relatively higher user experience in mobile devices. From the three major micro blog apps listed in Table 1.7 (i.e. Tencent Weibo, Sohu Weibo and Sina Weibo), the average user rating was 3.4 out of 5.

- Convenience

Blogs normally demand the considerations for page layout and logical flow of expressions, whilst micro blogs do not place requirements for the arrangements of the languages and texts. Each micro blog message consists of no more than 140 characters, inherently claiming less technical resources compared with blog articles. This form of shorthand communication therefore allows and promotes a more contracted style of communication, as users can publish and share their information in any environment that has a mobile (or WiFi) signal reception. The high level of convenience stimulates impromptu productions whenever and wherever users choose to. An example could be sharing live news at a major event.

- Back-to-face communication

In traditional blogs, each user carries an individual identity who can publish and comment on others, and hence to this degree each interaction is a form of face-to-face communication. In this context, however, some users may feel reluctant to publish comments as this would make their profiles and opinions directly visible to others. By contrast, micro blogs promote more of a *following* culture, where the environment is comprised of a few, key opinion leaders who are ‘followed’ or subscribed to by a comparatively larger body of audience-type users. The input system for each micro blog message can be in the form of a repost, comment or thumbs-up (i.e.

like), as opposed to necessarily that of a lengthy commentary or reply in blogs. The communication between opinion leaders and their audiences (or followers) therefore takes place in the form of a 'back-to-face' mode, where opinion leaders have the knowledge of the number of followers and their basic reactions, but do not have to be concerned with reacting to each and every response. A metaphor can be used to analogise this scenario: a man is playing a video game in front of a computer, whilst many people walk by and watch him playing behind him; he does not feel the need to proactively talk to his audiences, nor does he have the default knowledge of people behind him. Conversely, followers can merely express simple responses towards opinion makers rather than express detailed comments about their attitudes and beliefs. Even though it is totally feasible in the technical sense for both micro blog makers and their followers can check out each other's profiles, the emphasis of micro blog publishing is put on the dissemination of information. Such forms of communication can also be of one to one or one to many in micro blogs, as users can repost and tag as many users as they wish. Such nuances therefore render micro blogs as a somewhat more flexible form of interaction as compared with traditional blogs, often demanding much less of a typical user in terms of input and commentary.

- Dissemination: Width vs. depth

Despite their clear lineage, the nature of dissemination and the inherent compositions of blogs and micro blogs possess some inherent differences. Being essentially a multimedia diary, traditional blogs offered users the ability to express content in the form of text, pictures, audio and video. Such an environment therefore facilitated the production of detailed opinions and perspectives on a subject matter, representing the dissemination of in-depth information. By contrast, the greater emphasis on expediency, convenience and concision by micro blogs promotes the dissemination and consumption of information in width, that is, the scope of information coverage.

1.2.4.2 Tencent's mobile innovation

With the rise of the era of mobile Internet, software providers could no longer rely on providing services via desktop computers and laptops, but needed to embrace new expectations and methods of provision. As a consequence, makers of established social networks began launching mobile versions of their products in order to cater for evolving market demand, as shown in Table 1.7. Tencent was one of the first companies to address the growing needs of the mobile market.

Tencent's speedy response to market changes was, on reflection, quite remarkable during what was the emerging period of mobile Internet in China. With the issuing of Chinese 3G licences being made in January 2009 [46], Tencent launched the first mobile version of QQ for Apple's iPhone just 1 month later. To put this into context, this release was 8 months prior to the official release date of the Apple iPhone 3G in China (i.e. October 2009), which sought to address the needs of users who had acquired foreign iPhones via unofficial channels [52]. Similarly, Apple's first-generation iPad was released in March 2010, which Tencent coincided with the release of QQ's iPad version, QQ HD. These two examples illustrate Tencent's immediacy in embracing the market change and technology advancement, in this particular case being the emergence of the mobile era and the introduction of 3G technologies in China, which has led to the maintenance and growth of its user base.

As a matter of fact, Tencent's ambitions for digital mobile communication actually existed as early as 2001 in the form of, what was then, a futuristic concept named Mobile OICQ [53], which can be considered a true ancestor to Mobile QQ. Tencent collaborated with China Mobile, the biggest mobile telecommunication carrier in China, and secured service coverage for Mobile OICQ in seven provinces for its launch. The initial version of Mobile OICQ was designed as a simple communication tool between friends, catering for the basic needs of online chatting largely in the form of text messaging. With the evolution of colour screens and advancements in mobile platforms, newer versions of Mobile OICQ (along with its subsequent name change to Mobile QQ) were released in subsequent years. Even in the early versions of Mobile QQ, the service provision had already integrated conventional chatting facilities with news articles, entertainment (e.g. simple board games) and movies, amongst others. Thus, from the outset of its venture into mobile communications and social networking in China, Tencent forged a leading position with rapid entry into the market and sensitivity to technological changes and user expectations.

However, Tencent's ambitions in the Chinese mobile communications arena did not come unchallenged. Indeed, one notable competitor came from China Mobile in the form of Fetion (飞信) in 2007—the very company that Tencent had closely collaborated with just a few years earlier. Fetion was conceived as a comprehensive communication platform, which offered seamless connections between the Internet backbone and mobile Internet. In practise, this allowed users to register an account on either a desktop computer or a mobile phone, from where they can send unlimited texts between devices free of charge, as well as conduct IM with other users. The challenge presented by Fetion in the field of IM represented enormous pressure for Tencent. Even though the company had launched Mobile QQ app in 2009, the migration of this well-established QQ software platform could take time for a complete transition from the traditional desktop environment to the mobile environment. In essence, Tencent could not rely solely on updating Mobile QQ as a means of satisfying what was becoming an increasingly competitive marketplace. Thus, the company then decided that a more severe strategy of revolutionary change was required: rather than being defeated by others, they needed to question and change themselves as a means of overcoming the opposition [54]. This approach eventually sets the foundation for the creation of WeChat, which will be explained in Section 1.3.1.3.

Under this general backdrop of the bloom period of Chinese social networks, Table 1.7 also outlines the users' ratings for each mobile app, as indicated by the average rating (out of a maximum score of 5) for all versions of the app to date, and the total amount of users who contributed to the rating. All data were collected in December 2016 from iTunes and App Annie, a third-party database that collates historical versions and users' reviews of mobile apps [55]. The summary of data in Table 1.7 gives an indication of the three leading social network services in China and their current status (to be reviewed in Section 1.3.2), comprising of WeChat, QQ and Sina Weibo.

1.3 2011 to present: Current status

In 2011, several monumental changes took place in the Chinese social network arena that would define its current status and composition. As discussed in Chapter 1.2.3.1, the intense battle between Kaixin and RenRen culminated in a lawsuit for the *kaixin* domain name, Sina Weibo officially registered its exclusive use of weibo.com, whilst WeChat rapidly emerged via cunning strategies of innovation and the gathering of social network users. Collectively, these events had purged the market of numerous competitors whilst cementing the position of those who were able to continually address the needs of a rapidly changing technological and social space. This chapter will examine particular events that led to the elimination and rise of various Chinese social platforms, the outcomes of which may be used as practical case studies to determine success factors for future ventures into the Chinese market space.

1.3.1 Competition and elimination

1.3.1.1 Downfall of traditional SNS: Kaixin and RenRen

Kaixin and RenRen were considered as the strongest contenders to Facebook in China in the period between 2008 and early 2010 as explained in Section 1.2.3. Both platforms offered the core features that define SNS models, and thus could be considered to represent a more traditional form of social network in relation to more contemporary iterations such as WeChat and Weibo. Despite having achieved significant national success, Kaixin and RenRen were subjected to a new phase of development from 2011 giving rise to new challenges and implications for their creators that would eventually lead to their downfall.

Fig. 1.7 shows the world rankings of Kaixin and RenRen in terms of web traffic from their peak popularity in 2011 to the time of their demise in 2016, based on statistics obtained from international web analytics sources [56, 57]. Kaixin's rise to popularity involved a staggering 500% increase in just a single year, from 15 million users in 2009 to 90 million in 2010. However, as can be seen in Fig. 1.7, the popularity of both Kaixin and RenRen began to record gradual decline from the latter part of 2011, where in the case of Kaixin, became a dramatic free-fall in 2013 from which it could not recover. RenRen's decline, on the other hand, was somewhat less severe due to its IPO listing on 4 May 2011 [58], which allowed it to secure more substantial financial resources and thereby maintain some degree of foothold in the market. Such a severe fall from popularity experienced by both networks can be attributable to the status of Chinese social network space at the time, which by 2013 had entered a mature phase comprising of three dominant leaders—WeChat, QQ and Weibo (to be discussed collectively in Section 1.3.2)—who together eroded the user base that had been established by RenRen and Kaixin.

The effective defeat of Kaixin and RenRen in the social network arena led to a profound transformation of both companies in terms of their product offerings, which ultimately involved reducing the emphasis on their existing social network

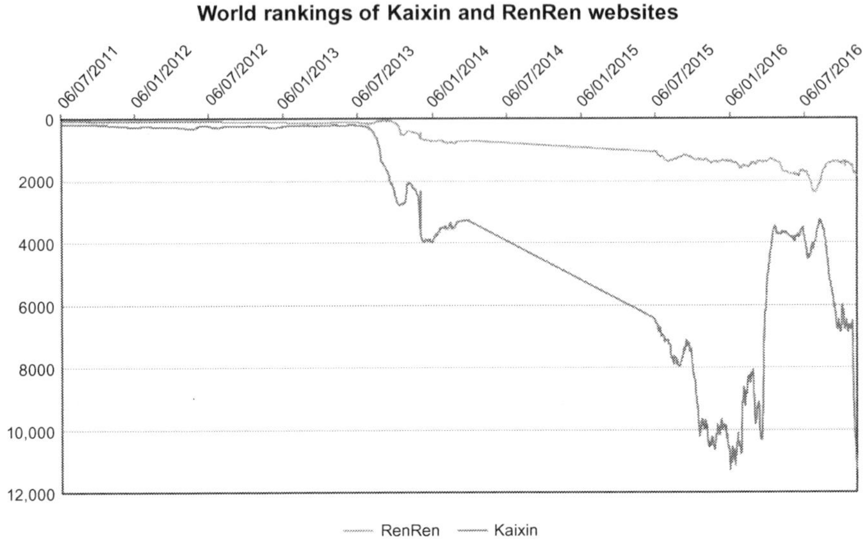

Fig. 1.7 World rankings of Kaixin and RenRen based on web traffic since 2011.

services. In the case of Kaixin, the company turned towards games development[18] (perhaps unsurprisingly given the platform's previous success with games such as Veggie Stealing), leading to a major increase in the company's ranking in 2016 as shown in Fig. 1.7. At the time of writing, Kaixin is in the process of being acquired by Shenzhen Sunwin Intelligent Corporation [59]. In quite marked contrast, RenRen gradually transformed into a social finance company[19] [60], and thus both Kaixin and RenRen have since distanced themselves from their roots in social network provision. The crucial element of these two cases, however, resides in the reasons for their failure and final departure from the social network arena, of which can be summarised under two main categories as presented follows.

- Declining enthusiasm for repetitive social games

Kaixin's social network model was largely dependent on social games to maintain users' enthusiasm for repeated visits. Its veggie-stealing game, as explained in Section 1.2.3.3, was perhaps Kaixin's most popular title, and led to several variations of similar games such as Qiang Che Wei (抢车位)—a game based on the idea of battling for parking spaces that was largely similar to veggie stealing. Such games had become an integral and vital element within social networks during the period between 2009 and 2012. Indeed, Kaixin's competitors at the time, such as RenRen, 51 Network,[20] Hainei Network (海内网),[21] Tencent and Sina, all followed Kaixin's

[18] game.kaixin001.com.
[19] licai.renren.com.
[20] 51.com.
[21] hainei.org.

example by providing similar types of social games within their respective platforms to preserve user interest and stimulate repeated visits.

However, the approach of providing comparatively similar games eventually represented a threat to the companies who provided them. Without greater attempts at providing novel and innovative games and other supporting features, there was the real risk of boredom growing amongst users. Compounding to this was the fact that, as compared to traditional computer and video games, games on social platforms had to be designed with different objectives in mind; that is, that they had to be built predominantly on the foundations of social interaction as opposed to the expansive and unrestricted nature of traditional games. This therefore represented a notable restriction to the general development and enhancement of games on SNS platforms. Binghao Cheng (程炳皓), the founder and CEO of Kaixin, underlined this issue in an interview in 2013 [61] where he stated that one of the major reasons for Kaixin's major decline was the periodic nature of games such as veggie stealing, and that users would lose interest after an initial novelty period. Even though Kaixin attempted to rejuvenate the gaming aspect of the platform with titles such as Happy Canteen (开心餐厅) in 2010 and Happy City (开心城市) in 2011, the success of veggie stealing was never replicated and thus contributed to the irreversible decline of user interest. Be that as it may, problems caused by the lack of creativity and innovation is not exclusive to Kaixin, as professional reviewers have openly criticised the monotony of the leading social networks, for example, a journal article [62] published in 2011 revealed the stagnation and fatigue of social networks in China and in the world including Kaixin, RenRen and Facebook.

- Fighting the wrong rivals

Beyond issues of creativity discussed earlier, another major reason for the downfall of Kaixin and RenRen was the undivided attention that both companies placed on battling each other to the neglect of emerging competition and market forces. The battle between Kaixin and RenRen can be traced back to 2010 as mentioned in Section 1.2.3.1, and persisted for many years thereafter. Tencent's interview with Binghao Cheng [61] shed light on key events that caused Kaixin's downfall.[22] The rapid rise of Kaixin between 2009 and 2010 meant it had positioned itself as the biggest rival to RenRen, and eventually led to the infamous lawsuit for the rights to the name of *kaixin*

[22] According to the interview [61] of Binghao Cheng, RenRen once offered to buy Kaixin but got declined. When the Kaixin team initially started their business, kaixin001.com was the only available domain name they could find. Later when they became more and more successful, people advised Cheng to buy the domain name kaixin.com, though the owner of that domain name asked for a couple of hundreds of thousands of dollars. As a founder of a startup company, Cheng turned down the idea of purchase. RenRen later bought the domain name kaixin.com and hereby built an SNS that is compatible with its existing RenRen network, meaning RenRen users and kaixin.com users can log onto both networks. According to the court decision in 2010, this was an unfair competition causing confusion to customers, and therefore RenRen was given a 0.4 million Yuan penalty by the court. However, Kaixin claimed a loss of 34 million customers and thus in 2011 appealed the court decision by asking for a compensation of 10 million Yuan from RenRen [63]. There are no official data yet reporting the result of this appeal.

The *kaixin* name and legal case provide potentially valuable lessons for entrepreneurs and startup developers. Binghao Cheng admitted two strategic mistakes regarding the use of the *kaixin* name: the first was the oversight of not having bought the domain name of kaixin.com during the time of the platform's inception and second was the company's delayed reaction (amounting to 6 months) to its alleged improper use by RenRen, and consequently losing the platform tens of millions of users. Even though Kaixin eventually won the lawsuit in 2010, RenRen had already achieved the purpose of substantially halting the rapid growth of Kaixin through their use of the fake *kaixin* domain, and paved the way for its IPO stock listing. According to Kaixin's claim in the lawsuit, RenRen's fake site had robbed it of 34 million users. Considered at another way, it could be said that RenRen obtained 34 million new users at a cost of just 0.4 million Yuan (in the form of a penalty charge imposed by the court).

In the midst of the growing battle between Kaixin and RenRen, Sina Weibo emerged and grew prominence. As an indication of the respect that Kaixin had garnered in the market, Sina's Weibo team sought the advice of Cheng (Kaixin's founder) on the operation of SNS during the initial period of Weibo's launch around the period of late 2009 to early 2010 [61]. Such a consultation was perhaps unsurprising given Sina's previously failed venture into the social network arena in the form of Friends (朋友), and beyond merely obtaining advice, Kaixin had granted Sina the right to import some of its user base to Weibo—a move that, in retrospect, indicates Kaixin's initial underestimation and disregard of the fledgling platform. Kaixin's early misjudgement of Weibo's eventual success was altered in late 2010, after Weibo experienced rapid expansion in the social network sector. In response, Kaixin attempted to launch a Weibo-type rival platform, but the outcomes from testing proved unsatisfactory and thus failed to materialise [61]. By early 2011, the Chinese micro blog market had undergone drastic changes, not least with Sina registering the solo use of the domain name weibo.com and thus began to monopolise the provision of micro blog services nationally (via its namesake platform). As for Kaixin's prospects for mounting a rival challenge to Sina Weibo (not to mention threats posed by other rapidly expanding services such as WeChat), it was a case of too little too late.

Similar to Kaixin, RenRen made similar mistakes of poor sensitivity to market changes and having invested too much time and resources on wrangles with Kaixin rather than dealing with emerging threats such as Weibo. Kaixin and RenRen both failed to grasp the nuances of how the market was changing under the impact of new technology and evolving user requirements. Such a combination of factors ultimately proved terminal for both companies, as witnessed by their eventual elimination from the sector.

Article in [64] publicly criticised the adverse impact the battle between Kaixin and RenRen had brought to the Chinese social network domain. Both Kaixin and RenRen were the first followers of the SNS models that Facebook created, however, instead of carrying on with learning from the good examples of Facebook's subsequent strategic moves, their continuous battles had brought oversight on the market and negative remarks from the public—RenRen was particularly criticised for its forged usage of Kaixin name and the neglect of network community orders.

- Losing the battle to Weibo

Kaixin Network was created and maintained by a typical technical team, who were lack of experiences in both business management and market creativity. On the other hand, the rapid growth of Sina Weibo originated from Sina's advantageous genes for news and business experiences. Sina's marketing strategy for Weibo has always been mature and steady, ever since its successful management of blog services in the early days—its appeal to celebrities and opinion leaders in various field indicated its rich resources and elite teams. The next section will explain how Sina gradually dominated the Weibo market.

Compared with Sina Weibo, both Kaixin and RenRen did not innovate and maintain a sustainable product in the social network field, and thus users gradually lost interests and turned to a newer form of platform—Weibo. Chapter 4 will fully discuss the features of Sina Weibo. Having established as a platform for the public to express and discuss their opinions, Sina Weibo implemented various innovative applications to cater for the growing demands of mobile Internet users. For all the reasons given earlier, many users from Kaixin and RenRen have started to migrate to Sina Weibo since late 2010 [64].

1.3.1.2 Dominance of Sina Weibo in micro blog services

As discussed in Section 1.2.4.1, after its emergence in the Chinese social network market, Weibo (the Chinese name for micro blogs) platforms quickly became popular in 2010 as all major Chinese web portals had all launched their respective Weibo services to act as newer replacements to more traditional blogs. 2010 was also the year when various Weibo websites were being rigorously tested in the market and improved as a consequence, whilst the competition that was created amongst rival companies helped to expand the overall user base for Weibo services. It was under this general backdrop that the domination of Sina Weibo appeared in 2011.

Whilst many Weibo service providers were still at the stage of exploring and establishing their respective marketing strategies for the social media space, Sina proudly announced their domain name of weibo.com for its proprietary Weibo service on 6 April 2011. Prior to this announcement, web portals had been using second-level domain names to attach their Weibo services to their existing websites, with examples such as weibo.sina.com,[23] weibo.sohu.com,[24] weibo.qq.com,[25] weibo.163.com.[26] Sina's registration of the weibo.com domain name was significant to their success in two major ways:

(1) It announced that Sina Weibo is not a subbrand of an existing web portal, but rather a dedicated and stand-alone product. Despite Sina's established presence as a web portal provider, Weibo was marketed and distributed as a separate entity from the company's

[23] Later changed to t.sina.com.
[24] Now as t.sohu.com.
[25] Now as t.qq.com.
[26] Now closed.

existing portfolio. This element of Sina's strategy therefore appealed to users from other web portals as they could register on Sina Weibo without requiring first to associate with a parent web portal. As a result, Sina Weibo was established and built purely for the purpose of social networking.

(2) The general term *Weibo* is the only pinyin[27] expression in Chinese language that refers to the notion of 'micro blogs'. Having learnt valuable lessons from the Kaixin and RenRen lawsuit (as described in Sections 1.2.3.1 and 1.3.1.1), Sina's adoption of the weibo.com domain effectively curtailed competition from rivals by preventing them to operate with the stand-alone Weibo title (unless being used as a second-level domain name, or perhaps with number postfix). This simple yet potent strategy of acquiring a key domain name paved the way for more users to join Sina Weibo and towards its eventual monopolisation of Weibo services in China. Such was the effectiveness of this strategy, Sina invested substantially in three main domain names: weibo.com.cn was bought in September 2009, followed by weibo.com in March 2010 and finally weibo.cn was acquired in August 2010 [65]. Sina's foresight and ambition for micro-blogging services is exemplified by the fact that when the weibo.com.cn domain was bought in 2009, micro blogs had only been in existence in China for approximately 1 month.

Be that as it may, the effective use of domain names was not the only reason that led to Sina Weibo's success. Several other major factors have also contributed to Sina's accomplishments, of which can be summarised as follows.

(1) As explained in Section 1.2.1, Sina had already established dominance in the traditional blog market. As the advantages of micro blogs began to prevail over existing platforms (as discussed in Section 1.2.4.1), Sina reacted by providing existing users with a seamless transition from their blog to Weibo service.

(2) Following the successful promotion and popularity of the *celebrity effect* feature on its blog platform (as described at the end of Section 1.2.1), Sina continued to develop this aspect on Weibo as a means of attracting and maintaining user interest. According to a third-party statistic source in 2016 [66], out of the 50 most popular film and television celebrities in China, 47 possess a verified Sina Weibo account, each attracting an average of 23 million Weibo subscribers. As a consequence, the *celebrity effect* has brought vast strength to Sina Weibo—an aspect that will be discussed in detail in Section 4.2.4.

(3) Sina is highly active in publicly promoting Weibo culture via a series of grand events, for example, the launch of a *Micro Novel Competition* (微小说大赛) [67] on 27 October 2010 that encouraged users to publish, comment and repost Weibo and other social activities. Since 2012, Sina has also hosted an annual grand ceremony, *Weibo Night* (微博之夜), that awards popular figures and events that have appeared on the platform [68].

(4) From the perspective of technical implementation, Sina has undertaken a gradual and consistent process of platform refurbishment and improvement for Weibo. Sina's platform was the first Weibo service to initiate the notion of an API-open platform amongst all Chinese web portal providers. Further to this, on 16 November 2010, Sina hosted a *China Weibo Developer Conference* (中国首届微博开发者大会) [69] as a means of gathering talents from around the country. This helped to advocate innovative ideas and applications on the use of Weibo's open platform, and to help define future development trends and opportunities for the broader Weibo sector.

[27] Pinyin is the official romanisation system for Chinese phonation.

(5) Sina was devoted to the optimisation of its branding strategy for Weibo. Since the early creation of micro blogs in China around 2009, Sina registered several key trademarks including '微博' (meaning 'micro blogs'), '围脖' (meaning 'scarf', but phonetically equivalent to 'Weibo' in Chinese) [70] and eventually 'Weibo' in its Pinyin form as explained earlier. When '围脖' ('scarf') was established, it became a popular greeting amongst friends, with expressions such as *Did you knit a scarf today?*, metaphorically implying 'Did you weibo today?' [71]. In March 2014, Sina's name was removed from the Weibo logo, thus separating Weibo from Sina's general web portal services and getting ready for Weibo's independent stock listing.

Taken collectively, the various content and market strategies undertaken by Sina proved decisive in establishing Weibo's leading position in the Weibo market. Fig. 1.8 shows the national penetration rate of various micro blog service providers in China by 2012. On 17 April 2014, Sina's independently Weibo brand went live on the IPO stock listing [72]. In direct contrast to Sina's success, and as will be discussed later, Weibo services offered by rival web portals were in a state of gradual decline.

163 Weibo NetEase Weibo (also known as 163 Weibo) once recorded an impressive user base of 0.26 billion in 2012 [74]. Since then, however, NetEase barely disclosed any further data about their Weibo service. Just 2 years later, in 2014, following Tencent's disbanding of their Weibo department, NetEase also announced the closure of their Weibo service.

Sohu Weibo Sohu's CEO, Chaoyang Zhang (张朝阳), despite declaring a goal of outperforming Sina, has not published a Sohu Weibo entry since March 2014, whilst the platform did not achieve the desired level of success to mount any sustained or meaningful competition to Sina Weibo.

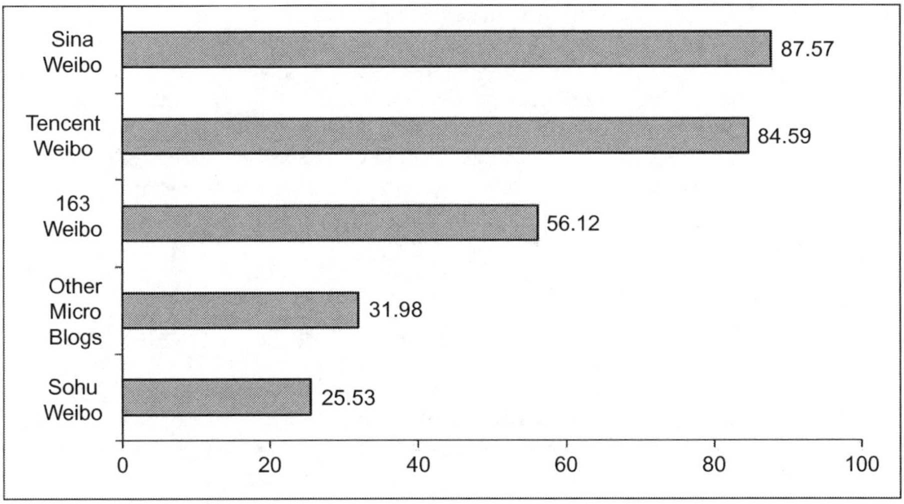

Fig. 1.8 Penetration rate of various micro blog services in China (2012) [73].

Box 1.3 Monthly active users (MAU)

MAU is an abbreviation for Monthly Active Users, which is a definition coined by Facebook in late 2008 [75]. MAU measures the number of unique users within a monthly period. Prior to this, the success of a web service was normally measured by the total number of subscribers, total active users or total simultaneous online users, as have been used in this chapter so far.

Tencent Weibo By 2010, QQ had amassed 0.9 billion registered users with over 0.3 million MAU (see Box 1.3 for the definition of MAU). Tencent's regular users were able to open a Tencent Weibo account with relative ease—a factor that ought to have served as a sound platform for competing with Weibo. In fact, Tencent Weibo was the only rival that could compete with Sina Weibo, as shown in Fig. 1.8. But despite the company's early ambition in the Weibo market, Tencent was gradually ousted by the competition and has thus reverted to its two main sibling products—QQ and WeChat. The initial ambitions, development and subsequent demise of Tencent Weibo are aptly reflected in Tencent's official statements in their annual financial reports [76]:

- Report 2011: *Tencent Weibo has experienced large-scale increase. We aim to be the largest Weibo service in China.*
- Report 2012: *As the slow pace of Chinese Weibo user growth, we are seeking an integral point for Tencent Weibo and WeChat, so as to manifest our characteristics.*
- Report 2013: No meaningful reference to Weibo could be found.

In July 2014—spanning a total period of just 4 years—Tencent adjusted their network marketing strategy and merged their in-house Weibo team with the web team, announcing the company's exit from the Weibo market. The failure of Tencent's Weibo competition with Sina can be summarised in a few aspects:

(1) The ongoing endeavour on renovating its flagship product QQ has led to the neglect of the micro blog market. Tencent Weibo was launched in April 2010, which was 8 months later than Sina Weibo (i.e. August 2009). In the phase of rapid market change and fierce battle amongst social networks in China, especially during the period of 2009–11 when social networks are subject to the impact of mobile technologies (as explained earlier in Section 1.2.4), the early entry to the market has added weight to Sina's competitiveness.

(2) The product design and user experience of Tencent Weibo had been reviewed as relatively poor compared to Sina Weibo [77].

(3) The massive user base of QQ did not necessarily bring impact on the micro blog field. As reported in Ref. [78], as there was a pop-up window in QQ reminding users to join Tencent Weibo, many QQ users consequently opened an account without even knowing what micro blog service stood for, especially for those aged user groups. Therefore, there have been a large portion of *zombi fans*[28] in Tencent Weibo. This

[28] Refers to those accounts that are opened but have never or rarely been active.

also explains why recent social network models tend to use MAU as a statistic to measure the success of user base, as described in Box 1.3.

(4) There is a high level of superposition of Tencent Weibo with its existing social network outlets such as Qzone. Existing users were quite often confused with the overlapping functionalities when they had signed up for Tencent's social network products. Furthermore, after a user published a micro blog in Tencent Weibo, the post would automatically appear in the Qzone space as well. The synchronous process has causing redundancy to users' communication.

(5) Tencent did not regard its micro blog service as a core product for the company, and has been deploying a defensive strategy to follow competitors in the market rather than leading [79]. Sina, on the other hand, has been largely devoted to innovate and promote its micro blog services as explained earlier.

1.3.1.3 Rise of WeChat

As briefly mentioned at the end of Section 1.2.4.2, QQ's drive to innovation came arose from the growing impact of mobile Internet and the growth in smartphone uptake. Even though Tencent had launched the Mobile QQ app in 2009, the migration from the traditional desktop environment to a more contemporary platform to fit the capabilities offered by smartphones could take time. Meanwhile, QQ and its competitors were facing substantial growth and changes in the IM market, that were caused by various innovative IM products, which essentially led to a new generation of IM as explained in Box 1.4. Beyond QQ, several other notable national and international IM platforms were in existence during the period between late 2010 and early 2011, as listed in Table 1.8.

Box 1.4 Mobile IM: New generation of IM

As a new generation of IM service, Mobile IM has revolutionised the concept of IM in the mobile Internet age, delivering a seamless and expressive communication experience, whilst enhancing the social features of traditional IM software. Beyond the core components such as text and picture messaging that featured in traditional IM software, mobile IM incorporates the following key innovations that were created over a series of iterations within various platforms.

- *Cross-Platform Support*: This feature allows users to link their profiles and interact regardless of the proprietary hardware and built-in operating systems within their smartphones. Although several traditional IM services, such as ICQ, MSN Messenger and QQ, had already provided cross-platform support, the feature became increasingly important in the new IM era where pervasive services and connectivity were of utmost importance. The crucial role of cross-platform support also excluded device- or brand-specific services such as Apple's iChat (later changed to iMessenger) as notably restricted in comparison.
- *Auto Index of Phone Book*: This allows a user's phone contacts to be automatically detected and seamlessly used to establish connections within the IM app. The feature was initially devised by Kik Messenger in October 2010, and was one of the main

(*Continued*)

Box 1.4 Mobile IM: New generation of IM—cont'd

reasons for the platform's rapid growth in popularity, registering one million users within 15 days of its launch [80].

- *Voice Messaging*: This feature provides an additional element of convenience by allowing users to record and send voice messages as opposed to the more traditional approach of text input via a virtual keyboard. Voice messaging was invented by TalkBox in January 2011, which quickly attracted one million users shortly after its launch [81]. The significance of this feature is exemplified by the previously cumbersome steps required to record and send voice messages. For example, in earlier versions of WhatsApp prior to TalkBox's implementation, sending an audio message involved a minimum of six main steps: Menu → Record → Finish → Compress → Send → Upload [82]. As a result of TalkBox's innovation, most if not all modern IMs can record and send voice messages within a single step.

Table 1.8 **QQ's competitors in the IM field (late 2010 to early 2011)**

IM app	First release	Achievements
Skype	2003	Acquired by Microsoft in May 2011
Fetion	May 2007	
WhatsApp	Feb. 2009	
Kik Messenger	19 Oct. 2010	One million users within 15 days of release
Miliao	10 Dec. 2010	
TalkBox	18 Jan. 2011	One million users within 1 month of release

Being highly sensitive to market changes, Tencent anticipated the turbulence of the IM market in this period of evolving and marked mobile development. Rather resting on its laurels and rely on its successful and proven QQ platform, Tencent focused on the need to revolutionise in the midst of emerging technology by stimulating internal competition, thus paving the way for the creation of WeChat in 2011. Tencent's founder and CEO, Huateng Ma (马化腾), explained several key reasons for creating a separate WeChat platform whilst retaining Mobile QQ, instead of modifying Mobile QQ into the current WeChat form:

(1) First, further innovation of Mobile QQ was difficult due to the internal organisation of Tencent. On this, Ma said: *Any product fault could be caused by internal organisations.* Mobile QQ, Desktop QQ and QQ Space (a.k.a. Qzone) are three independent departments within Tencent, who work collectively as peers rather than in a hierarchical structure. Consequently, it would be challenging for one department to obtain the support and coordination from neighbouring departments for new ideas and developments. Although Tencent subsequently made changes to its organisational structure to address such an issue, it proved significant in preventing notable advancements within existing platforms as in the case of QQ.

(2) Second, Ma was a firm advocate of driving internal competition within Tencent. This, he felt, would be a more effective way of creating a sustainable approach to dealing with fierce competition rather than rely on progressive updates and improvements to an existing platform. Thus, instead of reacting to external pressures, the company's strategy was to create revolution from the inside.

(3) Third, QQ's success had led to the establishment of stereotypical impressions of the platform amongst users. This was partly brought about by popularity of QQ's add-on products such as membership privileges, mailbox and games, of which eventually overshadowed the impact of the platform's core IM service. Due to the inherent hardware limitations of mobile platforms, the composition of the QQ mobile app could not rival the sophistication and range of functionalities that are presented in the desktop version. Thus the initial versions of Mobile QQ received numerous negative reviews on aspects of poor usability, as users' expectations on Mobile QQ app were still based on their previous experiences with Desktop QQ. This backdrop cemented Tencent's decision to develop an entirely new product from scratch, and that would accurately fit the needs and expectations of a specific sector of the market.

WeChat was thus created and released on January 2011, with an all-new feature set designed and customised for the then new generation of IM software for smartphones. A summary of its core features is listed in Box 1.4. WeChat 1.0 was released on 21 January 2011. As compliant with Tencent's strategy outlined earlier, this initial version of WeChat abandoned the majority of supporting functions that were present in QQ, allowing for basic functions such as importing QQ contacts and text messaging. This approach rendered a clean and simplistic appearance, as shown in Fig. 1.9. WeChat 1.0 was designed as an elementary IM software that could only import QQ contacts and allow for basic messaging via texts, which did not create much impact on the market.

Subsequent updates in the form of versions 1.2, 1.3 and 1.4 gradually adopted new features such as auto-index (see Box 1.4) and more sophisticated text inputs, allowing the platform to expand its user base to four million [80]. WeChat 2.0 expanded services again by implementing voice messaging, from where the platform's popularity experienced sharp increases. Following the release of WeChat 2.5 in August 2011, the number of users increased to 15 million which, by the end of the year, increased more than threefold to a staggering 50 million users [80]. Fig. 1.9 shows the momentous growth of WeChat in relation to the various key releases within the first year of its initial launch (a more detailed consideration of the leading role of WeChat in the IM and social network sectors in China is provided in Chapter 2). During this period of sustained and tremendous growth, previously notable rivals to WeChat (as listed in Table 1.8) were also gradually eliminated from competition. Some key cases are discussed next.

- Fetion and Skype: The Case of Previous Generation IMs

The contemporary IM market space consists of dominant platforms such as WeChat, WhatsApp, QQ and Facebook Messenger (this having become an independent IM app since 2014 [83]), who have all gradually embraced services consistent with the new feature-set as outlined in Box 1.4. By contrast, two platforms that represent previous generation IM in terms of features and functionality are that of Fetion and Skype. Apart from providing cross-platform support, both are distinct in terms of their comparative

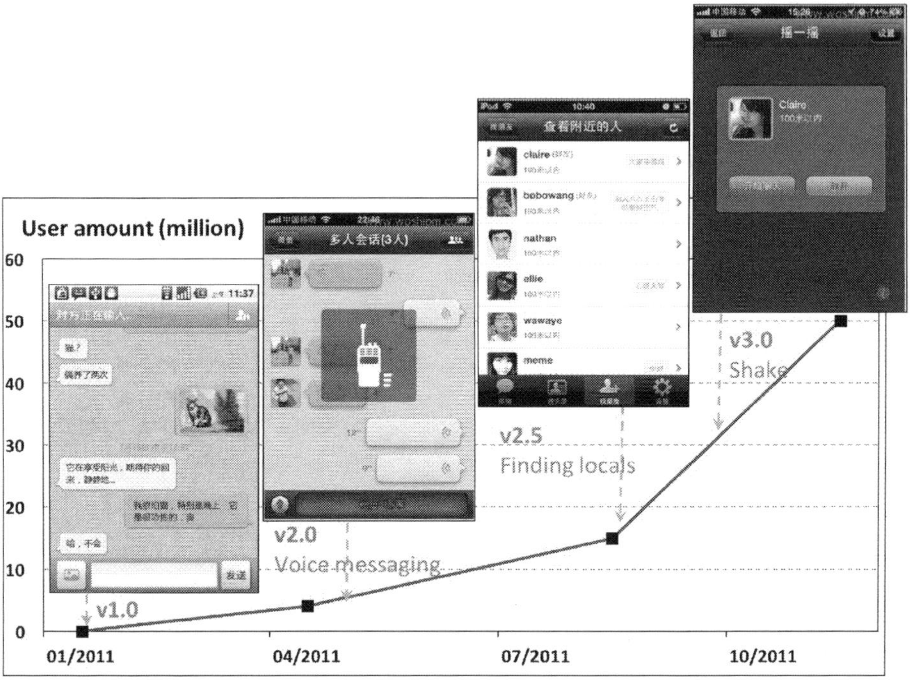

Fig. 1.9 WeChat's early versions and growth in 2011.

lack of features, which in the perspective of this analysis, serve as interesting examples of established platforms that are likely heading towards either eventual elimination or an alternative user base.

Fetion was released in May 2007, during the era of 2G mobile communications. As briefly mentioned at the end of Section 1.2.4.2, Fetion catered to users by providing a low-cost alternative to traditional mobile texting by linking PCs to mobile phones. By August 2008, Fetion had secured over 100 million subscribers, thus imposing a direct threat to the then IM leader, QQ, which had a total of 300 million registered users at the time [84]. However, Fetion's market performance started to decline due to internal company issues, not least by being owned by China Mobile, a state-owned company that is heavily influenced by bureaucratic and political matters that deeply affected Fetion's pace of innovation and change [85]. By August 2011, Fetion's total subscribers had dropped progressively to 80 million as announced by China Mobile [86], whilst in the same period QQ still led the market with 140 million simultaneous online users and the fledging WeChat began to carve its position by attracting 15 million users after just 7 months after launch. Since 2012, no user statistics for Fetion have been published, whilst China Mobile expressed the possibility of abandoning Fetion entirely in 2015 [87]. This was followed by a subsequent announcement that China Mobile's intention of revising Fetion at the end of 2016 [88]. Whatever the case may be, Fetion is a prime example of how a platform can quickly descend into obscurity and great uncertainty despite having established solid foundations in user base and delivered technological innovation to market.

Skype was founded in 2003 and rapidly gained user base and popularity for its Voice-over-IP (VoIP) service [89], leading to an average of 124 million connected users per month in the second quarter of 2010 [90]. Shortly after, in May 2011, Skype was acquired by Microsoft and later used as the substitute for the disbanding MSN Messenger service. In the western markets where Skype, WhatsApp and Facebook Messengers are popularly used, Skype is the only IM app that allows for real-time video and voice calls. Despite holding a leading role in the delivery of VoIP services, Skype is facing increased competition from progressive developments in the Chinese market. This is witnessed by the fact that both QQ and WeChat have implemented real-time video and voice calls (more details on these functions will be considered in Section 2.3.6.2), and thus represent plausible alternatives to Skype's previously unchallenged position in the VoIP market. Skype is also disadvantaged as a potentially broader application by its relative lack of social networking functions.

- The rapid rise and fall of Kik Messenger and TalkBox

Early IM apps that pioneered features that would become a cornerstone of modern IM services were gradually phased out of the market in the advent of new technology and new platforms. Kik Messenger was created in October 2010, offering innovative features such as cross-platform support and auto-indexing. It attracted one million users within 15 days of its launch. Despite this early success, Kik Messenger was removed from the app store just 1 month after its release due to controversial issues [91].

Another example of a pioneering platform is TalkBox in the form of the voice messaging function within IM. TalkBox was launched 3 days before WeChat 1.0 and had acquired one million users within a month of release. TalkBox's brisk success led to imitations of its voice message function by various Internet companies, two of which were Tencent [81] and Miliao [92]. TalkBox's innovations and popularity also attracted the interest of investors—before the birth of WeChat 2.0, Tencent made an offer to acquire TalkBox, of which was turned down [81]. Nevertheless as in the case of numerous other companies of the time, TalkBox failed to capitalise on its early success due to a relatively inexperienced team and poor marketing strategy, which led to its demise after just a year after its initial emergence.

- A short battle from Miliao

Another notable rival that existed prior to WeChat was Miliao (米聊),[29] as also listed in Table 1.8. Miliao holds particular historical significance as it was the first mobile IM app developed by Chinese developers in Mainland China. Miliao reached its peak period of popularity after adopting the voice message function in May 2011, culminating in a user base of three million [93]. However, despite what ought to have represented a significant challenge to WeChat, Miliao failed to secure a sustained

[29] www.miliao.com.

and leading role in the IM and social network arena. Miliao's parent company, Mi,[30] currently focuses on producing low-cost mobile phones in which Miliao is provided as built-in software. Reflecting on Miliao's disappointing performance, Mi's CEO stated three underlying reasons for the platform's failure [93]:

(1) *Poor product orientation and strategy*. Since its creation, Miliao never fully acquired a clear identity and position within the IM market. By contrast, Tencent was clear at the outset with what it expected from WeChat in terms of service and strategy (as explained earlier in this section). Whilst Miliao wrestled with decisions on whether to focus on providing an acquaintance community or promoting links between unknown users, WeChat was already firmly on the path of capturing a firm user base via niche features such as finding locals, shake and drift bottles. The issue of poor strategy and indecision mean that the market had already been permanently lost to WeChat by the time Miliao attempted to recover its lost ground.
(2) *Inadequacies in technology development and support*. Several technological challenges were imposed on Miliao's youthful development team, who could not acclimatise to the platform's rapid expansion in user base. The drastic increase in the number of users at the time of initial release was not matched by improvements to server infrastructures and service support, whilst subsequent software iterations suffered from a lack of testing. All this amounted to a flawed development process and poor user experience, thus further eroding Miliao's potential for expansion.
(3) *Weak promotion*. As one of the leading Internet companies in China, Tencent has regularly attracted significant Internet traffic to its core website that could be served as a key channel for promoting WeChat. Coupled with its strong financial position and experience in publicity, Tencent has created strong awareness and interest for its platform in a way that Miliao simply could not compete.

- WeChat vs. WhatsApp

WhatsApp was founded in 2009 and originally devised as previous generation IM app for smartphones. Later iterations gradually adopted innovative features for addressing the emerging mobile IM market, from where it subsequently attracted the attention of and later acquired by Facebook in 2014. Despite the persistent ban of its parent network, Facebook, WhatsApp is officially available for use in China. WhatsApp has experienced steady growth since its launch, rising to the status of the World's second most popular social network behind Facebook with one billion MAUs worldwide [94]. Despite its global success, WhatsApp has failed to dominate in the Chinese market for three main reasons:

(1) Even though WhatsApp was released two-and-half-years before WeChat, it was originally set at a price point of $0.99 in app stores, which significantly limited its expansion scope in China. By the time WhatsApp converted to free-to-use status in June 2011 [95], the Chinese IM market was already firmly occupied by new-generation IM rivals such as WeChat and Miliao. Therefore, WhatsApp's first-to-market status did not ultimately serve as a notable advantage in China.
(2) In terms of evolution, WhatsApp was comparably slow to react to new developments by competing platforms and changes in user demand. For example, WeChat initiated direct

[30] Mi, *small rice* (小米) in Chinese, stands for mobile Internet (www.mi.com).

input (i.e. a single button command) for recording and sending voice messages in April 2012 [96], yet the feature did not appear on WhatsApp until over 1-year later [97].

(3) WhatsApp's simplistic design remains focused on core IM functions whilst WeChat, despite possessing similar features during its initial release, has evolved into an expanded ecosphere for a vast range of services such as finding locals, WeChat Pay and taxi ordering. IM apps that are similar to WhatsApp in terms of simplicity and comparable functionalities have since been eliminated in the Chinese market due to the lack of expansion and innovative features. Thus, WhatsApp's poor performance in China is due in large part to its inability to provide distinct and improved elements relative to its competitors in the region.

Thus, with the demise of its key rivals (as listed in Table 1.8) for one reason or another, WeChat was able to solidify and further strengthen its leading role in the IM and social networking sector (more detailed explanations about WeChat's subsequent ventures are provided in Chapter 2).

1.3.2 Three current social network giants

Following from the developmental phase of the social networking market in China, the sector has moved into a period of relative stability with three dominant platforms: WeChat, QQ and Weibo. China's 4G licenses were issued in December 2013 [98], and since then the mobile Internet has entered a new phase of development in the Chinese territory. Weibo was created in the context of 3G mobile Internet in China; as the mobile technology kept advancing WeChat emerged to compete with Weibo; in the meantime, QQ has been continuously innovating itself to sustain its market value. The three platforms are the current social network giants in China. This section aims to provide a brief outline of the overall structure of the social networking market in China, with particular focus on the leading players and notable characteristics of service provision.

A report produced by Kantar [66] revealed that by early 2016, WeChat's user base is keeping growing although the acceleration speed is showing down, and other social networks and media is keeping dropping although the declining rate is slowing down as well. As can be seen in Fig. 1.10, despite the presence of new and established competitors such as Friends, Douban, Momo and LinkedIn, their market occupancy lag far behind the leading platforms. With social networks flourishing in the Chinese territory such that by 2016, China is third in the world in terms of the penetration ratio (being 56%) of social networks and social media, behind the United States (62%) and Brazil (58%) [66].

The growth of social networks in China has also impacted the country's broader Internet ecosphere. As a way of reacting to innovations led by social network providers, many websites have made the process of new-user registration optional (this being vital to appeal to social network users who may otherwise not spend the time to register an entirely new account), and offered additional options for logging-on via third-party accounts (such as a user's social network profile). These features promote the ease of registration and enhance the potential appeal of a new service provider to the vast quantity of users from social network platforms. Several examples of this in practise are shown in Fig. 1.11, spanning a shopping website to an online library service. These services are all independent from social networking platforms, yet they can all be

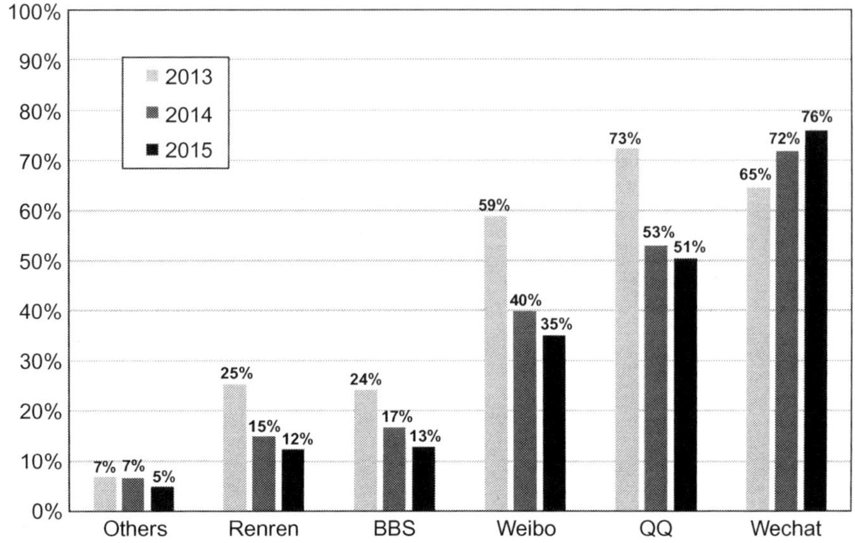

Fig. 1.10 The most used social networks in China by early 2016 [66].

accessed via a user's preexisting social network account. Thus, the present operation of Internet services in China is dominated by associations with BAT (Box 1.5).

Box 1.5 BAT: Three Chinese internet giants

BAT is the abbreviation for the three leading Internet companies in China: Baidu, Alibaba and Tencent [99].

- *Baidu* is China's most popular search engine and invests in a wide range of innovative developments in the sector. Baidu's dominance can be attributed in large part to Google's ban in China since 2010.
- *Alibaba* owns China's biggest e-commerce website, Taobao (an equivalent of eBay) and several other sibling products. In April 2016, Alibaba was announced as the world's largest retail business platform [100].
- *Tencent* is a provider of multifaceted services across social networking, games and the media industries.

The prosperity of Chinese social networks in the recent development history might have posed two major and related implications: the first being that users are faced with excessive choice in terms of the vast number of services and platforms and, second, the market is not sufficiently refined such that services or platforms serve distinct roles for users. The former issue can be a direct cause for the latter, whilst greater market refinement through the process of elimination in the normal course of competition can help to resolve issues of excessive choice. Having undergone a process of emergence,

Fig. 1.11 Many websites allow for login with third-party accounts (mostly social networks). (A) An online shopping website. (B) A web portal. (C) An online library. (D) A media and video website.

development, competition and elimination, today's Chinese social network arena can be considered as being of a mature state comprising of clear divisions amongst key players. On a broader scale, as shown in Fig. 1.12, the global social network market is dominated by essentially one company—Facebook—which comprises the main platform along with WhatsApp, Facebook Messenger and Instagram. By contrast, the Chinese market can be considered as a more competitively driven environment, consisting of an oligopoly of at least three notable players: QQ, WeChat and Weibo.

The notion of multisocial networking (whereby users possess any number of accounts spanning numerous platforms) is flourishing across the world as revealed by GWI Insight [101], where the average Internet user possesses the equivalent of 5.5

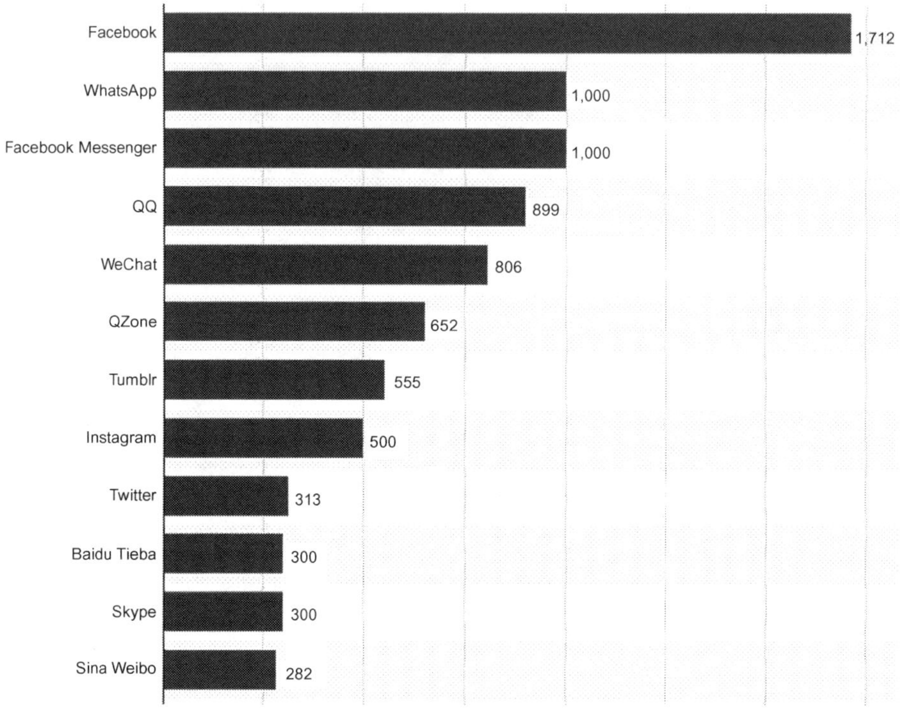

Fig. 1.12 Global social network/media ranking based on MAU (2016) [94].

user accounts and are active across at least three platforms as of early 2015. With the increasing provisioning of social network software, it has become increasingly vital for each platform to consolidate their user base via distinctive features and services in the midst of greater choice. Whilst there may be overlapping amongst the leading social network platforms in terms of functionalities and user base, each platform should play a different role in users' social network lives, which is the case in the current mature status of China.

Research by CNNIC [102] sheds further light on the nature of users by outlining some core reasons for the use of particular platforms despite their apparent overlap. The results from this study revealed that WeChat is commonly used for communicating with acquaintances, Weibo for the acquisition of news and information, whilst QQ (as a longstanding platform) for its broad assortment of contacts. Each social network amplifies a specific facet of user's characters and personalities, as they are being used in different ways. Nevertheless, these findings remain far from being definitive classifications or the reasons for the use of alternative yet similar platforms, as they each offer their own mix and style of service provision and thus cater to the specific needs of an individual at any particular moment. The following three chapters are dedicated to an individual examination of each of the leading platforms in China so as to shed light on their distinctive characteristics and reasons for success.

WeChat

2

2.1 The miraculous growth

Devised by Tencent, WeChat is the sibling product of QQ. WeChat is available as a free-to-download app on Android, iPhone, BlackBerry, Windows Phone and Symbian devices, whilst nonmobile, web-based OS X and Windows versions also exist. Similar to other IM and social network applications currently available in the market, WeChat offers an expansive range of services including text messaging, hold-to-talk voice messaging, broadcast messaging, video conferencing, games, photograph and video sharing and location sharing. A user's personal contacts can be shared with nearby users via Bluetooth, whilst additional social features allow users to be contacted by strangers should they wish (such as in the case of new acquaintances who have not established friend status on the platform).

Beyond basic forms of communication, WeChat allows users to post images and text, share music and news articles as well as submit comments and register 'likes' in a dedicated page, namely *Moments*, serving as an additional personal space within its social community. User privacy is an extremely important component in WeChat. All users must have mutual friend status in order for them to see each other's contributions. The platform's Official Account is a distinctive feature that enables additional features such as enabling push feeds to subscribers (i.e. followers), interacting with subscribers, and providing users with e-commerce services (this latter element will be considered in more detail in Section 2.4). WeChat also supports an integrated payment and money transfer system, allowing peer-to-peer money transfer and electronic bill payment.

Since its launch in 2011, WeChat has become the synonym of mobile Internet for many Chinese users [103], as a culmination of the platform's miraculous growth over the past few years (see Table 2.1). Based on the latest report on mobile statistics by the Chinese Government [104], the total number of mobile phone users in China reached 0.66 billion in June 2016. Tencent's official impact report indicates a total of 0.69 billion WeChat users in February 2016 (an increase of 39% from 2015), amongst which 0.65 billion are active users every month [105]. From these figures it can be seen that the ratio of total mobile phone users versus the number of WeChat app users is approximately 1:1, with the number of WeChat users exceeding the number of phone users. This statistic reveals two likely patterns of usage: that every mobile phone user in China is an active user of WeChat, or greater still, some mobile phone users are

Social Networks in China. https://doi.org/10.1016/B978-0-08-101934-4.00002-9

Table 2.1 **WeChat development history**

2011	WeChat launched	0.05 billion users
2012	Moment and Official Account launched	0.19 billion users
2013	WeChat pay launched	0.40 billion users
2014	WeChat enterprise account and city services launched	0.50 billion users
2015	First trial of adverts in Moments	0.65 billion users

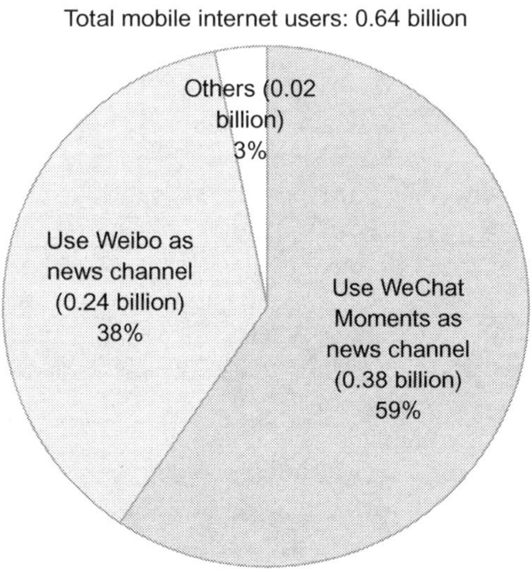

Fig. 2.1 WeChat as a major news distribution channel in China (2016).

actively using multiple WeChat accounts. Either way, this points towards a very high national penetration of WeChat usage in China.

As shown in Fig. 2.1, WeChat has also become a leading channel for news distribution in China. Out of the 1.3 billion Chinese population, approximately 0.64 billion are mobile Internet users as of June 2016 based on the Chinese Government's National Internet Usage report [104]. According to Tencent's official statistics, 58% of WeChat users frequently browse and publish in Moments. With 0.65 billion active users each month, this equates to over 0.38 billion users who are in regular use of WeChat as a channel for information acquisition and sharing. Comparatively, WeChat's main rival in China, Weibo, has an active monthly user base of 0.24 billion [106]. Taken collectively, WeChat and Weibo hold a substantial portion of the amount of time spent online by Chinese users.

As a leading Internet company in China (see Box 1.5), Tencent has placed WeChat at the core of its future development. The platform has implemented numerous additional features following the success of the core WeChat platform, with games representing a key avenue of expansion and source of profit. Other notable features include online videos, taxi on demand (a comparable service to Uber) and take-away food ordering. In its present guise, WeChat can be considered as Tencent's base platform that allows users to acquire a broad range of built-in services which, in turn, has strengthened the integration of WeChat into the day-to-day lives of Chinese users. This can be illustrated by WeChat's usage statistics [105], revealing 94% of WeChat users log onto the platform everyday, whilst 61% open the platform more than 10 times a day (this being an indicator of repeat visits for checking updates and accessing built-in features). The statistics also show 36% can be considered as 'heavy users', that is those who open WeChat more than 30 times a day. Over half (55%) use it for more than a total of 1 hour per day, whilst 32% use it for more than 2 hours a day. Thus, both frequency and duration statistics of WeChat reflect the persistent and sustained use and appeal of the platform.

WeChat offers users a continuation of the social space that originated from traditional networks such as QQ Space, Renren and Kaixin (as introduced in Sections 1.2.2.2 and 1.2.3). Some users have also compared the role of WeChat to Minecraft[1]—a game of autonomy where players can freely determine and act upon their creative expressions. WeChat holds a similar philosophy in that friends determine the attractiveness of a friend circle in the form of its Moments feature. As a reflection of personal life, WeChat provides different forms of friend circles amongst users, thereby changing the nature of the social pattern between strangers. For example, instead of spamming users with flood of advertisements, WeChat users can choose what kinds of ads they wish to receive by subscribing to the Official Accounts of the promoting companies (this will be explained in Section 2.4). Tencent exerted careful control of spam messages and adverts in WeChat. Commercial advertising was introduced to Moments 4 years after WeChat's launch, which resulted from a careful decision following a long-term consideration. Detailed aspects of spam control are provided in Section 2.3.5.3.

2.2 Substitution for traditional mobile telecom services

WeChat, as a successful example of a new-generation IM and mobile app, implemented several key innovative features that have impacted on a range of traditional mobile telecom services including short message service (SMS), multimedia messaging service (MMS) and even mobile telephone calls. This section will briefly introduce WeChat's IM functionalities and how they contributed to WeChat's continued success.

In terms of its core functions, WeChat's communication service is centred on its messaging service that includes text, voice, emoji, pictures, videos and geographical information. The notification system of WeChat messages operates in real-time, unless otherwise configured by the user. The instant messaging service in WeChat is therefore largely similar to that of existing mobile SMS, with the exception that it offers a broader range of transmittable content. As an indication of the extent to which Chinese users consider WeChat as a genuine alternative to SMS, a survey conducted by university graduates discovered that 88% of users have used WeChat as a direct substitute for mobile phone calls and SMS [103]. Additional studies [107, 108] by

[1] minecraft.net.

academics and industry experts also predict that WeChat could ultimately become the biggest rival or permanent replacement to SMS. WeChat's growing status and threat to traditional mobile phone services can be attributable to four main reasons, as outlined next.

The first major factor in fuelling the uptake and prominence of alternatives to traditional SMS is the widespread adoption of smartphones and penetration rate of 3G and 4G networks in China. Official statistics from Chinese Government [104, 109] reveal the uptake of mobile phone users reached 94.1% across the country in early 2016. This represents 660 million mobile broadband subscribers of which 162 million are also 4G subscribers. This data indicated that approximately half the Chinese population have access to broadband via their phones, whilst over 10% of the population are connected via 4G. Table 2.2 outlined the key statistics mentioned earlier based on a Chinese population of 1.36 billion as at the beginning of 2016. The penetration rates for both smartphone adoption and data access therefore serve as a key foundation and necessary condition for the pervasiveness of platforms such as WeChat.

The second reason is that, as also characteristic of its competitors, WeChat is free-to-download and -use in WiFi environments. Even in the absence of WiFi, the cost of sending text and pictures is markedly lower than using SMS or MMS via traditional phone networks, therefore serving as a real price advantage for users. In China the average length of SMS sent via mobile phones is 70 characters [110], which equates to 140 bytes. Taking China mobile as a comparative example (being the largest telecom carrier in China), the cost of sending an SMS is set at a fixed price of 0.10 Chinese Yuan (or 1 Jiao, the equivalent of approximately 0.015 dollars) [111]. Although the charge for mobile data can vary depending on subscription packages and carrier promotions, the cost of data usually falls into the range of 0.000000002–0.000016 Yuan per byte. The cost of sending the same 70-character text message via WeChat using a provider's mobile data service will cost between 0.00000028 and 0.00224 Yuan (thus, beyond being a negligible amount, is also considerably less than the price of sending a standard SMS). Similarly, using the same calculation, it costs 0.90 Yuan to send a picture of 50 KB (the maximum size allowed) via MMS, and only 0.0001–0.8 Yuan to send via WeChat using a mobile data service. In addition to the marked price difference between sending SMS and WeChat messages, WeChat also has the advantage of allowing users to send notably larger images of up to 20 MB for each MMS.

Third, as compared to SMS, the nature of WeChat facilitates a much larger scope for information propagation, and thus represents a key reason for its choice as

Table 2.2 Summary statistics of China mobile phone users as at the beginning of 2016

Category	Quantity	National penetration (%)
Mobile phone users	1.28 billion	94.1
Mobile Internet users	660 million	48.5
Mobile 4G users	162 million	11.9
WeChat users (active)	650 million	47.8

a distribution platform by numerous organisations. Broadcasting messages through the traditional SMS platform require the knowledge of target users' mobile phone numbers, and thus act as a natural limit in terms of the number of people that the message can be delivered to, not to mention the inherent difficulty of obtaining the unknown numbers of persons who may be relevant to a particular message, but with whom a user is unacquainted. WeChat, on the other hand, provides an Official Account feature to allow the broadcasting of information (further details discussed in Section 2.4). The feature operates under strict controls for spam, information quality and frequency as a way of safeguarding potential concerns that users may have about receiving unwanted information. Furthermore, redelivering an SMS will incur an additional cost that will restrict the possibility of information repropagation—a problem that does not exist in WeChat as users in WeChat are more likely to promote and repost messages based on interest or word of mouth. For organisations, therefore, this technique of information propagation represents a more effective and economical way of boosting awareness and exposure.

Last but not least, the interactivity permitted in WeChat also acts as an appealing feature in comparison to a conventional SMS format. Although both SMS and WeChat serve similar purposes with respect to point-to-point communication between users, the text provision of SMS is distinctly simplistic compared to the rich formats available through contemporary social network platforms. WeChat offers a broad range of content that can be sent in an instant via the chat window, including photographs from gallery, capture and send new photos via camera, Sight (take and send a 15-second live video), video and voice call, Red Packet (the Chinese custom of sending a monetary gift to friends and family), contact details, current location, favourites and coupons.

2.3 Design highlights

2.3.1 Minimalism design

Western perspectives on WeChat tend to regard it as a combination of Facebook and WhatsApp [112, 113]. Whilst this may be true to an extent, a comparison of the menu structures of these three platforms (as shown in Figs 2.2–2.4) reveals that WeChat's design structure, and indeed philosophy, is evidently different from that of Facebook and WhatsApp.

The design philosophy present within WeChat can be attributed in no small measure to Xiaolong Zhang (张小龙), the creator of WeChat and Vice President of Tencent, who is a strong advocator of a minimalism aesthetic (see definition in Box 2.1). Examples of how minimalism has been applied in the design of WeChat are explained next.

- Despite being equipped with wide-ranging features, WeChat's most important features are always displayed in the most noticeable positions on the screen. For instance, being an influential add-on product of social network platforms and Tencent's endeavours on this aspect of the platform (to be explained in Section 5.1), games can be accessed from the main Discover page within WeChat, as shown in Fig. 2.2. By contrast, the mobile game feature

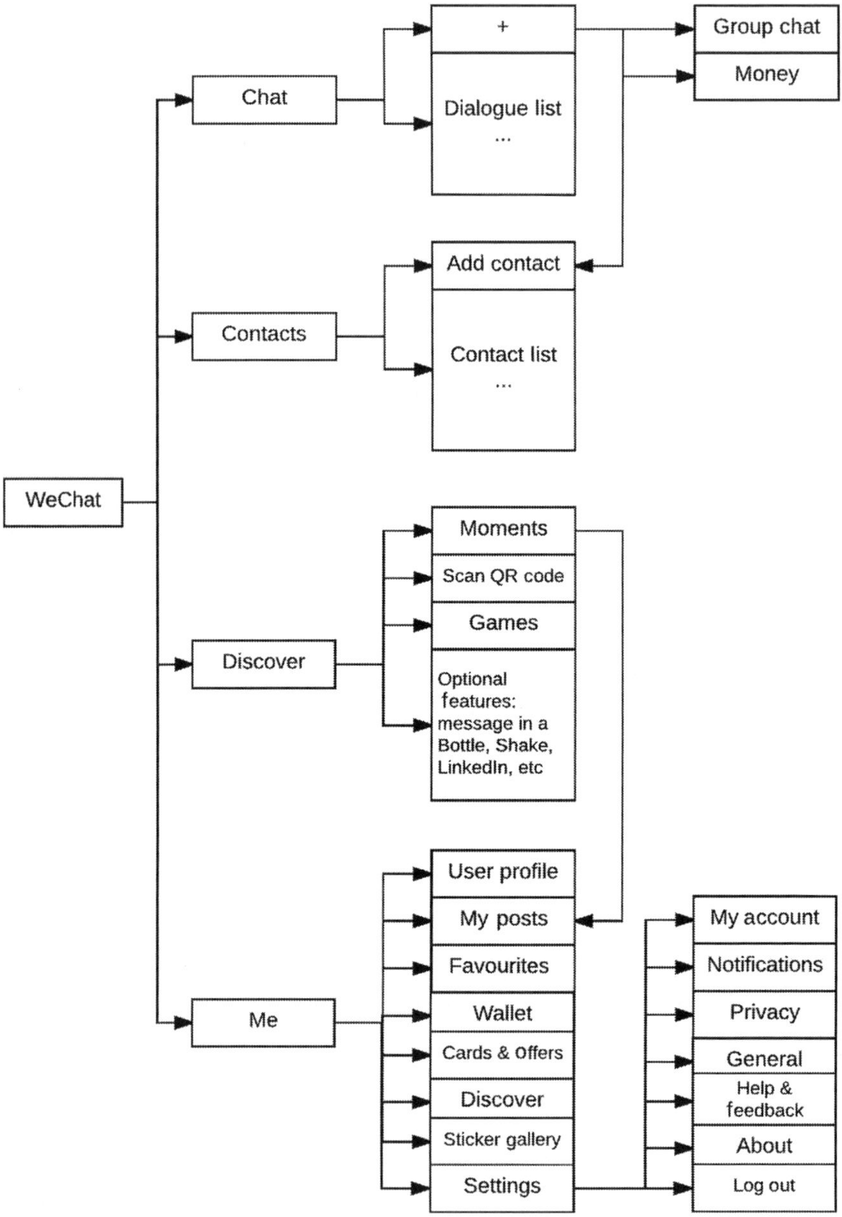

Fig. 2.2 Interface structure of WeChat user interface (as in 2016).

does not exist in WhatsApp, whilst it can be difficult to locate in the equivalent Facebook app where to do so, users need to go through several step which may not inherently be obvious: *More* → *See More...* → *Apps* → *Games*. Another example is the direct entry to the Scan QR Code function in the main page, as shown in Fig. 2.2—a frequently used feature that

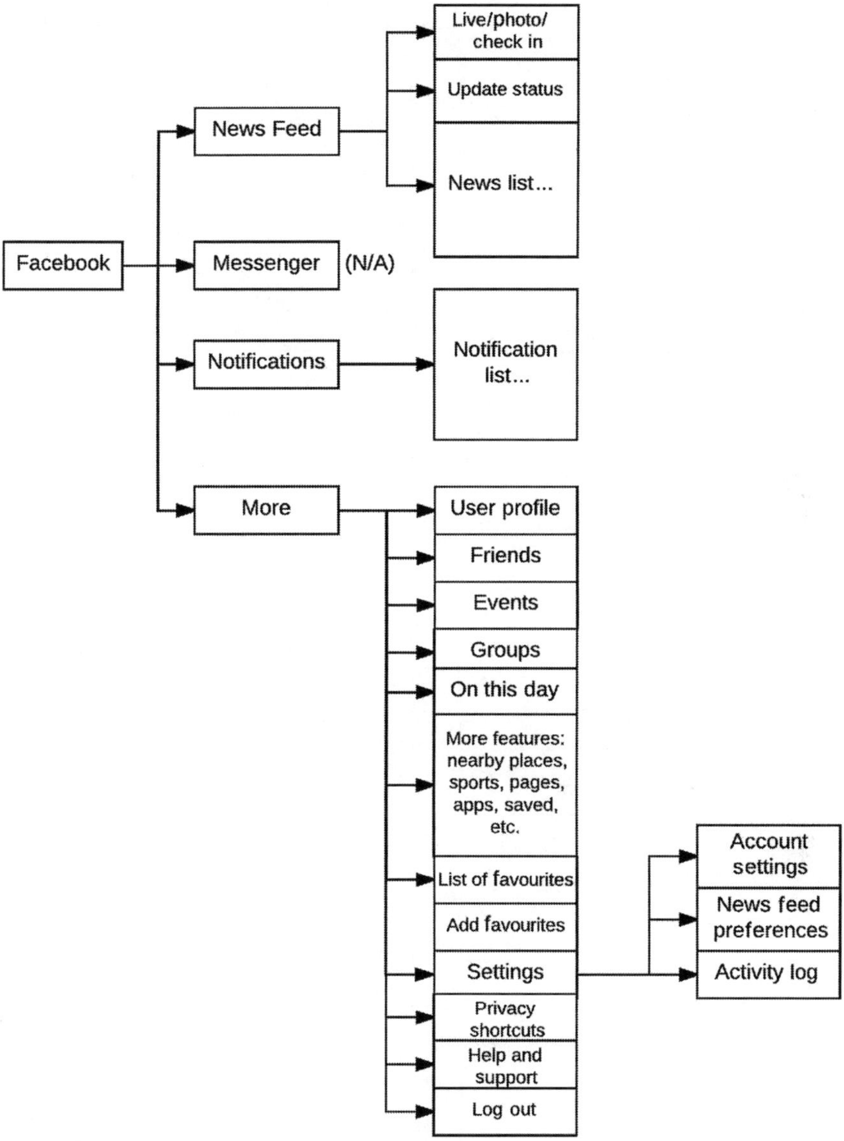

Fig. 2.3 Interface structure of Facebook Mobile App user interface (as in 2016).

saves users from having to carry out functions via manual typing (to be further explained in Section 2.3.4).

- The minimalism design theory is also applied to Moments, a fundamental component of WeChat where users share content and post personal updates. Article [117] claims that WeChat encourages the publication of photographs over texts for the reasons of user

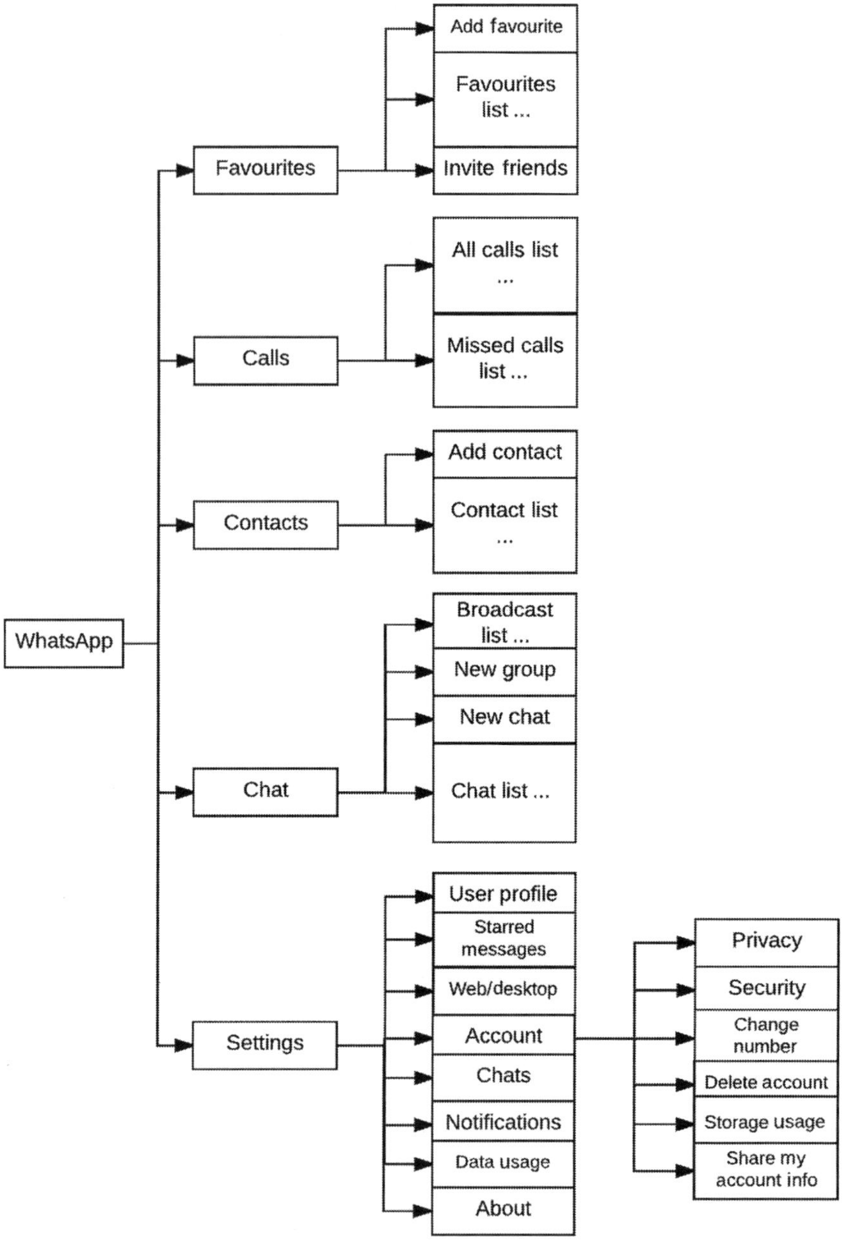

Fig. 2.4 Interface structure of WhatsApp user interface (as in 2016).

experience analysis—photographs can be easier to publish than text in the context of mobile devices. Therefore, the button to publish pure text in WeChat is notably absent from the main interface—an aspect to be discussed further in Section 2.3.5.1.

Box 2.1 Minimalism aesthetic

Minimalism first appeared in the art and culture field representing an art faction since the emergence in the 1960s [114], which has four main characteristics as described following.

(1) Departures from the nature of the object (or product).
(2) Reduces excessive expression in formalities and subjective awareness of authors.
(3) Leaves open space for the concept of art, and invites observers to participate in its construction.
(4) Contains a certain level of extremism.

A typical example of such practise in the digital age is Steve Jobs who fuelled a design revolution of Apple products with an aesthetic of minimalism [115, 116].

- Zhang also designed *Moments* as a 'clean' and clutter-free territory, free from unwanted spam and adverts. This decision, however, did not come unchallenged. Article [117] reported various groups within Tencent who were keen to incorporate commercial promotions in WeChat to generate profit, although Zhao persisted with the minimalist approach. More details on minimalism design in Moments will be presented in Section 2.3.5.3.

The minimalist approach is also reflected somewhat in the company's promotional strategy for WeChat. Indeed, the platform's rapid growth in China is believed not to be a result of Tencent's own advertising, but a consequence of the word of mouth from users [117]. As such, Zhang is firmly of the view that users are the best channel for dissemination in the mobile era, where high-quality products will lead to more satisfied users, who in turn act as the drivers of dissemination.

2.3.2 Digital ID: QR code

Each WeChat user has a personal QR code that serves as a digital ID. Whilst a username and password system is essential for establishing an account in numerous social networking platforms, this is not required in WeChat. A user's unique QR code exists regardless of whether a WeChat ID has been established. A preexisting QR code is already present in the user's host machine even in the absence of any WeChat ID. Scanning the QR code via WeChat's in-built QR facility will allow the user to connect instantly to each other, as opposed to having to navigate a text- or search-based system as is commonly the case on other platforms.

The ease of use provided by the QR facility is further encapsulated in the Official Accounts feature of the app (to be discussed in more detail in Section 2.4), allowing the QR ID to be used by business users as an avenue for promotion and publicity. Scanning the QR code of an Official Account will lead the user to the associated commercial page. Fig. 2.5 shows several examples including a job fair, shopping mall, wedding-hosting business, supermarket and cinema. The WeChat QR code feature has provided companies with the opportunity to access the platform's substantial user base as well

Fig. 2.5 Business promotion using WeChat QR code.

as the ability to direct specific forms of advertising and promotion. This, in turn, has triggered a growing wave of such forms of social marketing in China [118].

2.3.3 *Linking contacts*

There are several ways for users to add new contacts in WeChat. Table 2.3 compares the options for adding friends in WeChat with two of its most direct competitors, Facebook

Table 2.3 Options for linking contacts in WeChat, Facebook and WhatsApp as in 2016

Methods		WeChat	Facebook	WhatsApp
Adding friends	By user ID	✓		
	By name		✓	✓
	By mobile number	✓	✓	✓
	By email		✓	✓
	Hands-free operation (e.g. scan)	✓		
Indicating friends	By mobile contacts	✓	✓	✓
	By mutual friends		✓	
	Finding people nearby	✓		

and WhatsApp. As a direct derivation of the mobile Internet era, the design of even what would, at first, appear a simple feature reveals that WeChat has placed its main emphasis on the nature of mobile phone usage and on offering convenience. Unlike Facebook and WhatsApp, adding friends via email or name is not an option in WeChat. Instead, WeChat users must do so using mobile numbers or via the QR function as described earlier.

In WeChat, potential friends are recommended based on the user's address book on their phone. Alternatively, there is a dedicated Add Contacts page where users can input a specific WeChat ID or mobile phone number, or use an assortment of options to locate other users: Friend Radar, Join Private Group, Scan QR Code, Mobile Contacts and Official Accounts. Friend Radar enables a nearby geographical search of WeChat users (a feature that can also be performed using WeChat Shake, as explained in the next section). The equivalent functions for adding friends in Facebook and WhatsApp, despite similar appearances, possess quite different modes of operation. As mentioned earlier Facebook makes recommendations based on existing users of the platform, whilst WhatsApp relies predominantly on existing mobile phone contacts.

2.3.4 WeChat Shake

The WeChat Shake feature allows users to randomly select and interact with friends and other WeChat users in a surrounding area. Users are matched with others who are also using the feature at the time by shaking the phone or pressing the shake button. The result shows a preview of profiles of nearby users as well as their distance from the current user. Depending on a person's privacy settings, varying levels of information can be displayed prior to any further connection (such as establishing a friendship) between users. Such a feature therefore provides an added layer of interaction and expands the potential use of the app beyond conventional methods.

WeChat Shake also includes other culturally specific and location-specific functions such as 'Red Packet' (a Chinese cultural feature that will be discussed in Section 5.2.2) and finding local amenities such as shops, restaurants and other services. Due to the diversity of its features, many business organisations have employed WeChat Shake as a promotional tool. For example, a supermarket can distribute coupons to customers who will receive these coupons randomly by shaking their mobile phones, and a shopping mall can host a prize draw where winners are determined by WeChat Shakes.

The Shake function has also been widely used in the media industry, with one prime example being the Chinese New Year celebrations in 2015. WeChat Shake established new trends of interaction in TV media via its connectivity, as evidenced by statistics in Ref. [119], which reveal 11 billion Shakes took place during CCTV's New Year Gala—this being one of the major televised events in China during the festive period. WeChat Shakes reached a peak of 0.81 billion Shakes per minute at 22:34 during the night of the Gala, and thus the newfound collaborative possibilities between TV broadcasting and mobile interactions have led to new forms of interaction and user involvement within the media industry [119].

2.3.5 Moments: Friends circle

WeChat's Moments is a page where users can post their updates and share articles with friends. Friends of users can comment on posts, or give a thumbs-up (点赞) which is the equivalent of the 'like' feature in Facebook. Moments is expressed in Chinese as 'Peng You Quan' (朋友圈), translated as 'friends circle'. As in the case of many other social platforms, the Moments feature serves as an essential component of WeChat. Brief chronology of the developmental history of Moments is follows:

(1) 19 April 2012: The release of WeChat 4.0 incorporated the then new function of Moments, introduced in response to the example set by Instagram, to allow photo-sharing.
(2) 22 August 2012: Users can post replies to comments and customise the set-up for the visibility of posts.
(3) September 2012: Users can choose not to see the updates of chosen people, and make private pictures public.
(4) 9 August 2013: Users can mark posts, dialogue and Official Accounts as favourites.
(5) March 2014: Users can attach location information when publishing new posts.
(6) January 2015: The first three commercial advertisements ever on Moments were published as a trial: Coca-Cola, Vivo smartphone and BMW.

As mentioned in Section 2.3.1, one of the distinctive characteristics of WeChat Moment is its minimalist design and philosophy, which is reflected in three facets of the platform: image publishing, privacy settings and spam control. This section will examine these three aspects in more detail. As perhaps WeChat's most significant global competitor, Facebook will be mentioned here for the purpose of this comparison.

2.3.5.1 Emphasised image publishing

Facebook's operation emphasises the giving and receiving of updates to and from friends, and as such, provides clear options for posting live videos, photos and check-in-location. Immediately below this is a designated area (*What's on your mind?*) for users to publish a pure-text comment, followed by another prompt (*Are you currently at... ?* as a means of encouraging information and status sharing. The overall structure of a Facebook page is that there is no notable bias towards publishing any particular type of information (be that video, photos, status, comment or such like), because all forms are equally catered for.

In contrast to Facebook, the Moments in WeChat, as mentioned earlier, was initially inspired by Instagram. As a consequence, WeChat focuses more on encouraging the publication of photos than pure text, perhaps on the assumption that the former is easier to publish than the latter within a mobile environment. The button to publish in Moments appears solely as a camera icon located at the top-right corner of the page, indicating the clear significance of photo sharing in this feature. Once clicked, options include Sight (i.e. to record and publish a live video of up to 8 seconds in length), Take Photo and Choose from Photos, whilst no option is provided to post in pure text. Indeed, the ability to publish text without pictures is somewhat concealed, and is performed by pressing and holding the camera button, which then leads to a separate text-input facility. In addition to being a relatively hidden function, it is also not a feature that users could conceivably grasp easily.

Another design detail reflecting the emphasis on images in WeChat is the general layout of the Moments page. A considerable portion of the screen is dedicated for the user's cover photo followed by a smaller thumbnail image of the user's avatar. In Facebook, a user's cover photo can only be viewed under their profile page under the *More* tab. Thus, in comparison, WeChat consists of a notably more image-heavy and -focused style of presentation, whereas Facebook is more expansive in its provision of a multitude of formats for submitting status and content updates.

2.3.5.2 Privacy settings

As with other social networking services, privacy represents an important consideration for both users and providers, although in the case of WeChat, privacy also represents a vital element of its core operation. In many social networks, and as also the case in WeChat, users can only see each other's posts and activities if they have friend status. WeChat extends on this baseline privacy feature in Moments by also applying it to comments on posts, that is, only users with friend status can see each other's posts and subsequent comments on a particular activity.

Fig. 2.6 can be used as a likely scenario, where the arrows represent established friendship links between two users. Assume person B has published a post, which persons A, C and D have all responded to in the form of a text comment. The privacy setting in WeChat's Moments will mean that A will not be able to see the comments made by C and D as they are not A's friends. C and D can see each other's comments on the post that B published due to their friend status, but will not be able to view A's comment, either. This contrasts with Facebook where in this scenario all of B's friends (A, C and D) will be able to see all comments on B's post regardless of status.

Furthermore, Facebook users can share their friends' posts on their own pages, which means A, C and D can each republish B's posts should they wish to. This function is strictly prohibited in WeChat, that is, there is no such option except for external content such as web pages, and as such, renders the level of content propagation in Moments as being highly limited. To circumvent this, many users post weblinks or URLs instead of text or pictures to obtain higher levels of content dissemination.

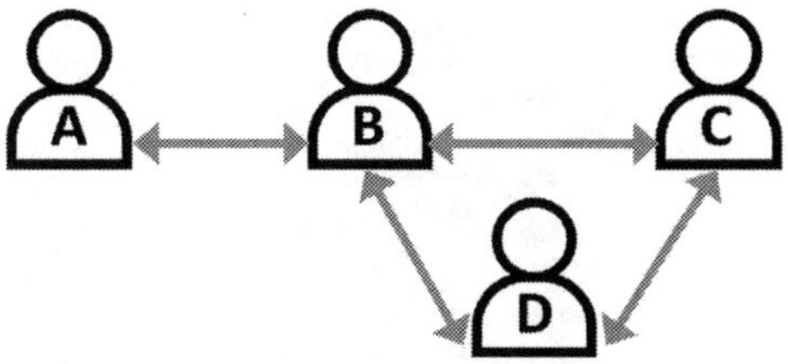

Fig. 2.6 A likely scenario to explain WeChat's privacy settings.

Facebook is therefore designed in such a way that encourages a greater degree of interaction and linkage between users than what is present in WeChat. Regardless of whether or not one user is a friend with another, they can interact by discussing or commenting on a post that they can both see. WeChat's approach differs as users are more strictly confined to information that they are permitted to see and have interest in. One conclusion from this comparison is that Facebook offers more in the way of the dissemination of information, whilst WeChat is biased more towards the personalisation of information and interaction.

WeChat's privacy settings cannot be altered by the user, and have been firmly enforced since the birth of Moments. The privacy options available to users include those for adding friends, managing blocked users as well as a binary setup for sharing (or not sharing) and hiding (or unhiding) Moments from selected friends. The most expansive option comes in the form of allowing Moments to go 'public' (i.e. viewable by all), although even with this option, other users will only be able to see a user's 10 most recent posts. Despite the apparent restrictive nature of WeChat's Moments configuration, it is one of the contributory factors for the platform's success and popularity, as issues of network security and privacy have become an ever-growing concern in the Internet age. By contrast, Facebook offers a wide range of privacy settings that can be customised by users, as shown in Fig. 2.7.

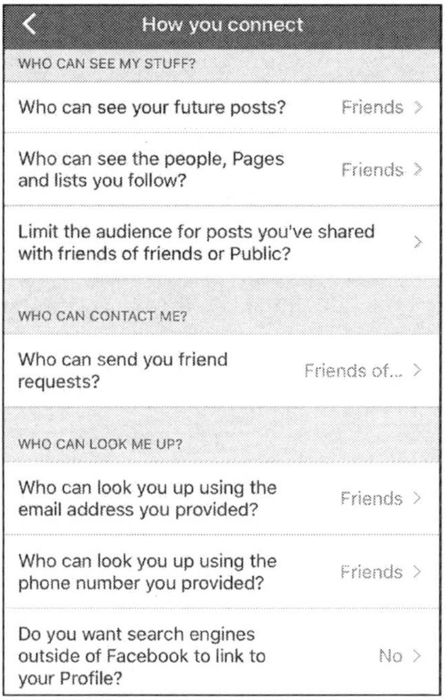

Fig. 2.7 A wide range of privacy settings in Facebook.

2.3.5.3 Spam control

In addition to the privacy settings outlined earlier, and as consistent with its minimalist design approach, WeChat also imposes several spam control measures. Spam commonly refers to unsolicited or undesired electronic messages [120], which can include the receipt of unwanted advertisements and/or irrelevant information, which can commonly appear in mainstay provisions on social network spaces.

Before examining spam-control issues in more detail, it is worth first to consider how Facebook and WeChat, respectively, deal with the dissemination of relevant and irrelevant information to users. In addition to the publication of user updates and shared articles, Facebook's News Feed also includes a range of additional content such as Suggested Posts (commonly comprising of advertisements), People You May Know, Suggested Groups and friends' activities (e.g. a reply to a post—such a feed also applies to the activities of a friend). Facebook's News Feed may also contain repeated information in a default status, such as in the case of a post that has received a comment or reply. In this case, the post (whether it be from the user or a friend) will appear multiple times on the feed, which can be a source of annoyance for some users [121].

By contrast, WeChat's Moments page displays only two types of feed: users' own posts and friends' posts. Posts are displayed chronologically, each of which will appear just once, followed by associated comments from friends or the user. WeChat's Moments page is therefore comparatively clutter-free and contains no repeated information.

As in the case of privacy, WeChat has rigorous control measures in place for controlling spam and unwanted advertising. Any potential advert needs to undergo a strict verification process (as outlined next) before it can appear in Moments.[2] In fact, WeChat's inclusion of advertising appeared in a relatively late stage of the platform's development—this being 48 months (or 5th year) after its initial launch, in spite of the tremendous growth in user base (0.19 billion users after 1 year of launch, as shown in Table 2.1). In comparison, Facebook and MSN Messenger initiated advertisements after 35 [122] and 18 months [123], respectively, after their initial launches.

WeChat's strategy for positive marketing promotions in Moments is an example of highly targeted advertisements within a local domain or business group [124]. For example, a local bakery retailer can upload adverts that will be distributed to consumers within a 5-km radius or to other businesses in the catering industry. This technique of a more stringent dissemination of commercial content can therefore increase the likelihood of adverts reaching relevant and interested receivers. In January 2015, the first three advertisements went live in Moments including Coca-Cola, Vivo smartphone and BMW, which were selectively distributed to users based on WeChat's set algorithm. As such, it remains the case that some WeChat users may have never received any advertisements on the platform to date.

[2]ad.weixin.qq.com

WeChat has well-established systems to prevent users attempting to circumvent the platform's restrictions and controls on advertising by delivering unsolicited information or adverts for products and services. Some examples are given as follows:

(1) In order to suppress group-sent[3] adverts, WeChat imposes a limit on the number of shared links. In the case of sharing weblinks (such as to websites or adverts for products or services), users who exceed the fixed allocation will be halted and given the message *You have shared too many links in a short period of time. Please try again later.*
(2) WeChat also imposes regulations on posting advertising contents in Moments. For example, if one user sought to publish a post in Moments that is essentially an advert for a branded product, this may be rejected with the following error message: *Failed to send due to inappropriate contents in the text.*
(3) WeChat also has systems in place to detect and halt accounts that are established and used for spam purposes. An account may be temporarily suspended as a result of spam behaviour reported by other users.
(4) When users decide to follow a likely spam account or accept an invitation from a spam account, WeChat will display a warning message: *He/she has no friends in frequent contact. It is advised to verify his/her identity first.*

2.3.6 World-leading IM functions

As arguably the most direct form of interaction between users in the context of a social networking app, the instant messaging service represents a core and essential function in both WeChat and WhatsApp. Chat page is a main tab in both WeChat and WhatsApp mobile apps. By contrast, Facebook requires the installation of a separate, stand-alone messaging app in addition to the primary Facebook app. Although Facebook CEO Mark Zuckerberg has explained that the primary purpose of the Facebook app is to provide News Feeds rather than messaging [125], a substantial quantity of users have voiced deep dissatisfaction and dismay with the two-app approach [126].

Beyond messaging, several other features in WeChat are worthy of note due to their effective design and user-friendly interface, which together contribute to enhancing user experience. The following section will present some of these notable functions in the perspective of usability, including voice messaging, switching between video and voice calls, group chatting and emojis.

2.3.6.1 Easy-to-use voice messaging

The 'hold-or-slide' voice messaging feature in WeChat was implemented since the app's inception in 2011, and soon became one of the platform's most appealing features. Such a feature preceded Facebook Messenger and WhatApp's equivalents by 2 years (both released in 2013) [127, 128], and both of which continue to experience ongoing stability problems [129, 130]. To this extent, some critics argue that WeChat has represented an important source of inspiration for Facebook in terms of new features and developments [131–133].

[3]Group Send: means one member of chatting group broadcast a piece of information to everyone in the group.

The nature of WeChat's voice messaging feature is not designated for real-time communication, but rather a system of leaving prerecorded messages that do not require live conversation. This is partly comparable to the voicemail function that has been in existence since the late 1990s on traditional mobile phones, although it did not achieve widespread use in China for various reasons [134]. WeChat's introduction of voice messaging therefore seized the opportunity to increase the widespread adoption of voice messaging within the Chinese context.

The procedure of sending voice messages in WeChat involves the use of a dedicated button in the bottom of the chat window to switch input from text to voice. The voice message can then be recorded by holding the *Hold to Talk* button—a sizeable area that is designed to be easily used. The recording can be cancelled by performing an upward-swipe whilst holding the Hold to Talk button.

The voice message feature has also proved a popular feature amongst older users who may be less technologically savvy. Research by Tang and Liu [135] showed that the *tap-and-shout* style of voice recording in WeChat is one of the easiest functions for older users in WeChat as compared to other common functions such as sending pictures or forwarding posts. The research also found that familiarising with new technology and features can reduce older users' sense of loneliness, as well as raise their level of awareness and perception. As such, WeChat has been able to offer suitably practical and easy-to-use features, such as in the form of the voice messaging system, towards attracting a broad user base beyond what may traditionally be reserved for younger, more technologically minded users.

2.3.6.2 Simple switch between video and voice call

Due to the critical significance of both video and voice call functions in WeChat, Tencent has invested a great deal in designing a simple mechanism to switch between the two. When there is an incoming video call, the user can accept this by pressing the green button or accept solely as a voice call by pressing the option above the green icon. Alternatively, the user can also switch to the voice mode during an existing video call. The button to switch is presented with the same level of significance as the *Hang Up* and *Switch Camera* functions, which reflects emphasises the importance of making the switch between voice and video call as easy as possible. Similarly, the user can also activate the loud speaker by tapping the *Speaker* icon.

These important yet simple features have not currently been implemented in other world-leading IM platform including Skype, WhatsApp, Facebook Messenger and QQ. There are three practical reasons why the ability to easily switch between video and voice call is important for users:

(1) In the event where users are without WiFi or a speedy mobile Internet connection, WeChat will still send invitations for video calls but this may not result in acceptable voice and/or video quality. The ability to easily switch between the two modes is therefore an important option to allow a user to spontaneously decide which type of call is best suited to their current network circumstance.

(2) The option also gives the user flexibility depending on other personal circumstances (e.g. running out of mobile data allowance, engaged in private matters) such that a video call would not be appropriate. The ability to seamlessly transfer to voice mode can therefore alleviate any concerns posed by a video call.

(3) In a public environment, users may not wish to conduct a video conversation for privacy reasons (such as exposing their conversations to the people nearby), and hence the switch to voice call would allow for the same level of privacy as that of a normal mobile phone dialogue.

2.3.6.3 Ad hoc style group chat

Unlike platforms such as Facebook where chat-groups are normally constituted on the basis of members' interests, backgrounds or news subscriptions, groups in WeChat are determined by the nature of chat or conversation contents. WeChat users can create and dismiss a chat group based on the conversation requirements, the details of which are explained next.

(1) As shown in Fig. 2.2, a chat group can be established by accessing to the main chat page and clicking '+' → Group Chat → select participants.

(2) In many cases, a group chat can easily be initiated from a one-to-one chat. Users who wish to invite more people to join their conversation, can do so by tapping on the person icon on the top-right corner of the screen to bring up the chat details page. From here, clicking the '+' button will allow users to be selected and added to the group, leading to a new but similarly structured chat window.

(3) Clicking the top-right group icon in the group chat window will bring up the group setup page where options are available to customize certain aspects of the group-chat screen. Members can also be easily removed by clicking the '−' button, though this option is only available to the founder of the group.

(4) Members can only see information about the group from the moment they join, and hence cannot view chat history prior to membership.

2.3.6.4 Customisable emojis

Emojis can serve a number of appealing roles in the context of online conversations, as pictographs can quickly convey a range of emotions within a text-based system. The presence of emojis can also influence the choice of communication channel for particular types of mediated conversation [136], and hence the significance and role of emojis in online messaging services cannot be underestimated. On 31 December 2013, WeChat 5.0 was launched with a new feature called Emoji Store, where users can download a rich assortment of emojis. Accessing the Emoji Store can be made by a simple two-click procedure.

Two years later, in 2015, WeChat built on this component by establishing the WeChat Emoji Open Platform (微信表情开放平台),[4] allowing artists and hobbyists to design and submit emojis to the platform. Although WeChat has many emoji styles that are internationally well-known, designs that possess native Chinese characteristics are also warmly received by users [137]. The Open Platform has therefore led to a

[4] sticker.weixin.qq.com.

substantial body of creative input by users via the emoji store. WeChat has also made subtle improvements to the way in which emojis can be added and used within the chat window. Users can add an emoji posted by another user to their own library by simply pressing and holding on it, then tapping the 'Add to Stickers' option.

2.4 Official accounts

2.4.1 Features

The WeChat Official Account is a key component on the platform that any individual or organisation can use as a dedicated channel to communicate with target audiences, which is an e-Commerce business model that neither Facebook nor Twitter has ever attempted. The Official Account can be considered as a powerful mobile interface, yet compact in size and operation. Official Accounts are built on the premise of WeChat's Public Platform (微信公众平台), a function module that Tencent added to WeChat's foundation 1 year after its original launch, and has since undergone rapid development. Accounts created on the Public Platform are called Official Accounts, of which there are three types: subscription account, service account and enterprise account. By February 2017, Tencent's company report revealed 10 million Official Accounts had been registered on the Public Platform, from where 0.7 million group-send messages were being delivered per day [105].

A friend status is established once a user is connected to an Official Account as a follower. Official Accounts appear as one category within the user's contact list. Tapping it will open the full list of all Official Accounts that the user currently follows. Using Guandong Unicom as an example, tapping it will bring up the main page of the company's Official Account, which is essentially in the form of a typical dialogue page, where all operations and communications take place. The bottom tabs on that page offer a customisable menu, where options vary across the different types of Official Accounts (these will be summarised later in Table 2.4). Users can send messages directly to the Official Account in the dialogue window. The Guandong Unicom Official Account can be quickly accessed from the main chat list in WeChat without having to navigate through the steps via the contact list. In the case of Subscription Accounts, the dialogue will be grouped within the category of Subscriptions in the chat list. This, then, represents the fundamental structure and source of operation for all Official Accounts.

Information from Official Accounts is exchanged as a means of conversation between account holders and followers, which may take the form of text (or rich text), weblinks, predesigned web pages, audio and videos. WeChat also provides a template for account holders allowing for the customisation of the dialogue page for desired functions. Users can even develop their own interface based on the current platform provided they have the relevant expertise. Such is the growth and popularity of the Official Accounts, it has led to the emergence of a new community in the IT field dedicated to the research and development of WeChat's Official Accounts platform

Table 2.4 **Comparison of the three WeChat official account types**

Components	Subscription account	Service account	Enterprise account
Target customers	Media or individual	Enterprises, government and organisations	Enterprises, government and organisations
Purposes	Disseminate information	Provide services	Mobile OA
Message display	Within the subscription folder	Displayed on the top of the friend dialogue list	Displayed on the top of the friend dialogue list
Broadcast limit	One message per day	Up to 4 messages per day	Maximum 200 messages every minute
Followers	Any users can join	Any users can join	Invitation or verification needed
Customisable menu	Supported	Supported	Supported
Advanced interface	Not supported	Supported after account verification	Supported
Customisable app	Not supported	Not supported	Supported
WeChat payment	Not supported	Supported	Supported

(e.g. http://www.zbj.com/wxptkf/). WeChat has also tried to assist this community by providing an official development library.[5]

2.4.2 Three types

Subscription account

This account is typically used to deliver news and information about products and services. After an account is verified, only one group-send message per day is normally permitted. The main objective of the Subscription Account is to allow for the establishment of relationships with account followers for promotional purposes, such as for brands and their products. Whilst Service Accounts and Enterprise Accounts are, by contrast, developed specifically for enterprises, Subscription Accounts are available to all users.

Service account

Service Accounts are designated for service interaction, which function in a similar way to those offered in telephony banking services, as well as nationally available phone query services in China such as 114 (the equivalent of 118 in the UK). After an account is verified, up to four group-send messages are permitted each month.

[5] https://mp.weixin.qq.com/wiki/home/index.html.

Service Accounts can be widely used by enterprises and business sectors. It can not only function as an information source for a company's services, but also provide organisations with a greater administrative outreach to customers and options for user management.

Enterprise account

This account is mainly used for internal communication within organisations, and can only be used following a verification procedure. The Enterprise Account was launched in September 2014 following strong promotional efforts, aiming to provide a mobile application for enterprise users across a broad range of functions. Whilst traditional communication channels in organisations can be fragmented in both time and space, WeChat's Enterprise Account allows users to conduct meetings, conversations and share content via their mobile devices, all within the common platform of WeChat. Other administrative duties such as employee assessment, reimbursement of expenses and staff supervision can also be carried out via an Enterprise Account. Indeed, one of WeChat's core objectives for its Public Platform is to bring users to an era of mobile office automation (OA), whereby staff can perform duties with anything, anytime and anywhere.

Individual or organisation users can therefore choose a suitable official account depending on their requirements. If they simply wish to deliver information feeds to achieve publicity, then subscription account will be sufficient. If they wish to conduct sales of products and other commercial transactions, then service account is advised. If the intention is to manage internal employees or team members, then enterprise account can be used. It should also be noted that a subscription account cannot be upgraded to a service account, and hence a separate registration process is required. Table 2.4 summarises and compares the core features of the three accounts.

2.4.3 Case studies

WeChat Official Accounts are widely used by a wide range of enterprises and organisations. As of March 2016, 73% Official Account users are enterprises and organisations, amongst which 28% are in the field of culture, media and entertainment; 21% are in the service industry; 17% are in IT, Telecom and Internet sectors and 10% are in business services [105]. The following case studies demonstrate the range of usage of WeChat Official Accounts, serving as a testament to the strong and unique position that WeChat holds as a mobile Internet platform for Chinese users.

2.4.3.1 Subscription account example: Weather network

An example of WeChat Subscription Account is Hangzhou City Weather Network. The landing page is essentially in the form of a conventional chat screen. The landing page shows news feeds sent to followers, which in most cases are only displayed in a preview mode in the form of thumbnail pictures. The page is also comprised of four buttons at the bottom, with the first giving access to the virtual keyboard for the user to communicate with the official account holder, whilst the other three serve as menu access for *Forecast and Alerts, My Weather* and *Weather Services*, respectively.

Users can access the full information of each post by tapping on the message. There is also an extended feature, where by typing a response of '6', the user can receive automated updates on the air-quality index throughout the day (i.e. this is a function predefined by the account holder). Similar to the function of automated responses in telephone services, the automated response feature in WeChat accounts requires little or no manual operation on the side of the provider. It has therefore been adopted in the design of many Subscription Accounts and Service Accounts as a means of providing a consistent and reliable level of service to followers that would otherwise be impossible if users' queries were addressed on a manual and individual basis.

2.4.3.2 Service account examples: e-Commerce

- Online shopping

WeChat's Service Account provides more in the way of utilities as compared to the Subscription Account. An example of Service Account is JD.com—one of China's leading online shopping portals. As with the case of Weather Network, JD.com's landing page is also in the form of a dialogue screen, allowing the company to send regular promotional and advertising information to followers. As also with the previous example, there are four buttons/tabs in the bottom of the dialogue page, and the first button on the bottom pane is used to access with the virtual keyboard as the means of communicating with the company. The other three buttons lead to associated menus of *JD shopping*, *Followers' Bonus* and *My Service*. One pop menu (in the bottom of the page) brings up the main shopping catalogue as designed specifically for mobile devices, comprising of further menu options at the bottom of the page. This example reveals the extent to which a standard account can be transformed into a fully functional and dedicated shopping app. Tapping on any product on the screen will open the full information page for that item, whilst a built-in checkout and payment facility is available in the event of a purchase—the details of WeChat Payment will be discussed in Section 5.2.1.

- Financial services

Another example of Service Account is China Merchants Bank. On the pop menu there are options including: *View Statement*, *Payoff Balance*, *Pay by Instalment*, *Withdraw Cash* and *Activate Online Payment*. In the bottom tab it reads: *Statement, My Account* and *Merchants Bank Wonders*. In the dialogue section with green background, it shows a greeting message and some basic introductions of this official account, which is automatically sent upon joining.

One of the core steps of the account is that it uses notifications to remind customers to bind their WeChat accounts securely to their credit cards. Once complete, users can enter the landing screen to access their bank statements, check balances and loyalty points. Users can also pay off credit card balances, apply for payments by instalment and apply for new cards. A service operator is available on request to provide live assistance, whilst the account provides automated notifications of customers' transactions and reminders. As in the example of JD.com, the range of functionalities offered by the Bank via its Service Account have been custom-developed from what was essentially a base set of interfaces from WeChat's Service Account provision.

- Travel

The Service Account of China Southern Airlines is an example of Official Account offering travelling services. There is a popup menu offering options for: *Book Flight*, *My Bookings*, *Ticket Verification*, *Airline Status* and *Online Check-In*. The bottom tab reads: *Airline Services*, *Mingzhu Membership* and *Travel News*. The main dialogue section gives instructions on making queries via automatic messaging services. Here, customers can bind their loyalty card with to their WeChat account. Upon opening the service account dialogue, users can book flights, query bookings, check-in online, choose seats and print boarding pass. Additional information such as local weather and airline data are also provided via this account.

2.4.3.3 Enterprise account example: Store management

Here an example is given for an Enterprise Account held by Häagen-Dazs. As at the time of writing, there are over 300 Häagen-Dazs stores in China, spanning over 60 cities. The Enterprise Account serves as a standardised and mobilised facility for the company's management of routine day-to-day operations such as monitoring and patrol.

A range of functional menus are offered for one store: *Environment Evaluation*, *Customer Service*, *Equipment Maintenance*, and *Management Tool Evaluation*. The middle screenshot lists all items within the Environment Evaluation category, including 'outdoor signs', 'lighted box', 'lighting scenarios', 'advert posters', 'logo' and 'poster stand'. Tapping the first item displays the detailed assessment page (the right screenshot), including the description of standards and assessment forms (consisting of tick options in this case). When the company's patrol supervisors inspect various items based on their internal checklists, they can report existing problems to the management team in the form of pictures, texts or evaluation scores. These also be transmitted to the management instantaneously, followed by direct feedback from management to the store on solutions or actions to take. The Häagen-Dazs management team can also inspect inspection reports towards determining common issues and solutions for the company as a whole, whilst inspection supervisors can be managed and assessed on variables such as the number of patrols carried out, collected data and comments to management.

2.4.4 Values and impact

WeChat Public Platform was previously known as WeChat Official Platform and WeChat Media Platform, and is eventually advertised to users as a public platform. During its initial announcement, WeChat had already established a substantial user base of several hundred million users, serving as an ideal avenue through which to disseminate and expand the public platform. By February 2017, 10 million Official

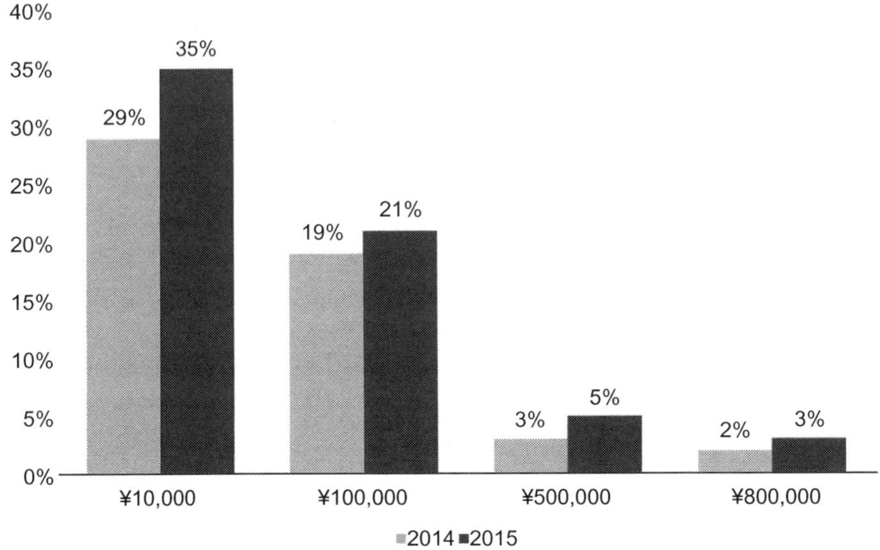

Fig. 2.8 Investment levels in WeChat Official Accounts by account holders.

Accounts have been registered [105], attracting growing investment from account holders as shown in Fig. 2.8.

WeChat Public Platform was designed to promote and maintain a positive eco-circulation within the WeChat community by offering high-quality and cohesive content. Today's WeChat Public Platform has become one of the mainstream forms of interaction for online businesses and the generation of media publicity. The value chain of WeChat's Official Accounts consists of information publication, marketing and promotion and customer interaction. Table 2.5 shows the range of functions used via Official Accounts [105].

As a major information propagation channel and media agency, Official Accounts are therefore used with increasing regularity in China. One of the main objectives

Table 2.5 Main usage of official accounts

Information publication	84.7%
Promotion and advertisement	64.1%
Interaction with customers	45.8%
Business consultancy and enquiry	21.0%
Platform for e-Commerce	18.2%
Client management	17.1%
Postsale service	12.4%
Big data analysis	12.2%
Recruitment	11.9%

Table 2.6 **Reasons for users to follow official accounts**

Reason	Percentage
To acquire news and updates	74.2%
To know the company state and trend, or promotions	41.9%
To use the services provided by official accounts	30.9%
To understand policies and relevant information	24.6%
To enquire about business and transactions	19.3%
To complain or give advice on governmental and public services	11.9%

for account holders is to increase the publicity of their accounts and to gain more followers. Table 2.6 lists the main reasons for following Official Accounts [105], where approximately three quarters of users do so for the purpose of acquiring information. As such, it is crucial for Official Account holders to offer valuable and engaging content to followers so as to maintain interest and persistent use.

Compared to Subscription Accounts and Service Accounts, Enterprise Accounts seek to provide internal usage within companies and organisations towards the realisation of mobile OA, with features such as human resource management, attendance checking, document sharing and real-time training. As an emerging technology, the Enterprise Account has been regarded as a revolution in the field of mobile OA [138], especially within the broader context of mobile Internet technologies and pervasiveness of smart devices, Traditional routine tasks that were once reserved for desktop computers and in fixed locations can now be provisioned via mobile devices, thus boosting convenience as well as management and communication efficiency. Table 2.7 outlines the most significant aspects of impact provided by the Enterprise Account based on statistics provided in Ref. [105]. The major users of Enterprise Accounts are also not, as may be expected, Internet companies, but traditional manufacturers, as shown in Fig. 2.9. Culture and media sectors have the lowest usage percentage, as Subscription Accounts and Service Accounts are perhaps more directly suitable for the nature of their respective businesses and operation.

Compared to subscription accounts and service accounts, WeChat enterprise accounts are targeted for the internal usage within companies and organisations in order to realise the vision of mobile OA, featuring human resource management, attendance checking, document sharing, real-time training, etc. As an emerging technology, WeChat enterprise account is regarded as a revolution in the mobile OA field [138]. With the vast development of mobile Internet technologies and the pervasiveness of smart phones, WeChat enterprise account proceeds to advance the intellectual

Table 2.7 **Impact of WeChat enterprise account**

Impact	Percentage
To improve the efficiency of internal operation and management	69.7%
To offer systematic forms of administration and enhance IT provisions	46.5%
To lower the cost of informatisation	38.2%
To simplify the work and business processes	35.6%
To enhance the efficiency of upstream and downstream cooperation	34.4%
To improve the efficiency of supporting services and marketing	22.8%

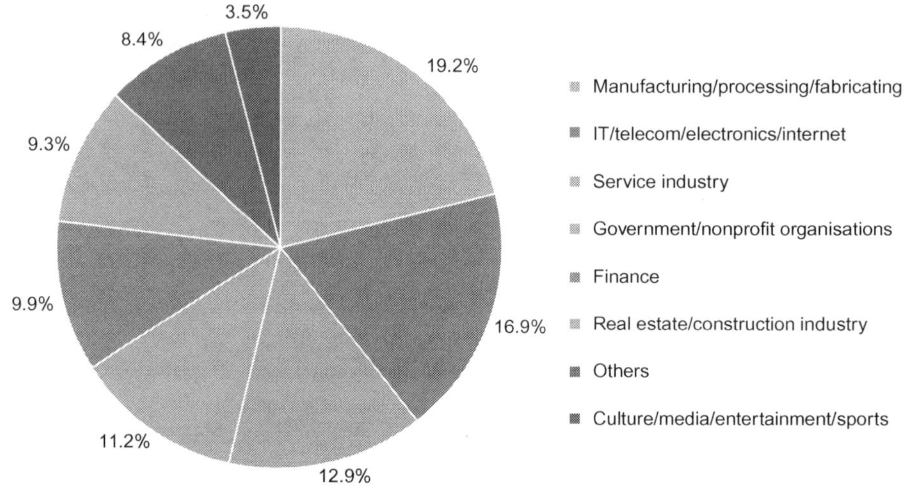

Fig. 2.9 Sector distribution for the usage of WeChat enterprise accounts.

mobile office operations. Traditional routine tasks that were taken place on desktop computers are now supported on mobile devices, which boost the management and communication efficiency. Table 2.7 shows the major impact of WeChat enterprise account based on statistics provided in Ref. [105]. The major usage of enterprise accounts is not Internet companies, but traditional manufacturers, as shown in Fig. 2.9. Culture and media sectors have the lowest percentage, as subscription accounts and service accounts are more suitable for the nature of their business.

QQ

3

3.1 Two decades of success

QQ is one of the most successful network products in Chinese Internet history. Since its launch in 1999, QQ has accumulated billions of users and, according to the official statistics [139], commanded 0.877 billion MAUs in 2016, the highest amongst all rankings for Chinese social networks. During the past decade, QQ has managed to withstand and cement its position in the digital communications sector in spite of sizeable changes and developments in the Internet landscape and associated technologies. QQ's longstanding position in the social network arena has contributed to the changing ecology of the Chinese Internet, influencing the lifestyle and the use of information technology of a whole generation [140]. As shown in Table 3.1, QQ has, along with ICQ, the longest history in the social network arena—an observation which is all the more impressive in view of its ability to maintain continuous growth and innovation.

QQ's creator, Tencent, currently possesses a market value of 185 billion USD and a brand value of 66 billion USD, positioning it as one of China's most valuable companies [141]. Tencent's creations, including QQ, WeChat and wealth of mobile games, continue to attract a huge share of the world's social media users, although the majority of their users reside in China. In terms of global rankings, 2016 figures by Statista, as shown in Fig. 1.12, show Tencent's two main platforms, QQ and WeChat, in second place behind those from the Facebook portfolio, that is, Facebook and WhatsApp.

As mentioned in Section 1.1.1, the name of QQ was initially inspired by ICQ, where its full name was originally that of OICQ, designated to mean *Oh I seek you*. In later years, the name was eventually shortened to QQ, whilst experiencing extraordinary growth and development, as can be seen in Table 3.2.

During the initial years of QQ's development, the number of subscribers was counted simply as the total number. Since the number of users exceeded 1 billion in 2010, a new statistic in the form of MAUs has been used to gauge the popularity of the platform. Even though the total number of QQ users has not been officially revealed in recent years, the unique QQ identifying number (as assigned to every unique user) is currently 11 digits, hence giving an indication that the total number of registered users is in the order of billions. Unlike Facebook which relies on a name-based system of registration, QQ's system permits a user easily to register for multiple accounts via different QQ ID numbers. However, regardless of which statistic is considered, it is

Social Networks in China. https://doi.org/10.1016/B978-0-08-101934-4.00003-0

Table 3.1 **Life span of major social networks in the world (as in Feb. 2017)**

	Beginning	End	Life span	Current users
ICQ	1996	Present (2017)	20 years	11 million subscribers in 2013[a]
QQ	1999	Present (2017)	18 years	877 million MAU
MSN Messenger	1999	2012	13 years	330 million subscribers in 2012
Facebook	2004	Present (2017)	13 years	1.7 billion MAU
Twitter	2006	Present (2017)	11 years	313 million MAU
WhatsApp	2009	Present (2017)	8 years	1 billion MAU
Weibo	2009	Present (2017)	8 years	282 million MAU
WeChat	2011	Present (2017)	6 years	846 million MAU

[a]Current statistics are unavailable.

evident that QQ's penetration level in the Chinese social network arena has reached a substantial level.

In the well-known domestic *3Q incident* of 2010–14 involving Tencent and Qihoo 360 (an established Internet security company in China) [142], QQ was accused of monopolising the Chinese social network market, although the Supreme People's Court judged that the platform did not, as of 16 October 2014, possess the status of market dominance. The feud that developed between the two companies became so toxic that the Chinese Government had to intervene to maintain the normality of network operations and service provisions, thus revealing the extensive influence that Tencent QQ has forged on Chinese society. Despite winning the legal battle, Tencent had received numerous criticisms for its deemed-to-be-monopolising style in the aftermath of the *3Q incident* from where Tencent has undoubtedly learnt valuable lessons. In 2010, Tencent initiated an open-platform strategy (available at open.qq.com) that permits direct contributions to the QQ platform from the wider development community. This new strategy helped QQ to improve internally whilst also encouraging the participation and improvement of others towards achieving a longer-term sustainability and evolution for the platform. To this extent, Tencent now functions as a central link for social organisations and enterprises [143], growing stronger not necessarily through competing and overcoming rivals with its vast user base, but by helping other companies to grow and give input to QQ's continuous cycle of improvement.

3.2 Endeavour for innovation

Table 3.2 highlights some of the QQ's core functions since its inception. As can be briefly seen in table, Tencent is constantly adding new functions to the platform as a means of broadening its versatility and delivering new user experiences.

Table 3.2 **Evolution of QQ**

1999	OICQ published	60,000 users
2000	Voice chat function	5 million users; 100,000 online simultaneously at 20:43 on 27 May 2000
2001	Tencent Explorer; Invisible Status; Mobile OICQ	50 million users
2002	Renamed to QQ; Video Call; QQ Group	0.1 billion users
2003	Personalisation; Ringtone; Screen Capture	0.2 billion users
2004	Network Drive; Distance Assistance; QQ Secretary	0.3 billion users
2005	QQ Pets; Qzone; QQ Address Book; QQ Music	10 million online simultaneously on 16 Feb. 2005
2007	Offline File Transfer; Window Shake	30 million online simultaneously on 13 July 2007
2008	Super Group	0.8 billion users; 40 million online simultaneously on 12 Mar. 2008
2009	Group Status; Impression of Friends	0.9 billion users; 51 million online simultaneously at 20:00 on 23 Feb. 2009; Ownership of over 400 patents
2010	QQ Skin Engine; Big Videos	0.1 billion users online simultaneously at 19:52:58 on 5 Mar. 2010; Chairman Jintao Hu visited Tencent on Sep. 5
2011	App Box; Group Video Chat	0.14 billion users online simultaneously *(WeChat was born)*
2012	QQ for iOS and Android	0.17 billion users online simultaneously
2013	Voice Message function	Tencent became the first Chinese Internet company with market value of over 100 billion USD
2014	Enhanced Chatting Interface	0.2 billion users online simultaneously (70% are mobile users) on 11 Apr. 2014
2015	File Display; Distance Learning	0.86 billion MAU
2017	Outlook Integration	0.877 billion MAU *(WeChat has 0.846 monthly active users)*

One of the fundamental reasons for QQ's perpetual success is their endeavour for innovation, especially in the context of adapting design and services to the continuously changing user requirements and technological development, as illustrated in Table 3.2. Although similar approaches were taken by other SNS providers, many were eventually eliminated from the market due to stagnated advancement, whilst QQ is still growing stronger. In the Global Mobile Internet Conference on 7 May 2013 [144], Tencent's founder and CEO, Huateng Ma (马化腾), commented on the rapid growth of the company's products and emphasised the significance of product innovation:

Frankly speaking, this is scary for us too. No matter how strong you are in the tidal wave of mobile Internet, you can be destroyed within a month if you are even slightly careless. Many big companies seem to be powerful, but in fact they are vulnerable. Therefore, being in awe of industrial innovation has forced us to do every little thing attentively.

3.3 Highlights of features

3.3.1 Overview

The interface structure of QQ is shown in Fig. 3.1, which reveals the major functionality blocks of the platform.

3.3.2 QQ number

QQ's unique ID system consists of a series of consecutive integers, the length of which has been growing in-line with the quantity of users. Early QQ users would likely have been assigned a five-digit ID, whereas a present day user will likely receive an ID with at least 11 digits. ID numbers are randomly generated by Tencent's servers upon the registration of new users, and hence there is no official mechanism for Tencent to control how numbers are distributed.

Somewhat unexpectedly, the QQ ID number has made significant impact on modern Chinese Internet culture. The following are some core reasons for this phenomenon:

(1) The QQ ID number has become a necessity for acquaintance amongst few friends, where the greeting of *What is your QQ number?* is often asked in friendly conversations [145, 146]. Since each QQ number is also affiliated with a unique email address that corresponds to the QQ number (e.g. a user with QQ a number of 123456 is automatically assigned an email address of 123456@qq.com), knowing a person's QQ number means that friends can be contacted either on the QQ platform or by email.

(2) Chinese culture places sensitivity to certain numbers where, for example, the numbers '6' and '8' are believed to be lucky, whereas '4' is regarded as unlucky [147, 148]. Given QQ's longstanding success in the Chinese social network domain, the nature of QQ numbers has and continues to be a hot topic in the Internet community, whilst the possession of, especially, 'lucky' numbers are highly valued by individuals in the community [149].

(3) Related to the last point, QQ numbers have long been regarded as a form of virtual property by Chinese Internet users [150, 151], although it has also been a controversial topic in the area of criminal law. The first legal case that drew national attention took place in 2006 when a series of 'lucky' QQ numbers were stolen and traded for profit (the number '98888' was once sold for 42,000 RMB, i.e. 6115 USD [152]). Although the principal offender was jailed for 1 year for the vandalism of telecom freedom, there has been on-going debate on whether the offence should instead be judged as one of larcenies [151, 152].

3.3.3 Management of contacts

QQ has in place a distinctly effective contact management mechanism. Unlike WeChat and Facebook where contacts are typically listed in alphabetical order by default, QQ

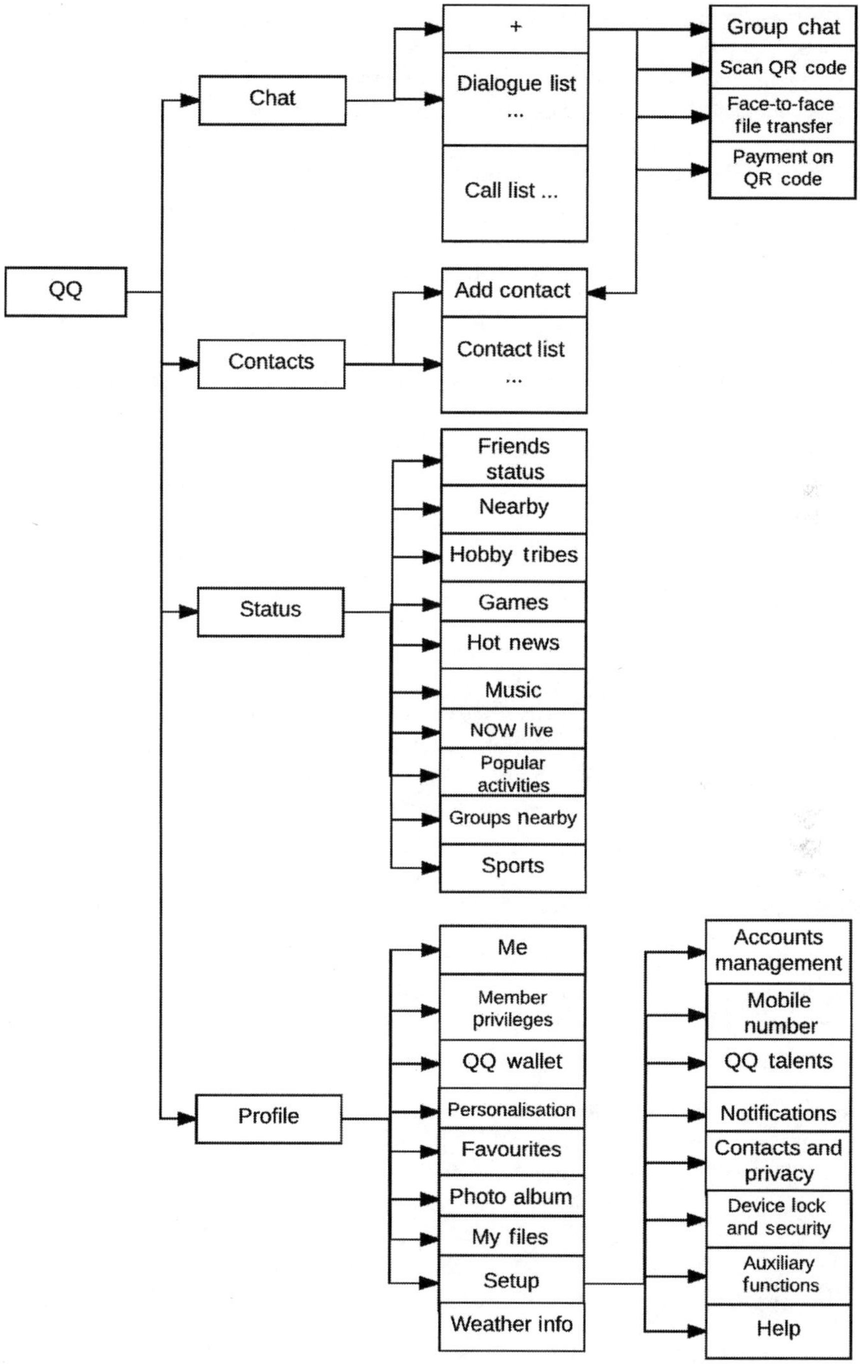

Fig. 3.1 Interface structure of mobile QQ app.

allows users to organise contacts into self-defined categories. These categories and associated contact members can then be displayed in an expandable tree structure, allowing a user to show and/or hide particular categories as they wish.

QQ's objective has always been one of maximising the social links amongst users, and as such, its contact management system operates on the assumption that a user is in possession of many contacts. Complimentary to Tencent's provision, there have also been numerous on-going discussions in QQ's user community in exploring alternative techniques for the batch management of QQ contacts [153, 154].

3.3.4 Mobile file transfer

Beyond messaging services, QQ offers several other utilities to complement its core provision. One such feature is the mobile file transfer facility, which can take place in two ways: the first being via the systems main chat window (this being available only between users with friend status), and the other is through a face-to-face connection (available between all users).

3.3.5 Qzone

Although QQ was initially designed as an IM platform, Tencent has since incorporated a social network space into the system so as to compete with rival products. This strategy was initially enacted in response to the threat posed by MSN's entry into the Chinese market, as explained in Section 1.2.2, which has evolved into the current status whereby both WeChat and QQ combine IM with social networking features. WeChat's social space is provided in the form of Moments (as discussed in Section 2.3.5), whilst that for QQ is known as Qzone.

As opposed to the WeChat's minimalism design approach for Moments, Qzone is broadly equipped with numerous attractive features as explained later, all of which provide users with opportunities to create and customise their personal space.

Content Variety In addition to commonly used rich-text formats, Qzone allows users to embed various types of content into their personal page in order to enhance its appeal, such as Flash modules, videos and background music.

Templates and Personalisation Qzone offers a wide range of themed templates that can be selected and used as the basis for customisation. This serves as an important feature to facilitate personalisation as it has become common practise, especially amongst younger users, to adapt their Qzone space to reflect personal taste and popular trends. Qzone's templates are further supplemented by a wide range of third-party offerings in the form of additional materials and resources for personalisation such as [155, 156].

Photo Album Qzone's provision extends to the facility of a relatively powerful and generous photo management system, allowing users to create up to 256 albums with each accommodating up to 512 photos. Photos can be uploaded in batches, with each photo retaining its original resolution without undergoing a compression process, with all users being provided with 30 GB of online storage capacity by default. The presentation of photos can be made in an assortment of styles, including dynamic photography, slideshow, personal album and avatar stickers.

Online Games As will be discussed in Section 5.1, Tencent is also the creator and publisher of numerous leading online games in China. With the successful precedent in the provision of online games via SNS platforms (see Section 1.2.3.3), Qzone represents one of the main distribution channels for Tencent's in-house games.

Apps Qzone's app centre[1] serves as the central hub for additional apps that can be added to Qzone, providing a one-stop service for users to obtain three main entertainment media: games, movies and digital books.

3.3.6 Membership and account varieties

QQ membership status and accounts come in an assortment of options depending on the requirements of the user, leading to what is essentially a rather complicated structure. However, broadly speaking, membership and accounts can be seen to reside under three main categories: VIP membership, titles for Qzone and Official Accounts.

- VIP membership

QQ's VIP membership was launched in December 2000 and remains one of Tencent's important profit-making add-on products. VIP members are offered a wide range of additional privileges across the range of QQ features such as Qzone, games, life and online shopping. As shown in the schematic in Fig. 3.2, user privileges can be increased horizontally and/or vertically, with the former representing the membership fee paid by the member, and the former referring to dynamic growth value that is calculated using an internal algorithm that takes into account various factors such as user activities, frequency of QQ usage and the user's impact on the QQ community.

QQ's VIP membership is a business model that has run over 16 years and is still continuously growing with profit. There have been regular promotional strategies from Tencent to improve VIP services to members. Two examples from Ref. [157] include:

(1) In early 2016, QQ collaborated with Burger King in offering discount vouchers to VIP QQ members, with an additional feature in the QQ mobile app helping users locate their nearest Burger King restaurant. The promotion attracted 1.5 million VIP QQ members to participate within a week of launch, thus significantly raising the profile and awareness of the Burger King brand during the period.

(2) In June 2015, QQ worked with a real-estate developer in Beijing by giving promotional offers to VIP QQ members. Over 1000 users used this privilege, of which 47 resulted in the

[1] http://qqapp.qq.com/.

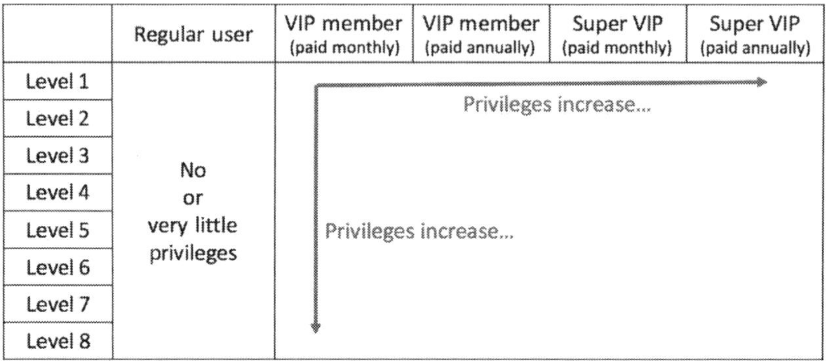

Fig. 3.2 QQ membership options.

purchase of a new flat leading to total sales amounting to approximately 70 million Yuan (or 10 million USD).

- Titles for Qzone

Qzone users have two options to help make their personal space stand out from the crowd. The first is to apply for the title of 'City Talents' (城市达人, *cheng shi da ren*). Becoming a City Talent will increase a user's opportunity of being promoted to appear on Qzone's community homepage, and thus to receive considerable exposure and the potential establish more social links. The City Talent title was initially reserved for users who possessed specialism in particular fields, but the requirements were subsequently lowered to attract application from a greater number of users. Current requirements include the upload of a personal photo and the submission of user information such as name, gender, age and area of residence.

The second option for raising awareness of a personal space is to seek verified status. A verified space will lead to greater functionalities and features than regular spaces, as well as indicate to followers of the account that its content comes from a trustworthy source. The verification status is an option that is often favoured by many organisations, media outlets, celebrities and brands given its added connotations of quality and having undergone an additional assessment process.

- QQ Official Accounts

Similar to the Official Accounts offered in WeChat (see Section 2.4), QQ also allows individuals and organisations to register for Official Accounts. Unlike WeChat, however, QQ does not provide Enterprise Accounts to assist the internal management of organisations. QQ offers four types of Official Accounts: verified Subscription Account, unverified Subscription Account, verified Service Account and unverified Service Account. Beyond some minor differences, the functionalities and features in these accounts largely resemble those found in WeChat [158]. Overall, the admission criteria for Official Accounts are set lower than those in WeChat, as they can be created without verification process so as to attract a greater quantity of users.

3.4 QQ vs. WeChat

Given the significance and market dominance of Tencent's sibling platforms, QQ and WeChat, this section makes a more detailed comparison between the two so as to illustrate the more salient features of their composition. Their most common elements as social network platforms include:

- Both are platforms designed and owned by Tencent.
- Both provide the combined services of IM and social networking.
- Both are notably successful social network platforms in China.
- Both feature an abundance of add-on features.

The following sections review the rationale for and core differences between the two in respect of Tencent's company strategy, traditional PC platform versus mobile devices, communication trends, social links, user interfaces, target users and revenue generation. These discussions will help to uncover why and how Tencent created two seemingly overlapping yet highly successful products.

3.4.1 Company strategy

Section 1.3.1.3 already explained the background reasons for Tencent's decision of creating WeChat when QQ was already an existing social network product. Both QQ and WeChat are available in the form of a dedicated mobile social networking app, designed and owned by Tencent. At first glance, the two platforms may appear to be repetitive with respect to provision and intent, although the precise purpose behind Tencent's strategy becomes more evident under closer scrutiny. Under the scenario where a company needs to address a specific market, in this case, namely the mobile communications sector, one of two solutions can typically be employed: the first being to consolidate similar products within a portfolio, and the other to divide market share between similar products. As a core and firmly established product in Tencent's repertoire, QQ has made great contributions to the success of the company during the advancement of the Internet in China since its inception. However, in the midst of more recent developments in mobile Internet technology and provision (including aspects such as the increasing availability of and access to mobile data, smart devices, mobile apps and communications platforms), Tencent could not afford to rely solely on QQ for adjusting to the ever-changing nuances within the market and user expectations. In essence, Tencent decided against subjecting QQ to a large-scale adjustment or major renovation, as the risk of such an approach was that the public may not consider a major revamp of a firmly established product to be sufficient for addressing the contemporary needs of a changing market. Consequently, the creation of WeChat represented a strategic move to occupy a specific market share in what was then the emerging mobile Internet sector.

In retrospect, Tencent's strategy with WeChat has been demonstrated to be one of optimal timing in capturing the company's resources and the various advantages and opportunities presented by the market at the time of its release, where it has become one of the dominant apps in the Chinese mobile sector. Critically, Tencent has demonstrated that despite certain inherent similarities, both QQ and WeChat can coexist under the continuing evolution of the mobile Internet era, where the contrast and distinction between the two platforms is expected to become more prevalent. For instance, WeChat's Public Platform (as discussed in Section 2.4) is one such feature where WeChat has carved a more unique identity, and of which has received unprecedented success. Tencent's founder and CEO, Huateng Ma, explained the rationale behind the mutual dependence between the two products in the Global Mobile Internet Conference on 7 May 2013 as [144]:

> *The relationship between Mobile QQ and WeChat is not to substitute one platform with another, but to complement each other's strengths. They are developing respectively with distinctive characteristics, targeting different markets, and catering for different needs.*

3.4.2 PC vs. mobile

As discussed earlier, despite aspects of similarity and the sustained growth of WeChat, it does not represent a designated replacement for QQ. Users of both systems have formed quite different habits and customs of usage, thus further underlining the distinction between the two platforms. Importantly, QQ's main strengths continue to reside within a PC desktop environment, allowing more sophisticated and complex tasks to be performed such as large file transfer, game invitations and group play, delivering screenshots in chat windows, as well as the ability to multitask between various operations, which would not be not be feasible in a mobile environment. The window-based interface of QQ operates as a central control panel where users can quickly access services including mailbox and personal space, serving as a connection centre as opposed to an information-acquisition platform.

Desktop QQ has also captured popular usage amongst the work environment as a communications platform between colleagues. Compared to the Enterprise Account in WeChat, which is specifically designed to assist internal operations within organisations and company communications, QQ is entirely free to use, even within the work setting. And although QQ contains less simpler features than those from WeChat's Enterprise Account, it has proved to be more than sufficient as a system for linking people within a corporate context. However, as in the case of other forms of personal media, many companies in China have nevertheless had to devise their own policies to regulate QQ usage at work in cases where workers may be addicted or excessive users of the platform [159]. In comparison, Mobile QQ is designed as a migration platform from desktop QQ to mobile devices. As opposed to WeChat which was conceived with the specific purpose of addressing the opportunities offered by mobile devices, Mobile QQ addresses the need for users to receive messages whilst not using their conventional desktops, thus allowing for a continuation of major QQ services including IM, personal space and mailbox, beyond a fixed location.

Conversely, WeChat is, from the very outset, devised for mobile devices where hardware resources and computing speed are both comparatively limited, thus imposing technical constraints on the types of duties that can be performed. Thus, differing to the design of Mobile QQ, WeChat is built on the philosophy of lightweight, flexible and simplistic design for mobile settings, culminating in a feature set that seeks to integrate functions in novel ways in order to cater to user preferences. This approach is evident in convenience features such as those involving motion gestures, such as shakes and QR code scan, along with communications via video and voice call, and the voice messaging feature, which have provided genuine and often cost-effective alternatives to traditional mobile networks. Other associated and popular WeChat features made feasible via mobile platforms include location-sharing, WeChat Pay, taxi ordering, mobile phone top-up and games. According to Xiaolong Zhang, WeChat's inventor and designer, the platform's simplistic aesthetics reside at its very core [160]:

> *Despite the huge variety of functions implemented in WeChat, the most important ones are, without exception, displayed in the most obvious positions, while secondary functions are always hidden.*

From this comparison, it comes as no great surprise that despite the apparent similarities between WeChat and QQ, as well as the expansion of Mobile QQ in ways that mirror the types of services available on WeChat, many users use WeChat as the dedicated mobile app of choice [161].

3.4.3 Concept of online

As mentioned earlier, the dominant and designated terminal for QQ remains the PC platform, whilst WeChat is that of mobile devices (typically mobile smartphones). Similarly, QQ may be considered as Tencent's IM tool devised for the PC era, and WeChat as that for the mobile Internet generation. With respect to online connectivity, WeChat functions in a permanent online state, irrespective of whether or not the user is actually connected to the Internet, and thus users are shown to be persistently online. Conversely, users of Mobile QQ will be automatically logged-off (thus appearing 'offline') after a period of inactivity.

The concept of *online status* in QQ originated from the nuances of IM operation in the PC era. Users must be located on their PC workstations and be of online status (i.e. being logged-in and visible) in order to send and receive IM messages or conduct real-time conversations. However, some users may not wish to be visible to others or be contactable whilst online, yet still be able to receive information. Users who prefer to be 'invisible' have attracted the nickname of *diving* or *divers* in the Chinese SNS community, meaning those who wish to see the activities of others yet choosing not to be seen themselves. To cater for this need, QQ put in place a series of status options, including *Online, Q me, I've left, Busy, Do not disturb, Invisible, Offline*, as well as the option to create a customised message.

WeChat, on the other hand, does not provide options for online or offline status, mainly for three reasons. First, as described earlier, WeChat focuses on implementing features solely for the purpose of mobile Internet, whereby the notion of being 'constantly online' regardless of the user's actual connection is essential for underlining the persistent nature of the platform and its mobile context. In practise, online status is not of great significance given the relative instability (or variability) of mobile data connections. Second, WeChat places little emphasis on the requirement for users to be simultaneously online in order to perform actions—an element that is reflected in its functionalities. Third, the asynchronous communication mode provided in WeChat means instant responses are not necessary for information exchange.

Given these general characteristics of both platforms with respect to designated terminals and connectivity, a conversation between WeChat users is most likely to be conducted between smartphones, whilst that in QQ is more likely to be made between desktop PCs or a PC and smartphone. As will be discussed in Section 2.3.6, platform characteristics have also dictated to an extent the type of communications features that can be conveniently offered, especially in the case of smartphones where WeChat's voice messaging function has drastically enhanced user experience. Being principally a PC platform, and aware of the distinctive possibilities residing amongst both platforms as well as their individual market positioning, Tencent has therefore refrained from occupying users' fragmented time slots in daily lives.

3.4.4 Social links

QQ connections are made on the basis of QQ numbers, whilst connections in WeChat are made in a variety of ways, including QQ friend contacts, mobile contacts and people nearby. During WeChat's initial introductory phase, contacts were mostly imported as existing QQ numbers (this being one of the notable benefits of operating as a sibling to an already established product in the form of QQ), as well as an instant recognition of conventional mobile number contacts. WeChat takes advantage of the fact that a user's mobile phone address book would more than likely contain the most expansive list of contacts. Upon creation of a WeChat account, the user is automatically presented with a list of matching friends that can potentially be added, including existing contacts within the address book of user's host mobile phone who are also WeChat account holders.

Given the long history of achievement, QQ's large user base has founded a powerful online community where a QQ culture is being promoted. QQ also offers each individual user an effective management system to sort out the contacts (described in Section 3.3.3), based on the assumption that each user will have abundant social connections in the QQ community. On the other hand, WeChat has given up the option of categorising contacts, instead is listing all friends alphabetically, which works in the same way as a mobile phone address book. Even though this may limit user's ability of organising contact list, this is compliant with the overall objective of WeChat to fit for the purpose of mobile Internet; furthermore, since WeChat delivers strict privacy and spam control policy, it is to be used amongst close friends; therefore, users are less willing to add any strange contact to their list.

3.4.5 QZone vs. Moments

QQ and WeChat both provide a complimentary feature beyond core IM facilities to promote information sharing and interaction amongst users. These appear in the form of QZone and Moments, respectively. This section will outline some of the core design differences between the two and how they lead to varying types of usage.

3.4.5.1 Privacy settings

Privacy settings are drastically different between the two platforms. In WeChat Moments, only friends can see each other's posts and related comments. In other words, assuming that A and B are friends, and B and C are also friends, when A comments on B's post, C can only see this comment if he/she is also a friend of A. On the other hand, QQ allows for a more open level of information exposure and interaction. QQ users can see posts published by friends in Qzone, and all comments made on such posts will also be visible to everyone who has access to the post and be able to make comment—consequently, friend status is not a prerequisite for viewing and interaction amongst users who have access to such content.

Qzone users can not only view friends' updates, but also repost them on their own personal space for wider dissemination. In direct contrast, Moments in WeChat does not permit a user to repost content by a friend, with the sole exception of web pages, which means the prospect for information propagation in Moments is nearly zero. On top of these features, Qzone will also display content from the platform's Official Accounts as a means of maximising information exposure, whilst this is not the case in Moments where users are firmly protected from potentially unwanted information broadcast. In conclusion, Qzone leans towards the role of community and information propagation in its social system, whilst Moments favours personalisation and strict privacy.

3.4.5.2 Publishing priority

Last but not least, due the platform-derived characteristics of QQ (PC) and WeChat (mobile), as have been discussed earlier, knock-on effects are also evident in terms of how information is published and the level of priority that is assigned to content. One such observable characteristic is that Qzone places priority on displaying text before pictures (this being in view of the fact that the PC environment centres predominantly on textual input), whilst Moments gives priority to publishing pictures over text.

The types of new contents that can be added to Qzone's include text, pictures, check-in (i.e. a location-based service) and videos. Here, the text option always appears first and is set as the default option. Conversely, WeChat Moments presents a noticeably different setup where the button for adding a new post comes in the form of a camera icon (on the top-right corner), which indicates the platform's emphasis on visual content. Clicking the camera icon will lead to a new menu with options for *Sight* (i.e. a short live video), *Take Photo*, *Choose from Photos* and, somewhat surprisingly, none for publishing pure text. Indeed, the option for publishing text without visual content is placed in a noticeably hidden location (by holding the camera icon for 2 seconds), almost as a way of discouraging users from publishing textual content.

3.4.6 Market and revenue

Tencent's company report [139] for the third quarter (Q3) of 2016 reveals a total revenue of 40.4 billion Yuan for that period (approximately 6 billion USD), representing a 54% increase from the previous year. This equates to an average daily revenue of 450 million Yuan (or 66 million USD). In the same period, Facebook reported revenues of 7 billion USD [139]. Thus, in comparison, Tencent's achievement is nothing short of astonishing, especially in view of the fact that Tencent's products are dominant only within the Chinese territory, whilst those of the Facebook group are leaders across many regions across the world (see also Fig. 7.1).

Of the 40.4 billion Yuan revenue for Q3 2016, Tencent's distribution of income channels is shown in Fig. 3.3. As can be seen, games and QQ membership (both add-on products within their respective platforms) serve as two major incomes' streams, collectively contributing 69% of the company's entire revenue.

Given the different product orientations of QQ and WeChat as explained in earlier in this chapter, the sibling platforms also have dedicated strategies for revenue generation. QQ mainly relies on its end users to generate income, whilst WeChat derives profit mainly from business users.

- QQ: Profit made from end users

The trend for mobile QQ app is expected to continue with developments in its style and settings for membership services, along with a healthy provision of privilege services to attract subscribers, as described in Section 3.3.6. Fig. 3.3 reveals QQ membership contributes 24% of Tencent's total revenues. This is supplemented by numerous other customisation features that appeal to younger user groups due to their low pricing structure, such as chat bubbles, personalised themes and add-on emoji

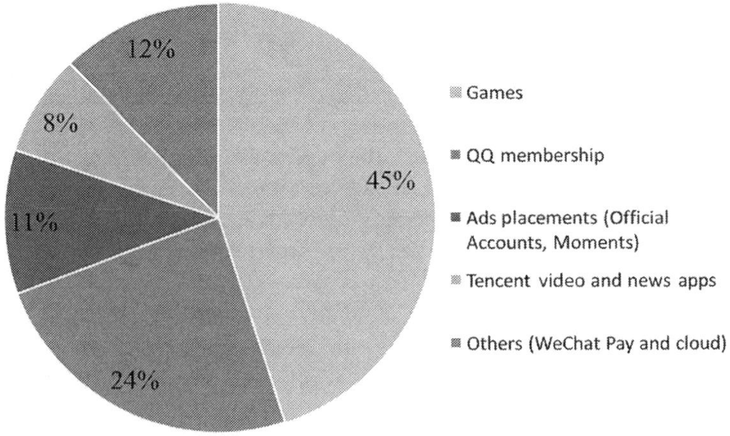

Fig. 3.3 Tencent's revenue distribution for Q3 2016.

apps. QQ also possesses a dedicated games platform, QQ Game,[2] which operates predominantly on a desktop environment. QQ Game was created in 2003 and continues to make significant contributions to Tencent's company profit each year. Tencent has also expanded in novel ways in terms of payment facilities as a means of generating additional income—QQ Token, the virtual currency system on the platform, which is used for in-game purchases and membership services [162].

- WeChat: Profit made from business users

WeChat provides ample channels for third-party businesses to communicate with existing and potential customers via the Public Platform, as explained in Section 2.4. Business users can create up to three types of Official Accounts, depending on their needs. General WeChat users can choose the kind of advertisements they wish to receive by subscribing to the Official Accounts of specific companies. WeChat's Public Platform therefore delivers mutual benefit for businesses and end users, representing an appealing investment channel for organisations to gain access to WeChat's substantial user base. Even though WeChat places strict controls on the distribution and content of advertisements in Moments, the platform is still able to contribute 11% of Tencent's revenues through Official Accounts.

[2] http://qqgame.qq.com/.

Weibo

4

4.1 The Chinese Twitter

4.1.1 Continuous development

Media analysts have referred to there being essentially two micro blog services in the world: Weibo and Twitter [163]. In Section 1.3.1.2, reasons were examined on how Sina defeated its local rivals towards becoming the dominant leader in the Chinese micro blog arena. Indeed, Sina Weibo has become so dominant in China that the term 'Weibo' (literally translated as 'micro blog') is, for all intents and purposes, exclusively used to refer to Sina's platform. Table 4.1 outlines the main events of Weibo's development journey according to statistics provided by Refs. [106, 164, 165].

Weibo's development was original based on the success and features of Twitter, where users can take the role as audience to receive information of interest and/or publish content for others. Similar to Twitter, the publication of posts in Weibo is restricted to 140 Chinese characters, although Weibo experimented with expanding the limit to 2000 characters in January 2015, which was subsequently implemented in full in February 2016 [166]. Weibo allows for the sharing of numerous data including texts, pictures, weblinks and videos. As with the provisions of similar platforms, Weibo's main characteristics are the ability for users to publish information rapidly and the swift dissemination of content.

As discussed in Section 1.2.4.1, Sina Weibo is a product arising from the influence of mobile technology advancement, particularly with respect to the proliferation of mobile data services (such as 3G and 4G) and smartphones which gathered pace from around 2009. Just a year later, Sina Weibo underlined its investment in the mobile Internet age—official Sina statistics for 2010 revealed an average of over 25 million tweets were made each day on Sina Weibo, 38% of which were performed on mobile devices [167]. Unlike WeChat which is designed specifically for mobile devices, Weibo possessed a broader remit by being offered across various desktop, browsers and mobile terminals.

4.1.2 Weibo vs. WeChat

The year 2011 represented a peak year for Sina Weibo's development. As explained in Section 1.3.1.1, not only did Sina Weibo defeat its two most significant competitors at the time (Kaixin Network and RenRen, who, at the time, were China's most successful equivalents of Facebook), Weibo also established its dominant position

Social Networks in China. https://doi.org/10.1016/B978-0-08-101934-4.00004-2

Table 4.1 Sina Weibo development history

2009	Sina Weibo launched	8 billion users in total
2010	Hosted the first *China Weibo Developer Conference*	75 million users in total
2011	Registered weibo.com domain name	73 million MAU
2012	Hosted the annual grand ceremony, *Weibo Night*	97 million MAU
2013	Daily active users reached 46 million	129 million MAU
2014	IPO stock listing	176 million MAU
2015	Extended word limit of posts	236 million MAU

Note: Statistics represent end-of-year figures.

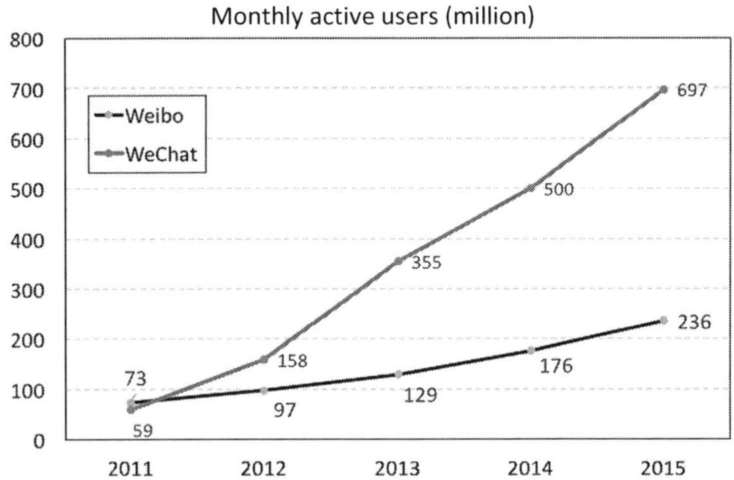

Fig. 4.1 Weibo vs. WeChat: MAUs.

through the implementation of key strategy as explained in Section 1.3.1.2. Following this prosperous period for Sina, rival services were gradually phased out and the term 'Weibo' became synonymous with Sina Weibo.

Despite this initial period of success, Weibo's growth was significantly halted by the competition from WeChat, which was released in 2011, 2 years after Weibo. Fig. 4.1 compares the MAUs for both platforms from late 2011 to the end of 2015 [168, 169]. WeChat's ability to mount a serious challenge to Weibo's dominance is attributable to two main reasons:

(1) As previously discussed in Section 2.3.5.2, user privacy is given utmost importance in WeChat. This has manifested in the form where, without exception, only direct friends can see each others' content on the platform, be it posts, comments or any other type of contribution. By contrast, Weibo's default settings allow all users to see all available content published on the platform, regardless of the relationship between users (e.g. as a *follower* or *followee*). Weibo's strategy therefore presents pros and cons: the advantage is that it can increase the speed of information dissemination, whilst the drawback is that Weibo users feel concerned with the violation of their privacy [170].

(2) WeChat designers followed a minimalism aesthetic philosophy (as explained in Section 2.3.1), and have implemented various spam control techniques (see Section 2.3.5.3) so as to ensure users are not disrupted with unwanted adverts, scams, commercial promotions or meaningless broadcast. Too much the contrary, Weibo has, over the years, introduced large-scale advertisements and commercial placements within its platform that users cannot opt-out of as a means of maximising revenue. For example, the launch page of Weibo's mobile app is invariably that of a commercial display. The main news and user content page is comprised of numerous unsolicited advertisements interleaved with friends' updates. Moreover, upon registering for a Weibo account, a new user is, by default, automatically enlisted as a follower to a potentially significant number of other users. A test was conducted in October 2016—upon the creation of a new Weibo user account, a total of 61 Weibo users were added to the new user's account to follow. These 61 users are examples of those who have paid additional fees in return for obtaining greater exposure on the Weibo platform.

4.1.3 Weibo vs. Twitter

Being originally constructed with Twitter as a basis, notable degrees of similarity exist between Weibo and Twitter. This section presents some of the most notable (as well as less obvious) distinctions between the two platforms.

- Interface structure

Figs 4.2 and 4.3 show the schematic diagram for Twitter and Weibo's interface, respectively. Mobile app versions for both platforms each comprise of five main pages, providing similar core functionalities necessary for micro blog services such as writing/commenting/reposting/liking posts, news feed lists, messaging, following friends as well as popular features such as search facility, scan QR code and listing of 'hot' news.

- Word limits

Twitter imposes a post limit of 140 characters, that is, one alphanumeric letter being one character, and which normally occupies 1 byte of memory space, although Twitter has its own formal and intricate definition of characters [171]): in context, with the average word length in the English language being 5.1 letters [172] plus a space character following each word (thus giving 6.1 characters), each Twitter message can convey approximately 23 intelligible pieces of information. On the other hand, despite Weibo's recent expansion of its word limit to 2000 characters for posts, Weibo users have generally maintained the habit of publishing within the original limit of 140 characters: though this being typically in the form of Chinese characters, each equating to approximately 2 bytes of memory [173]). The average length of a word

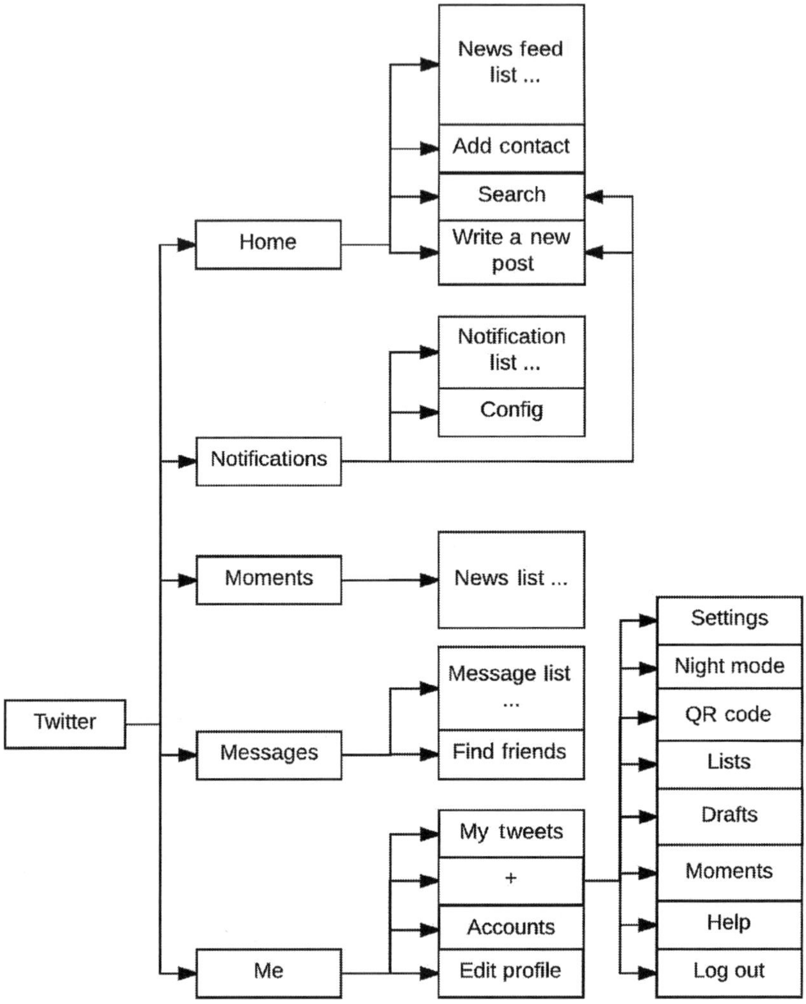

Fig. 4.2 Interface structure of Twitter (mobile app version).

in the Chinese language comprises of two characters [174]. Hence, each micro blog written in Chinese can express 70 pieces of intelligible information, which is nearly three times that of Twitter (see calculations next).

$$\text{Twitter:} \quad \frac{140}{5.1 + 1} \approx 23$$

$$\text{Weibo:} \quad \frac{140}{2} = 70$$

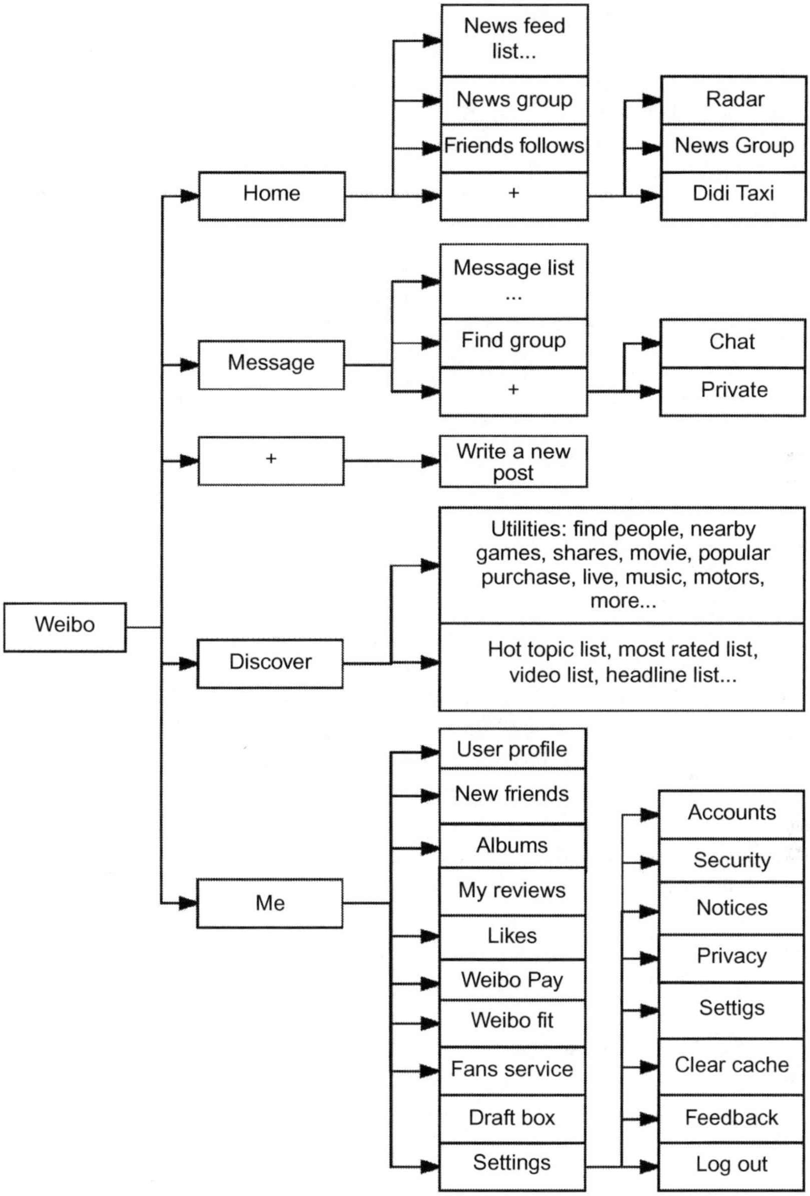

Fig. 4.3 Interface structure of Weibo (mobile app version).

- Functionality

As shown in Figs 4.2 and 4.3, Weibo has, over time, incorporated a wider range of functionalities than what is found on Twitter, such as News Group, Find People Nearby, Live and Motors. One general trend in Chinese social networks is that companies seek to devise and integrate add-on products to their core platform. Without exception, Weibo has done so via additional services including shopping, games, taxi and fitness, all of which will be discussed in more detail in Chapter 5. On the other hand, built-in functionalities in Twitter are fundamental rather than diversified extensions to its core service, although the potential for additional features on Twitter is made possible via external API development by third parties.

Another point of comparison is video and music services on both platforms. Weibo has a built-in service for users to upload and share videos, whilst Twitter users can only do so via links to third-party video platforms such as YouTube. Weibo's music application is an extremely popular feature, whilst Twitter suspended its music service on 21 Mar. 2014 [175]. One of main reasons for Twitter's unsuccessful music provision is the fierce competition from iTunes, where users have formed fixed habits of listing to and purchasing music from Apple's service. Weibo also benefits from the comparatively less rigorous systems of copyright in China, allowing it to provide extensive music libraries and access to content, whereas Twitter's service merely comprised of Spotify, Rdio and iTunes [176].

- Media nature

Twitter was founded by the then emerging company, Odeo, from where it gained increasing popularity over the years via a series of tests, updates and promotional activities. By contrast, the development and rise of Chinese micro blogs possessed unique advantages in terms of publicity as they were produced by well-established Chinese Internet web-portal companies such as Sina, Sohu, NetEase and Tencent (described in Box 1.1). Micro blogs developed by these companies were therefore built upon a wealth of existing knowledge and experience gained from parent networks and web portals [177]. And as such, the eventual Chinese micro blogs that were to emerge benefited from the company's respective experience with aspects such as media and content distribution, and user preferences.

Even though Twitter and Weibo have become leading channels for news acquisition for their respective user groups, research in Ref. [176] found that the usage of news media in Weibo is more substantial than that of Twitter. Fifty-one percent of Twitter users' behaviour pertains to obtaining and sharing news, whilst the equivalent for Weibo is 70%. This indicates that Chinese users place high emphasis on using Weibo as a source of accessing and sharing news and media stories. Weibo's role as a news channel will be further discussed in Section 4.3.2.

- Social impact

Aside from news and media story acquisition, Twitter is mainly used for entertainment purposes, of which comprise of three main activities: browsing, posting and obtaining friends' updates. Weibo users also regularly partake in these activities, on top of which Weibo is also used as a platform for users to express political and social opinions. Section 4.4.1 will discuss how Weibo has, by design or otherwise, made notable contributions to democratic voices in Chinese society.

A 2010 article [163] made a comparison between Twitter and Weibo in respect of the extent to which a post by a user with few followers could be disseminated to a large audience. The example provided in this case was that a Twitter user with 238 followers posted a tweet that eventually obtained over 95,000 reposts during 6 days spanning 5th to 10th September 2010. The extent of such vast information propagation was deemed by the authors to be impossible in Weibo. Section 4.4.2.1 will provide an example of a recent case to contradict the outcomes from Ref. [163], whereby a regular Weibo user with fewer than 1000 followers obtained the attention of users at the national level.

4.2 Design features

4.2.1 *Publishing*

As detailed earlier, a Weibo user can use up to 2000 characters for each post: this having been expanded from the original of 140 characters to allow for more flexible publication for users [166]. No restriction is placed on the content or style of posts, hence users can publish anything ranging from trivial matters to important news events. Weibo therefore places little requirements in becoming an author on the platform, and therefore any user regardless of background, education, wealth or social status can potentially become a source of information, news or commentary on Weibo.

One restriction that remains is that for photos, where a maximum of nine is permitted per post, of which associated thumbnails are aligned as a 3×3 grid below the text. This limit has stimulated creative efforts amongst users in the delivery of information.

As Weibo becomes increasing prevalent as news source (to be discussed in more detail in Section 4.3.2), Sina has continuously reminded users of exercising responsible reporting when they post news and updates, especially content that could be disingenuous or misleading to the public. Sina has also established a facility for users to report fake or dishonest information, which is available as a link on the bottom-right corner of each user's Weibo page: '举报不良信息' (translated as 'Reporting Unhealthy Information'). Based on Sina's own investigation [178], numerous fabricated news stories have been removed, for example, an explosion that was supposed to have taken place on 8 Mar. 2012, and a young boy selling flowers was reported to have been kidnapped on 26 January 2012.

4.2.2 *Messaging*

As concomitant with competing platforms, Weibo has a built-in function for private messaging, although in the face of competition from WeChat, Weibo has made progressive innovations to its messaging service. The original chat function in Weibo came in the form of a basic tool offering a pure text format, which has since been expanded to include features such as sending pictures, location, groups and Red Packets.

4.2.3 *The big 'V': Verified accounts*

Upon Weibo's creation, Sina offered a mechanism for verified accounts, which was initially designed for use by celebrities and organisations. Verified accounts have a 'V' sign (denoting 'verified') attached to the bottom-right corner of the respective avatars.

The sign was initially presented in gold colour and changed to red in late 2016. The previous verification process, being relatively strict and somewhat tedious, therefore gave users with the 'V' logo a higher level of status in the Weibo community. Being a verified account also means the user will bear a certain level of responsibility and liability for the information that is published. This element is particularly crucial for the marketing strategy of the celebrity effect, which will be discussed in the next section.

Over recent years, Weibo gradually extended the verification process to attract more users and organisations. The platform's current verification process has thus become relatively straightforward,[1] covering the following categories:

- celebrity verification
- website verification
- media verification
- university verification
- enterprise verification
- personal identify verification

Amongst these categories, the personal identification verification represented a key step for the establishment of an authentic, real-name identification system in the social network space. This feature is enacted by a user through uploading their national Chinese ID card photograph onto the system, from where their personal details are formally verified against their national credentials.

The number of verifications for organisations has increased dramatically, serving as portals for disseminating information to the public. Over 97% of central governmental departments, 100% of province-level governments and over 98% of local governments possessed verified accounts on Weibo. As of October 2015, there were over 280,000 governmental verified accounts on Weibo [179]. Such verified accounts allow official parties to communicate directly to the public, as well as to receive feedback. This form of direct and peer-to-peer communication service represents an important extension to the provision and delivery of public notices, since the government and organisations could only previously rely on comparatively static websites to disseminate information. Weibo therefore serves as a notable public service for distributing national information as well as being a source of help for those wishing to obtain more information about particular national events or policies. Sections 4.4.1.2 and 4.4.2 will address these aspects in further detail.

4.2.4 Celebrity effect

As explained in Section 1.2.1, Sina started promoting the notion of the celebrity effect during the company's earlier venture with Sina Blog, way before the establishment of Weibo. As in other cultures, celebrities in China can include movie stars, reputable writers, TV presenters, sports men and women, established entrepreneurs and leaders of industry, who may each hold a significant fan base. Sina had made concerted efforts

[1] http://verified.weibo.com/verify/.

at the outset on establishing links with and attracting celebrities as a way to encourage them to use Sina's blogging platform. This mutually beneficial strategy served to raise Sina's profile well as further increase the platform's subscriber base, along with the associated benefits of enhancing the profile of individual celebrities. The use of celebrity blogs to promote blog services can be considered a unique characteristic of the Chinese online space, which has caused notable disturbance in the Chinese Internet industry. As the popularity of blog services began to diminish in China, Sina persisted with promoting celebrity blogs on its micro-blog service. As explained in Section 1.3.1.2, the *celebrity effect* was one of the most important strategies conceived by Sina to distinguish itself from the competition.

According to 2016 statistics [66], out of the 50 most popular film and television celebrities in China, 47 possess a verified Sina Weibo account. Each attract an average of 23 million followers, and amongst the 300 celebrities listed in the entertainment and sports sector, 278 have opened a Sina Weibo account. This tremendous degree of uptake has therefore brought vast exposure and value to Sina Weibo. For example, Jackie Chan had been using Sina to host his blog service (as mentioned in Section 1.2.1), and following the recession of blogs he has continued to use Sina to host his Weibo account where he regularly publishes news and interacts with his fans.

As China's social media ecosystem continues to evolve, Weibo has become an immensely popular platform for the public to discuss celebrity news and activities. Based on Ref. [66], over 110 million discussions were made in respect of the top-50 celebrities on Weibo in 2015 alone. One popular category is that of boy bands, where four members of the band TFBoys occupy four respective positions on the top-50 celebrity list—one band member is shown in Fig. 4.4—whilst for another band, EXO, current and former members of the group occupy a total of six positions on the list. Typically, the popularity of a Weibo account is assessed by factors such as the number of followers, total number of posts and the quantity of interactions (such as reposting and comments). However, measuring the popularity of a celebrity involves other metrics such as the amount of times the person is mentioned online. For example, although Chinese celebrities such as Jay Chou (周杰伦), Wallace Huo (霍建华) and Shuang Zheng (郑爽) do not have Weibo accounts (or equivalent accounts on other platforms), they all appear on the top-50 list of the most popular celebrities due to the frequent propagation of their names on online platforms.

In 2015, a total of 15,000 posts were published by the top-50 celebrities on Weibo, which together attracted a total of 650 million interactions (such as reposting and comments), meaning that each post recorded an average of 43,000 interactions. In fact, many posts by celebrities contain trivial content that possess little or no meaningful content, but are often short, stand-alone statements about the person's status (see, e.g. Fig. 4.4). Despite the basic nature of such material, posts like these prove that they serve to satisfy the public's insatiable appetite by attracting significant attention from followers. The fourth example in Fig. 4.4, for instance, shows the case of one celebrity posting a 'Good night' greeting with three supporting photographs that were casually taken. Within two days this post recorded over 1 million reposts, over 253,000 comments and over 669,000 likes. Similarly, the third example in Fig. 4.4 shows a

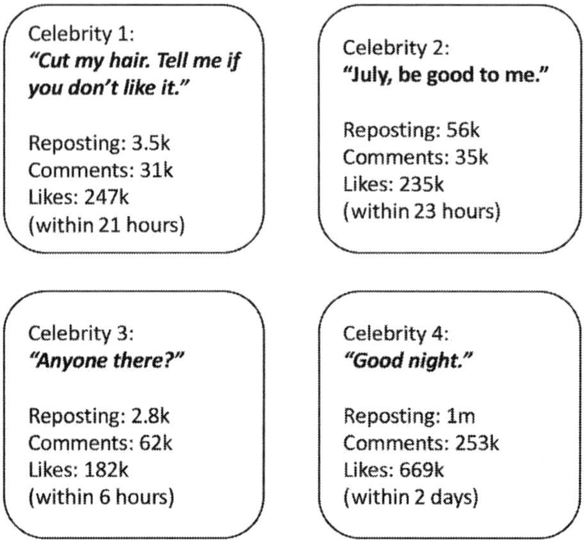

Fig. 4.4 Example of notable Weibo interactions with celebrities' posts about trivial matters.

celebrity asking if anybody was online which, within 6 hours of posting, received 2852 reposts, over 62,000 comments and over 182,000 likes.

Examples such as these demonstrate the massive contribution of the celebrity effect on Weibo's ecosystem, which has inevitably permeated similar blogging and social networking services in China [180]. The combined effect of such activities, trivial or otherwise has enabled Weibo to build its reputation by serving as an avenue for users to engage with celebrities. This system of celebrity information propagation, however, possesses certain benefits and implications, some of which are highlighted next.

4.2.4.1 Benefits of celebrity effect

- Celebrity Weibo has broken the mould of a fixed propagation model where celebrities could only broadcast information via traditional media and press channels.
- Content published by celebrities can be regarded as the most genuine source for a particular person. A celebrity can use Weibo to personally clarify rumours disclosed in other press, inform followers their activities and make official announcements.
- In response to the rising popularity of the celebrity effect, Weibo introduced a series of new features allowing for users to engage directly with celebrities. The most notable of which is that followers can make comments on a celebrity's Weibo page, and thus offered a direct communication mode between fans and idols.
- Research in Ref. [66] commented that young, handsome and multitalented male icons who were born in the 1990s to 2000s have become increasingly popular in the past year, and one of the main reasons for their success has been the 'fan power' being the driving force for celebrity endorsement on Weibo.

4.2.4.2 Implications of celebrity effect

- Given their potential influence and extent of following, comments and attitudes by celebrities are likely to have a notable effect on the mindset of fans and followers. There is therefore an expectation on celebrities to act and behave in an accountable and responsible manner on platforms such as Weibo, especially given their ability to disseminate information to a mass audience, as a failure to do so could lead to a negative impact on society.
- The authenticity of a celebrity's Weibo account can be limited to an extent, irrespective of its appearance or official status. For example, it is often commonplace to find that a personal assistant is hired to produce posts on behalf of a celebrity, which when discovered, is considered as an act of deception by followers [180].
- As with other comparable platforms, Weibo can be used for acts of deliberate malice. The platform has recorded frequent cases of violations of privacy and issues of reputation rights.

4.3 Network and media services

4.3.1 SNS model

As previously shown in Fig. 1.4, some distinctive differences exist that distinguish social networks from social media models. Weibo's predecessor—Sina Blog—is classified as a form of social media in this context, but Weibo remains difficult to categorise despite the availability of the aforementioned classification features. Part of the reason for this is that, being a still relatively new form of SNS platform, Weibo contains a substantial quantity of features associated with social media, whilst also possessing elements that do not fit within this mould.

Fig. 4.5 shows the full semantic network based on a search of the term 'privacy' in Weibo, produced by research in Ref. [181]. The sizes of the nodes are proportionate to the number of nodes linked to them. The distance between the words on the graph reflects the strength of relationship between each concept: that is, the frequency with which words are linked. Concepts with strong relationships appear closer together, whilst concepts with weak relationships are further apart. Even though the research examined the issue of privacy, the findings revealed the top-three related keywords used most frequently in Weibo: 'individual', 'Weibo' and 'information'. This result is consistent with the characteristics depicted in the social media model (see Fig. 1.4), where information sharing and dissemination are based on the emphasis of the individual.

4.3.2 News channel

Weibo's media function has extended its importance as a channel for Chinese Internet users to obtain news on national and international developments. As shown in Fig. 4.3, the Discovery section is one of the core pages on Weibo app, which when accessed, provides a list of hot topics, and thus provides a convenient way for users to browse current and popular news stories and information.

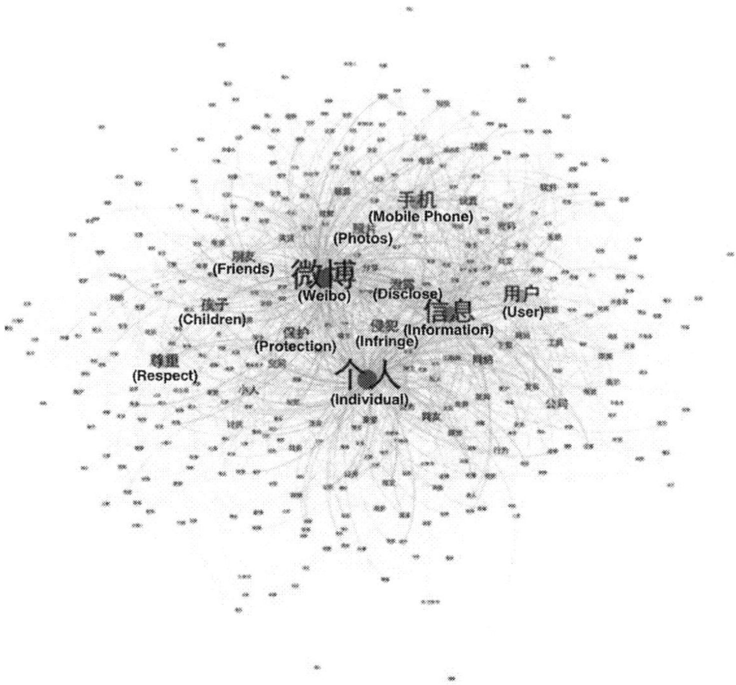

Fig. 4.5 Semantic network of Weibo using index 'privacy' [181].

One recent example is the coverage of the UK referendum on EU membership, which was shown on the hot-topic list. As on 25 June 2016, the statistics showed that the article was read a total of 0.73 billion times and received over 252,000 comments from users. The topic is ranked the second hottest topic in the sociology category. Weibo also promoted interaction and interest by inviting users to participate in a simple poll. To inform users of hot topics, Weibo displayed a default message in the search field on the Discovery page of: 'Everyone is searching: UK leaves EU'.

Another example is that of the 2016 Rio Olympics. In modern Chinese culture, the Olympic Games have been constantly capturing the attention of the entire nation [182]. In the list of Weibo's hot topics, there were at least three entries on the Olympics during the period of Olympic Game in 2016. Weibo placed various highlights of the topic on the main Discovery page, including a default term of: 'Everyone is searching: The 20th Gold Medal' in the search field, an *Olympics Video* utility, '中国田径女队被出局' (China's Track Team is Out), and highlights of the latest stories from the Games.

4.3.3 Live broadcast

One niche application within Weibo is that of Weibo Live (微直播),[2] a video broadcast platform developed by Sina for live reporting. As with normal posts, a user can

[2] zhibo.weibo.com.

participate in an existing live broadcast by commenting or displaying content with the host and other users, as well as host their own live events. Weibo Live therefore serves as an innovative broadcast system that extends on the more traditional services provided by social networking platforms. The advantages of Weibo Live mainly include:

- Weibo Live is convenient to use comprising of a one-press action to initiate the process.
- The function supports a wide range of terminal devices, including computers, tablets and even TVs.
- There is no need to upload videos as a separate process as users can simultaneously record and broadcast.
- A live broadcast can potentially attract a large audience as concomitant with other forms of publishing on the platform.

An example is shown in Fig. 4.6 of a promotional activity in Beijing in July 2016. The event was presented by a host and captured live via a camcorder. The live video was broadcast via Weibo Live and displayed on large LCD screens at the venue, hence also drawing the attention of passers to the event. The host also displayed live messages via Weibo from where followers could make additional comments and interactions, all of which were displayed on the screen in real time in conjunction with the live video. The event received fervent response from the audience—both those present in person and online—whilst the Weibo message board refreshed at a rapid pace indicating the large quantity of users and interactions.

Another example of Weibo Live is an application scenario where celebrities can use the feature to engage with followers by simply using a smartphone or tablet device.

Fig. 4.6 Embedded Weibo usage in a live event in Beijing (July 2016).

Celebrities can host Q&A sessions with the followers who could raise questions by posting to the session. These messages were displayed in real time on the bottom half of the screen. The celebrity was therefore able to answer questions and interact with fans directly.

4.4 Social impact

4.4.1 Democratic voices

The 35th item on the Chinese constitution states: *Citizens of the People's Republic of China have the freedom of speech, publishing, gathering, socialising, parading and protesting.* In the case of traditional blogging platforms, as emphasis is placed on the voice of the individual rather than social connections (as described in Section 1.2.1), users could be reluctant to post certain content or opinions due to the potential exposure of their identity. By contrast, a platform such as Weibo facilitates a rapid transmission of information by any individual, which is often independent of their level of knowledge, status and identity. An opinion voiced on Weibo is done so on a level playing field with all other users, and thus represents potentially one of many contributions within a system of peers. Many critics such as Refs. [183–185] have therefore regarded Weibo as having played a major social role in China's democratic voices. The characteristics of Weibo's provision that enable it to contribute in such a way is reflected in two aspects: the grass-roots nature and public scrutiny.

4.4.1.1 Grass-roots nature

Grass roots (草根), as defined in the Chinese modern dictionary, is: 'common citizens who act as a public majority at the base level of society' [186]. The term created in reference to those in direct contrast to persons possessing political power, wealth, a high level of education/qualifications and/or social influence. Thus, in the context of Weibo, if celebrities and big 'V' users (the mainstream) represent one major faction, grass-roots users (nonmainstream) would represent the other. As a self-sufficient media platform, Weibo functions on the default position of cultivating interaction between mainstream and nonmainstream users. Article [187] defines the dissemination of information from mainstream users to grass-root users as the *resonation effect*,[3] whilst dissemination from the grass root to the mainstream is defined as the *overflowing effect*. This section will focus on the latter concept.

Knowingly or otherwise, Weibo has provided a powerful voice for Chinese grass-roots users. In parallel with Weibo's increasing prominence, many grass-roots users have become recognised as popular news distributors on the platform. Based on the theory of Six Degrees of Separation [188], everyone can be connected with anyone else in the world with no more than six links. Weibo's reposting mechanism allows

[3]Discussed in Section 4.2.3, The Big 'V'—Verified accounts and Section 4.2.4, Celebrity effect.

users who are entirely unknown or unconnected to each other to form 'weak ties' (see Box 1.2 for definition), and thus enhancing the travel of information from grass-roots users to the mainstream. The mainstream users can further repost these information therefore multiplying the dissemination speed and scope, thereby multiplying the speed and scope of dissemination and hence increasing the impact of grass-roots users. The case studies that will be presented in Section 4.4.2 are typical examples of such impact.

4.4.1.2 Public scrutiny

The ability to express opinions in Weibo that can garner large following or interest from the community has therefore stimulated other facets connected to the democratic voice. One such element is the propensity for users to engage in the scrutiny of public affairs and acts of government. Well-known examples of such public scrutiny are the *Weibo Anti-Corruption* (微博反腐) wave that has taken place since 2011, which is defined by Baidu Baike [189] (the equivalent of Wikipedia in China) as:

> *Weibo Anti-Corruption refers to a social phenomena where Internet users scrutinise, criticise, and reveal corruption behaviours relevant to public power and social force, via a specialised form of new media—Weibo.*

The Weibo Anti-Corruption wave in China reached peek levels during 2011 and 2012. At the time, Sina Weibo just took over the leadership in the micro blog arena,[4] where its features and, in particular, the ability to quickly disseminate information were not immediately obvious to the Chinese public. Indeed, it was not uncommon for users to confuse Weibo as being a direct alternative to more traditional social networks at the time, such as MSN Space and QQ, where privacy plays a more dominant role. As such, some users, including government officials, disclosed indecent behaviour or acts of bribery on Weibo without anticipating that it would lead to stark condemnation from the public. Some notable examples of such behaviour are outlined following [190]:

- *The flirting scandal.* In June 2011, the Head of Sanitary Bureau in Jiangsu province mistook Weibo for a private chatting tool and used the platform to flirt with female whilst revealing elements of bribery that he was involved in. This quickly drew the attention of numerous Weibo users and eventually the Chinese authorities. The city's standing committee subsequently called an emergency meeting and suspended the job of the Official.
- *The erotic picture scandal.* In July 2011, a post entitled 'Found a memory stick—seems to contain erotic videos of a Kunming city government official from Development and Reform Commission' was widely disseminated on Weibo. Consequently, the Development and Reform Commission of Kunming city confirmed the identity of the person in the videos and suspended his role 1 month later.
- *The showing-off scandal.* In March 2012, the Vice Chief of Xiqing District in Tianjing city was under investigation for the reason that his daughter regularly posted photographs on Weibo showing off her collection of luxurious and designer goods. Users on Weibo also led to expose several privileges that she possessed due to her father's position in government,

[4]Discussed in Section 1.3.1.2.

which were deemed unfair to society. These included a school transfer with insufficient qualifications and admission to the National Land Bureau without having passed the required examinations.

- *The watch scandal.* In August 2012, the Head of Safety Supervision Bureau in Shanxi province, Da Yang, was photographed with a smile during the inspection of a severe car accident. These photographs were quickly reported on Weibo and reposted several thousand times. Yang's depiction led to huge backlash on the platform, with users voicing their anger over his flippant and unsympathetic attitude towards the severe accident scene. Public attention on this case of the *smiley Head of Bureau* led to more serious revelations, including the numerous expensive watches he had worn on various occasions, one of which had an estimated value of over 300,000 Yuan as reported by Weibo users. Under mounting public pressure, Yang gave an interview on Weibo to explain his source of income, but the watching public deemed his answers to be unsatisfactory. One month later, following an official government investigation, several of Yang's official duties were revoked.

As Chinese users became more familiar with Weibo's dual characteristics of being a social media and network platform, the anticorruption phenomena waned somewhat as many officials became more careful about what they disclosed on the platform. Report in Ref. [190] comments that many officials now refrain from wearing watches, and have become cautious with the type of items and brands (such as cigarettes and clothing) that may be particularly visible and open to scrutiny and backlash. Some officials do not possess a Weibo account and forbid their family members from using it. Despite this, Weibo anticorruption phenomena are still very much in operation, serving to represent the voice of regular citizens on matters of public affairs that may not be otherwise represented in traditional avenues of media.

4.4.2 Public helpline

To serve a role of an effective social press, Weibo has been widely used as a public information helpline by Chinese Internet communities. The real-time, interactive and convenient characteristics of information dissemination on Weibo (especially via mobile platforms) exceed what can be provided through traditional media channels such as TV, newspapers and websites. Whether information pertains to major events around the world or local incidents, Weibo users are able to report events, express opinions and obtain comment from other users. This section will present two case studies that demonstrate how Weibo has been used as a public helpline in aid of the general public.

4.4.2.1 Case study: Assault incident in Rujia hotel

At 00:06 on 3 April 2016, a Weibo user 'Wanwan_2016' (弯弯_2016) published a post reporting an incident that happened just minutes before:

> *After checking into Rujia Heshuo hotel, I was followed by a male stranger who later caught hold of my hair and pulled me away. I suspected he was attempting to drag me to an area where there were no surveillance cameras. Hotel staffs heard my scream*

but thought it was a quarrel between a couple, and therefore did not intervene. I finally managed to escape after another female hotel guest interfered.

Over the following 2 days, Wanwan reported her experience in more detail on Weibo, including about how she approached the hotel management and police about the crime and potentially catching the perpetrator. She reported that the response from the hotel, despite being a nationally recognised chain, was nonchalant and unhelpful, whilst the police did not investigate her case with adequate actions.

Despite the passive response shown by the hotel and police in the first instance, Wanwan's report of the incident on Weibo created tremendous following and interest, and eventually became a hot topic not only on Weibo but also across numerous other social media and networking platforms in China. The topic of 'Heshuo Hotel Girl Got Assaulted' (和颐酒店女生遇袭, 'Heshuo' being the hotel name) gathered pace on Weibo where, within a matter of days since the original post, it was ranked number 1 on the list of hot topics. At 19:30 on the 6th April (just 3 days after the initial post), the topic recorded 1.5 billion visits, 1.9 million comments and 53,000 followers. Public comments were generally comprised of sympathy for the victim, condemnation of the crime and criticisms of the hotel and police. The significant degree of attention that was created eventually imposed pressure on the hotel and local police station, where on the afternoon on the 6th April, a public apology was made to the society in both a press conference and formal statement on Weibo by the senior hotel management. Even a well-known Chinese travel company, Ctrip (who provided Wanwan's hotel booking service) made a formal apology to the public on Weibo. The local police also sped up their investigation and arrested the perpetrator of the attack on the 7th April [191].

The summary of this event can thus be made as follows. The victim Wanwan reported the crime to the police immediately after the attach, but failed to obtain a satisfactory response. She then persistently reported the incident on Weibo through text and video content, which led to substantial levels of interest from the public just days following the incident, of which resulted in a profound effect on the pace and will of the official parties on the handling of the case. Thus, in the eyes of many Internet users and the general public, it has been commented that publishing information on Weibo can lead to more effective outcomes than solely relying on the actions of the police [192]. This perspective holds water where, given the penetration of social media and networks will continue to expand in China, more people will likely resort to such platforms to seek help and assistance when official bodies fail to address their needs. Wanwan's case is a poignant example of how public pressure and awareness, as made possible via Weibo and similar platforms, contributed to a rapid resolution and application of justice.

4.4.2.2 Case study: Posts for missing persons

Requests for information on and calls for missing persons are also quite common in Weibo. Such cases are usually one of two types: someone looking for a missing family member or someone who has been found and seeking home. The purpose of such posts is typically that of advertising the identity of the missing person as well as contact information. Posts can be rapidly disseminated by Weibo users, and in the case where an original post is reposted by users of verified accounts, the dissemination effect becomes even stronger.

In a similar vain, Weibo has also been used to raise awareness of natural disasters and times of public need. Following the Yaan earthquake on 20 April 2013, Weibo users had made over 640,000 posts on aspects such as search parties and missing persons, which collectively recorded over 30 million readers within 24 hours of the event. Subsequent charities that were promoted on Weibo for the earthquake relief reached 0.1 billion Yuan within 5 days of the disaster [193]. Some commentators have thus referred to Weibo as one of the most convenient and important channels for hosting and enacting a range of public services and initiatives [193].

Add-on products

5

Unlike Facebook or Twitter who promote open-APIs for third-party developers to produce add-on applications and features for their platforms, WeChat, QQ and offer both core functionalities and added features as in-house, proprietary services. This is owing to the trend of Chinese social networks in offering an integral platform to cater for the needs of users, especially in the context of mobile Internet. Therefore, as irrelevant as some may first appear on an SNS, this chapter will explore several adjuncts yet important add-on products developed by platform providers, including mobile games, electronic payment facilities, fitness applications and taxi services. As will be seen, such add-on products have brought vital complimentary benefits in strengthening the core provisions of a platform, as well as enrich the broader functioning of the Chinese SNS ecosystem.

5.1 Mobile games

Stimulated by the increasing penetration of Internet connectivity on smartphones, the number of Chinese mobile-game users has expanded rapidly in recent years. The rapid acceleration of the Chinese mobile market has attracted game developers and investors alike, the value of which rose from 16.9 million RMB in the third quarter of 2012 to 108.5 million RMB in the second quarter of 2015 [194–196]. As consistent with other parts of the globe, social networks have become a cornerstone of mobile game distribution in China. At the time of writing, over two-thirds (66.9%) of Chinese players access mobile games via social network channels, as reported by CNNIC [197].

5.1.1 Genres and ranking

There are various media channels and platforms in China that publish, rank and assess mobile games, most of which consistently categorise mobile game genres into the same eight major genres, including Leisure and Quiz, Sports and Racing, Chess and Card, Action and Adventure, Management and Strategy, Fly and Shooting, Role Playing and Network Games. A shown in Table 5.1, the two largest genres are Leisure and Quiz and Sports and Racing, which have a market occupancy of 28.5% and 23.8%, respectively. Chess and Card and Action and Adventure genres also occupy significant portions across all games. The two smallest genres are Role Playing and Network Games, which have a combined occupation of 6.3%. One possible reason for this is that games from these latter two genres are subject to greater limits in hardware

Social Networks in China. https://doi.org/10.1016/B978-0-08-101934-4.00005-4

Table 5.1 **Chinese mobile game genre classifications (2015)**

Rank	Genre	Market occupation (%)
1	Leisure and Quiz	28.5
2	Sports and Racing	23.8
3	Chess and Card	16.9
4	Action and Adventure	11.0
5	Management and Strategy	6.9
6	Fly and Shooting	6.6
7	Role Playing	3.3
8	Network Games	3

Table 5.2 **Most downloaded games across all genres (2015)**

No.	Game title	Developer	Genre	Downloads (million)
1	WeRun	Tencent	Sports and Racing	1097
2	Temple Run 2	Imangi Studios	Action and Adventure	512
3	Chinese Poker	Tencent	Chess and Card	434
4	Drift	Tencent	Sports and Racing	425
5	Fun Fest	Happy Wind	Leisure and Quiz	398
6	Rhythm Master	Tencent	Leisure and Quiz	295
7	WeMatch	Tencent	Leisure and Quiz	260
8	Thunder Fighter	Tencent	Fly and Shooting	207
9	WeFly	Tencent	Fly and Shooting	185
10	Space Hunter	Yinhan Games	Network Games	162

performance and network provisions on mobile devices, and thus restrict the degree of complexity that can be provided. Hence despite the popularity of these genres in PC and console platforms [198], games from these categories are experiencing fewer downloads than those from other genres.

In terms of mobile game rankings in China, the total download counts can give a relatively accurate reflection on the penetration and popularity of individual games over a longer-term basis. Table 5.2 shows the top-10 most downloaded games across all genres at the end of 2015. Of the 10 Chinese titles, 7 are developed by Tencent, thus indicating the prevailing success of Tencent despite the presence of over 23,000 mobile game developers in China for the period between 2013 and 2015 [199].

5.1.2 Business strategy

This section presents the example of WeMatch (天天爱消除) as a case study for four main reasons: first, the game is situated firmly within the top-10 most downloaded games in China, as shown in Table 5.2; second, it belongs to the leading Leisure and Quiz genre and may be considered as one of the most successful clones of Bejeweled;

third, it is developed by Tencent—the largest and most influential social network company and game developer in China and fourth, it faces direct competition from rival title Fun Fest, developed by Happy Wind—an independent company specialised in mobile games—employing similar gameplay features and rules.

This game will be analysed on three aspects. The first concerns how the game attracts players, which entails importing new players and offering a smooth and trouble-free download experience, which can together be assessed by the download count. The second aspect is how the game retains players once they are engaged. This is determined by the appeal of the game, such as the visual design and playing experience that may be influenced by local cultures and gamers' expectations. Another component for retaining players is to employ strategies for saving player data such as via scoreboards, progress and playing time. The extent of player retention can be assessed by active user counts over a given period. The third and final feature is how the title generates income. Fundamentally, each game needs to entice gamers to play repeatedly with an appropriate payment mode in order to maintain healthy revenues for the game's creators.

5.1.2.1 Attracting players

WeChat's main 'Discover' page provides direct entry to the Games section of the app, thus helping to provide easy access as well as added exposure on the platform. Whilst a similar feature is offered in comparable platforms, it often requires a somewhat longer process of navigation before it can be accessed. In the case of Facebook on iOS, games are obtained via the following menus: *More* → *See More* → *Apps* → *Games* as shown in Fig. 2.3, and thus takes a greater number of steps than that in WeChat.

Upon entering WeChat's games section, users can see their player profile together with other relevant game promotions that are customised to their playing habits and preferences. Users can also see the most recent games that he/she has played, games that his/her friends have been playing (this therefore also serving as a subtle invitation to download those games), and other popular games in which the player may also be interested. Evidently, the platforms place notable effort in attracting players to download new games and/or to carry on playing existing games.

WeMatch was initially integrated within the WeChat app when it was first introduced in August 2013. This approach saved users from having to log into an app store, enter credentials and endure additional download times. This strategy led to a successful publication of the game, with 40 million registered users within 10 days of release [200]. As the game grew in popularity, more features were added and it was eventually separated from the WeChat app, although all original user profiles and data were kept intact.

5.1.2.2 Keeping players

Global-Mobile-Game-Confederation [199] revealed 54.5% of Chinese players would give up on a game if it lacks attractive contents. WeMatch is a representative example from the Leisure and Quiz genre, and offers a user-friendly interface and appealing graphics. Despite its simple rules (being largely similar to Bejeweled), WeChat can be played in either timer mode or adventure mode. The latter was introduced 2 years after the game's original release, offering additional features such as gadgets and bonuses. Via such a strategy, WeMatch reached 25 million daily active users as announced by Zhiping Liu (President of Tencent) in August 2013 [200].

The presence of a scoreboard can be a key strategy for stimulating repeated play. Research by Von Ahn and Dabbish [201] indicates Chinese players attach significant value on score rankings amongst friends, and is a feature that represents one of the most direct methods of stimulating repeated play. Additionally, research by CNNIC [197] shows 66.8% of Chinese players would watch and participate in a game's scoreboard, of which 65.2% of these players would compare their own rankings with friends on the scoreboard.

The scoreboard in WeMatch consists only of friends in a specific social circle who are playing WeMatch, unlike some other titles where rankings are shown for the entire player population, and therefore most other players are likely unknown to the player. WeChat takes a different approach by providing rankings based on a player's acquaintances, thus offering a more personal level of comparison. This personal level of customisation is consistent across other aspects of the game—for example, WeMatch cannot be played without first logging-on to the social platform (either WeChat or QQ), and thus operates under a specific set of criteria according to the player's profile.

WeChat also contains numerous features that facilitate sharing. For instance, after a player passes one level, the game will display the information of friends who have also passed this level along with their respective scores. The vast expansion of the Chinese economy in recent years has led to great increases in personal income levels across the country. With heightened levels of wealth, associated levels of growth have also been experienced in the consumption of luxury and designer goods as well as the notion of 'showing off' behaviour. Yuan [202] analysed the impact of what he terms as a 'showing-off style' of consumption (involving acts such as buying and displaying expensive consumer goods to friends to indicate personal wealth and achievement) and its impact on judgements of happiness amongst the Chinese population. The research outcomes of Yuan [202] revealed that showing-off consumption behaviour leads to higher levels of perceived happiness. In terms of gaming, such behaviour can be facilitated through sharing information about gaming achievements and progress via host networks. WeChat deploys a dedicated button that literally translates as 'show off' to allow players to advertise their success on a particular level to their friend circle.

5.1.2.3 Generating income

Once Chinese players establish a habit of playing a game repeatedly, their propensity to spend more money on the game increases. In WeMatch, higher levels in the game can become so difficult that players need to increase the chance of winning by acquiring special tools and/or gadgets. In some cases, it is simply impossible to complete a level unless gadgets are purchased and used. Players can purchase items such as extra power, weapons, gadgets and lives, where the cost of additional features is often set at very low prices to stimulate spending. The price of acquiring a handful of gadgets that would allow a player to easily pass an additional four levels in WeMatch is approximately 30 yuan—the same as the price of a chocolate bar in China. With such a design and pricing strategy, WeMatch generated an income of 1 million yuan per day [203].

5.2 Financial services

5.2.1 Payment system

All three social network giants in China have implemented payment services in the form of electronic wallet (or e-wallet) systems within their respective platforms. e-Wallets can be directly accessed from the personal page in various apps, and offer a broad range of services that mirror those commonly provided by traditional banks. Table 5.3 details a list and comparison of these services. Common functions include depositing funds into the e-wallet, withdrawing cash from an e-wallet to a designated bank account, direct money transfer between users, Red Packet service (to be explained in the next chapter), paying utility bills, mobile phone top-up, accessing trust funds or investment opportunities, viewing transaction history, giving charity and making donations and accessing online shopping systems.

In terms of online shopping systems, each platform offers an alternate form of implementation. In WeChat, e-shops and other forms of e-Commerce services can be opened with an Official Account, as explained in Section 2.4, and purchases can be made using the cash balance in the user's e-wallet. WeChat therefore provides an integrated and self-sufficient shopping utility. By contrast, QQ's provision comes in

Table 5.3 **Financial services offered by the three Chinese social networks**

	WeChat	QQ	Weibo
Deposit cash	✓	✓	✓
Withdraw cash	✓	✓	✓
Money transfer	✓	✓	✓
Red packet	✓	✓	✓
Pay for offline shopping	✓		
Pay for utilities	✓	✓	✓
Mobile top-up	✓	✓	✓
Pay off credit card balance	✓	✓	
Trust funds or investment	✓	✓	✓
Transaction history	✓	✓	✓
Charity	✓	✓	✓
Online shopping	✓	✓	✓
Online game credits	✓	✓	

association with JD[1]—one of the leading online shopping websites in China—where users have direct access to JD's shopping site via the QQ wallet page. And distinctive to the earlier two systems, Weibo hosts a 'lucky buy' service which functions in a similar way to Madbid [204], where users purchase credits in order to submit bids on discounted auction items.

As mentioned in Section 5.1, Tencent places great emphasis on gaming provisions, which has led to several highly ranked SNS games. Therefore, e-wallet facilities are also firmly integrated with gaming services where users can purchase game credits and associated game items for use in Tencent titles.

One other notable and unique function of WeChat's e-wallet is the ability for it to be used as a payment system in offline, day-to-day shopping scenarios, known as WeChat Pay. This operates as a contactless payment system used at the till of bricks-and-mortar vendors, and is largely similar to the Apple Pay system. As shown in Fig. 5.1A, when a user wishes to make a purchase, WeChat Pay produces a unique bar code within the app that is linked to the user's e-wallet. This is then scanned by the cashier's payment

Fig. 5.1 WeChat pay used for offline shopping. (A) Contactless payment. (B) Supermarkets promoting WeChat Pay and Alipay.

[1] jd.com.

Table 5.4 What are the reasons that make you want to use WeChat Pay?

46.2%	Simplicity—no need for cash and changes
44.9%	Convenience—no need to carry a wallet or purse
39.2%	Promotion—sellers frequently offer promotions or discounts for digital payment

system for fund transfer. Chinese retailers have therefore welcomed the system as it affords much greater convenience and speedier transactions than traditional cash- and card-based systems. Fig. 5.1B shows an example of a supermarket promoting WeChat Pay and a prominent competitor, Alipay. Research in Ref. [105] showed that amongst retailers who provide WeChat Pay and traditional cash payment options, 54% of users will choose to use the former for the reasons listed in Table 5.4.

Being built on WeChat's tremendous user base, WeChat Pay has experienced rapid and popular uptake in China since its introduction. By March 2016, more than half of all WeChat users had used its e-wallet service, where approximately 70% of all users record payments or transfers with an average value in excess of 100 yuan per month (equivalent of 15 USD or 10.5 British pounds)—more detail on the spread and value of payments and transfers is shown in Fig. 5.2 [105]. In comparison, none of WeChat's most direct competitors such as Facebook Messenger or WhatsApp offers a comparable service, of which is reflected in mobile revenues for the respective platforms. In the first quarter of 2016, WeChat generated 1.8 billion USD in mobile revenues, compared with WhatsApp's 49 million USD and zero for Facebook Messenger [205].

The penetration rate of WeChat's e-wallet is also impressive, where as mentioned earlier, over half of WeChat users have linked their banking credentials to the app. This is a notable achievement especially given the inherently distrustful culture in Chinese society and the associated risks with the Internet in terms of cybercrime, malware and

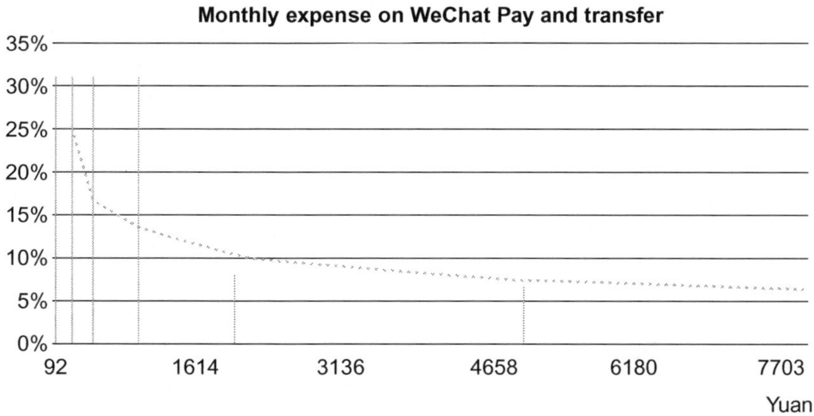

Fig. 5.2 Monthly expense on WeChat Pay e-wallet.

Table 5.5 The most frequently used payment functions in WeChat

Red Packets	84.7%
WeChat Pay	58.1%
Money transfer	56.9%
Receiving money	33.1%
Paying off credit cards	13.6%
Sharing payments between friends	12.8%

scams. Yet, being integrated with what has become a trusted brand in the form of both Tencent and WeChat, along with the provision of identity and authentication systems, Tencent has thus far been able to address certain reservations and concerns in the use of e-payment systems. This is perhaps in more stark contrast to Western platforms such as WhatsApp and Snapchat, which have yet to implement comparable payment systems.

Table 5.5 shows the ranking of various payment functions in WeChat in terms of usage [105]. Red Packets is the most frequently used payment option with 84.7%, and will be discussed in the next section.

5.2.2 Red Packets

Red Packets, also sometimes known as Red Envelops, have a long cultural history in China. Red Packets are defined as being of significance in two notable occasions in Chinese culture [206]: in Chinese New Year, where members of the senior generation in a family insert an amount of cash in red envelopes to give to children as well wishing, and the other, also involving cash-in-envelope, as a wedding present to the bride and groom. WeChat has pioneered the transfer of Red Packets onto social network platforms in digital format, alongside the numerous other add-on features discussed earlier. In 2014 WeChat launched a 'Red Packet' campaign, where users were able to send digital money to friends and family to celebrate Chinese New Year rather than sending cash in a red envelope, as is customary. Under this context, the gifting of Red Packets on social networks not only happens in traditional scenarios (i.e. from older generations to children, and for weddings) but also is extended between friends and colleagues, and even amongst organisations, which is an embodiment of an important element of Chinese relationships within a social network environment.

WeChat's Red Packet service went online on 26 January 2014 *quietly* without any official promotion or advertisement, and quickly spread throughout the country. Five days after its release, from midnight until 16:00 on the day of Chinese New Year, WeChat's Red Packet facility registered over 5 million users [207]. By March 2016, the user base expanded to 84.7% of all WeChat users and became the most widely used function in the WeChat payment facility, and approximately 70% users would pay or transfer a total amount in excess of 100 yuan (equivalent of 15 USD or 10.5 British pounds) each month [105].

The success of WeChat's provision of Red Packets can also be largely attributable to its well-thought design as much as the digitisation of a national tradition. Consistent with the minimalism principle as discussed in Section 2.3.1, WeChat's designers have focused on simplicity and usability over complexity and excess:

(1) The Red Packet feature is made directly available in the main chat window alongside other common facilities such as photos, voice/video call and location. User can choose the recipient of the Red Packet by opening the associated chat window.
(2) Opening the Red Packet feature will lead to a page where certain configurations can be set for the Red Packet. If this takes place in a one-to-one chat window, then the Red Packet only needs to set with the exact cash value followed by a greeting (such as *Happy New Year*). If the Red Packet is to be sent in a group-chat window, then its total value and the quantity of recipients can be defined (i.e. the total number of users who can open it—thus, for example, a packet can be sent to a group of 20 users but only the first 10 who open it can receive money).
(3) Once the packet is configured and sent, it will be displayed in the chat window. The recipient simply needs to tap the Red Packet icon to open it. The chat window will also display notifications of who has opened the Red Packet, with this information being available only to the sender. (The recipient can only see their own notifications, i.e. *You have opened xxx's Red Packet.*)

WeChat users can associate their e-wallets with their bank cards, and hence those who receive cash via Red Packets can withdraw the amount directly into their bank account. The ease of use and minimalistic interface has meant that the Red Packet component has become another significantly popular aspect within WeChat, even amongst older users aged over 55 who deliver Red Packets an average of 25 times per month [208].

Beyond interface design, Red Packet has also been transformed from a dutiful gift-giving into an exciting game that can be initiated by and played amongst a group of users. There are two ways of preparing Red Packets in a group-chat scenario. The first is to define an identical amount of money for each recipient (such as 10 yuan for each of the first 10 persons to open the packet), and the other is to let the system to assign a random amount for each recipient—the latter being more intriguing for play, and has led to a popular form of group play known as *Red Packet solitaire*. The game commences when one user in a group-chat window sends out a Red Packet containing a predefined number of recipients that is set to be fewer than the total number of members in the group. Since not all members of the group will be able to receive a cash gift, users will actively compete to open the packet (the sooner they open it, the more chance there is to acquire a packet). After the packet has been opened by the set number of recipients, all members of the group can view the result, which indicates the exact amount received by each person. The recipient receiving the largest payout of that round (denoted as 'Luckiest Draw') must then initiate the next round of sending a Red Packet via the same process. The game is repeated for as long as users wish to.

Red Packets in the form of solitaire has further fuelled the explosive growth in group-chat activity, especially during seasonal events such as Chinese New Year and national holidays. Fig. 5.3 shows the quantity of Red Packets sent and delivered for a range special occasions according to a variety of sources [209, 210]. The total number

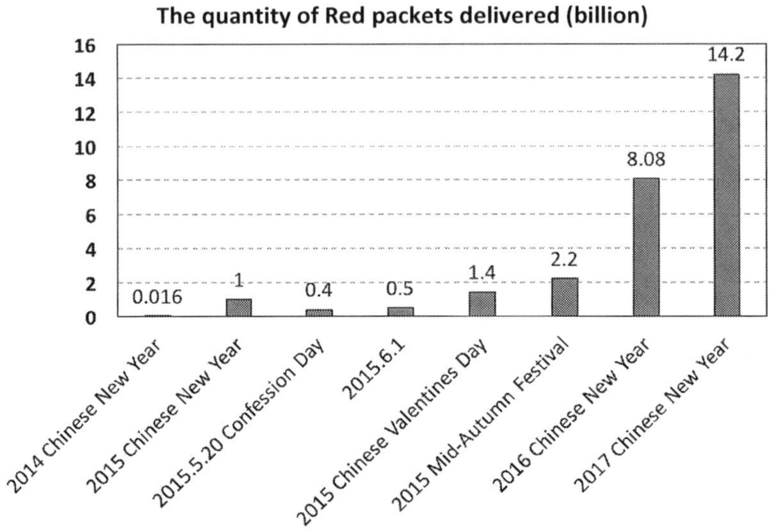

Fig. 5.3 The quantity of Red Packets delivered in special occasions.

of packets delivered on the day of Chinese New Year increased from 0.016 billion in 2014 to 14.2 billion in 2017, amounting to an 88,700% gain in just 3 years. Red Packets is also widely used in other festive occasions, as shown in Fig. 5.3, such as 20th May—Confession Day,[2] 1st June—Children's Day, Chinese Valentines Day[3] and Mid-Autumn Festival.[4]

5.3 Lifestyle services

Statistics from Ref. [105] reveal 62% of WeChat users have made use of the various functions provided in the platform WeChat to help with their daily lives. The following sections will detail some of the most notable examples of lifestyle features available across the leading social network platforms in China.

5.3.1 Fitness

Amongst the major sports and fitness activities, all the three leading Chinese social network platforms offer walking-related features. The rationale behind this is quite clear when considering the four sports in China that have the highest levels of participation for social network users: walking—46%, badminton—24%, running—22%

[2]The Chinese pronunciation of '520' is similar to '我爱你' (I love you).
[3]Namely *Qi Xi* (七夕), the 7th of July on the Chinese Lunar Calendar.
[4]Namely *Zhong Qiu* (中秋), the 15th of August on the Chinese Lunar Calendar.

and swimming—18% [66]. Since running can be tracked in a similar way to walking using smartphone apps, WeChat, QQ and Weibo have all provided built-in functions that can be used to monitor walking and running activities.

All three platforms offer a page showing the user's rank on walking and running activities among all friends who also participate, which is typically calculated on the total number of steps or total distance on a daily basis. Research in Ref. [105] showed 63% of social network users consider the greatest benefit of a fitness component on a social network platform to be the ability to keep track of daily exercise, whilst 40% like features allowing the comparison of exercise activities with friends, and 23% consider it a helpful tool for gaining awareness of health and wellbeing.

5.3.2 Third-party services

The provision of third-party services has become commonplace across the leading social networks in China, allowing users to obtain direct access to a variety of services including food ordering delivery, buying movie tickets, accessing travel services (such as hotels, train tickets, flights) and ordering a taxi. By February 2016, services such as these have been fully enabled across 17 provinces and 78 cities in China [105].

Even though services provided by third-party operators may often be hosted through other proprietary avenues such as other dedicated apps or websites, their extended presence on social platforms serves unique advantages over native apps and software. The following case study of Didi Taxi illustrates some of the more notable benefits to third-party providers in having their services hosted on a Chinese social network platform.

As a comparable equivalent of Uber, Didi Taxi is one of the leading taxi-calling companies in China. The service can be accessed via the company's dedicated mobile apps across various mobile platforms, but also in conjunction with WeChat through its e-Wallet page. Research in Ref. [211] showed that a large portion of Didi Taxi drivers spend 80% of their time communicating on WeChat, 10% chatting with passengers and only 10% on using Didi Taxi's native app. Despite being virtually identical to Didi Taxi's app in terms of interface design and functionalities, drivers thus demonstrate stark preference for WeChat's version. The reasons for this can be summarised as follows:

- WeChat allows drivers to develop their own customer resources: an element not possible in Didi Taxi's proprietary app. For example, one advantage of using an SNS platform such as WeChat is that drivers can establish a long-term social relationship with passengers and thus to promote repeated custom.
- Drivers can create and maintain their own community on WeChat (i.e. in the form of chat groups) to share information, offer help to peers and even share errands.
- WeChat helps to establish and cement the reputations of reliable and experienced drivers based on their relationships and rapport with customers. New and potential customers can also be linked via a friend's recommendation on the basis of previous experience and good service. Similarly, should a driver be unavailable, they can recommend trusted fellow drivers so as to also acquire and maintain a good reputation via any preexisting connection with customers on WeChat.

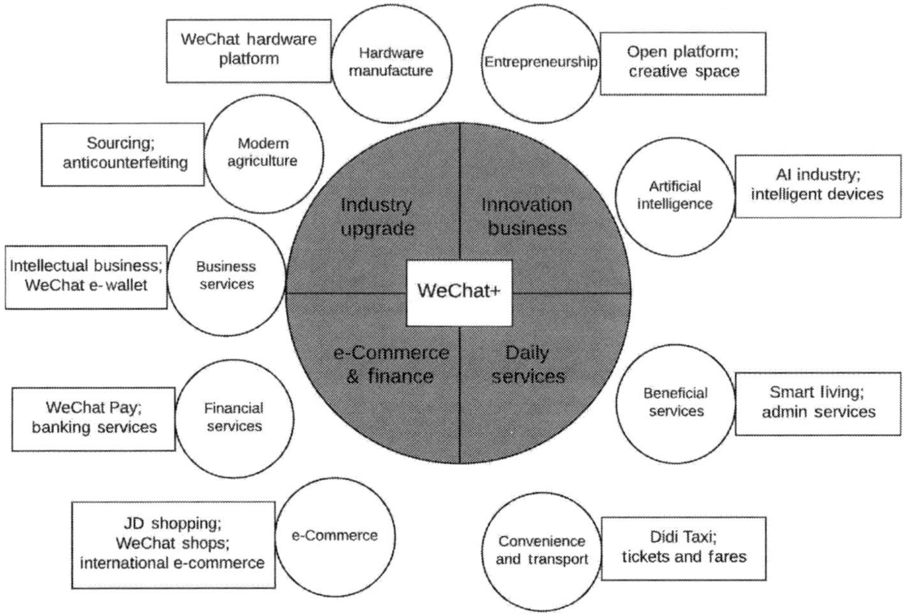

Fig. 5.4 Extended services (WeChat+) [105].

- Given the earlier emphasis on the need for drivers to establish and maintain good reputation amongst the taxi community and with customers, drivers will tend to be proactive in their use of taxi facility on WeChat in attracting customers. Conversely, Didi Taxi's native app is based on a passive service where drivers can only await calls from prospective passengers and submit bids in response.

As mentioned in Section 1.2.2.2, Tencent have made active and persistent endeavours in seeking and offering multifaceted services from its core social networking provision since 2003. This strategy and its success can be witnessed in WeChat's annual company report of 2016 [105], where Tencent proudly reports its platform as being a gateway for a multitude services including industry upgrades, innovation business, e-commerce and finance and daily services. Coined as WeChat+, this gateway platform (as shown in Fig. 5.4) will act as a connecting hub to allow service and product industries to come closer to end users. The ultimate aim is stated to be that of enhancing the performance of associated stakeholders such as hardware manufacturers, entrepreneurs, artificial intelligence provisions, transport, agriculture, business and financial services.

Orders and regulations

6

6.1 Governmental media censorship

The Chinese Government's stance on media and Internet censorship is one that continues to receive external criticism, rightly or wrongly, especially from the west, although it must also be stated that the country's policies on such matters are done so with national interest at heart. Four notable aspects of orders and regulations with respect to the operation of Chinese SNS platforms will be considered in this section.

6.1.1 Internet authorities in China

2012 was the 20th anniversary of China's connection to the Internet. Drastic advancements and the uptake of Internet technologies have also experienced significant advances over the past decade. As of December 2016, the national penetration of the Internet reached 53%, amounting to 0.73 billion Internet users in China, which equals the entire population of Europe [104]. Under this context, the Chinese Government founded the Office of the Central Leading Group for Cyberspace Affairs (中央网络安全和信息化领导小组) in 2012 (coinciding with the 20th anniversary) in order to coordinate network security and digital information across various key fields including economics, politics, culture, society and the military, as well as to perform macroscopic planning and devise development strategies for advancing national information security and nomocracy. Jinping Xi, the Chairman of the People's Republic of China, was appointed as the Head of Office, with Keqiang Li, the Premier of the People's Republic of China, acting as Deputy Head. The deputy execution of the office is run by the Cyberspace Administration of China (国家互联网信息办公室),[1] serving as the most powerful and authoritative organisation for Internet operations under the ruling of the central Chinese Government.

The Ministry of Industry and Information Technology (MITT) (工信部)[2] is a direct state department in China, MITT was founded in March 2008 with the remit of devising and executing industrial planning, field policies and standards, advancing technological innovation, managing telecommunication, supervising information construction and coordinating national information security. As an administrative department, MITT plays the role of guidance, policy management and advisor, and is not permitted to interfere with the operation and functioning of industries.

[1] www.cac.gov.cn.

[2] www.miit.gov.cn.

Social Networks in China. https://doi.org/10.1016/B978-0-08-101934-4.00006-6

As Internet technology continues to evolve, so too must the country's regulatory bodies. One new profession is that of the Internet police[3] [212], which is a direct outcome of pervasive computing as well as the rise of cyber crime, serving as the front-end force for maintaining law and order in the digital domain. Internet policing requires advanced computing skills and knowledge, as well as experience in handling different forms of Internet crime.

6.1.2 Content management

In November 2009, China's Ministry of Culture published an official document, *The Notice from Ministry of Culture Regarding Improving and Strengthening the Content Management of Online Games* (文化部关于改进和加强网络游戏内容管理工作的通知) [213], which listed several enforcement policies on the monitoring and scrutiny of online game content. This led to several high-profile consequences, including name changes to the well-known veggie-stealing games that contributed to the success of Kaixin Network and RenRen Network (as explained in Section 1.2.3.3). In this case, the Ministry of Culture deemed that the word 'stealing' in the game's title represented a potential negative influence on younger users and its explicit association with crime [40]. As a result, the name was changed from 'veggie-stealing' to 'veggie-picking'.

The Ministry's remit on content management also involves investigations into counterfeit information in cyber space, especially that concerning fake news. *China's Criminal Law, Revised Edition (9)* (刑法修正案(九)) published in 2015 [214] states that one who fabricates news about crisis, natural disaster, epidemic and policing or crime, and who deliberately disseminates counterfeit information online leading to social order disturbance will be sentenced to no more than 3 years fixed-term imprisonment, custody or surveillance. More severe offences can lead to the maximum term being increased to imprisonment for up to 7 years.

6.1.3 Filing of internet companies

The Chinese Government's efforts in managing Internet order extends to maintaining records of all Internet companies in the country towards sustaining and policing public order in online societies. By the end of 2016, there were a total of 91 listed Internet companies in China with a combined market value of 0.54 billion Yuan (approximately 80 million USD) [104]. In 2005, the MITT published the *Filing Management Policy for Non-Profit Internet Information Services* (Chinese: 非经营性互联网信息服务备案管理办法) [215], requiring all Internet and IT companies to report detailed company profiles with local authorities, including legal representatives, contact details and IP address.

[3] Its full name in Chinese means Professional Police for Public Information Internet Security Surveillance (公共信息网络安全监察专业警察).

6.1.4 Privacy protection

In December 2012, the National People's Congress of the People's Republic of China issued *The Resolution of Strengthening Online Information Protection* (关于加强网络信息保护的决定) [216], outlining 12 policies for enhancing the protection of online privacy for individuals. Examples of some of these policies include:

- Any organisation or individual must not steal or illegally acquire personal information of citizens, nor sell or transfer such information to others.
- Online service providers who collect personal electronic information of citizens must do so publicly under the rule of regulations.
- Online service providers must provide effective technological facilities to ensure the information security of their users.
- Governmental and official staff who acquire citizens' personal information as part of their duties need to keep such information confidential at all times. No disclosure, tampering, destruction, sale or illegal transfer of information is permitted.
- In the event of discovering any disclosure of personal information or violation of privacy, citizens reserve the right to demand that the relevant online service provider(s) delete their personal information or take necessary measurements to mitigate personal damage. The affected individual has the right to institute legal proceedings against the parties at fault.
- Failure to abide by the regulations will lead to varying levels of penalty, including criminal sanctions.

6.2 Public efforts

In addition to regulations enforced by government authorities, a plethora of effort is made by public entities including organisations, network communities and industries, towards improving order and the ecology in cyber space.

6.2.1 Seven bottom lines of online behaviours

In the 12th *China Internet Conference* hosted in August 2013, a consensus on Internet order, known as *Seven Bottom Lines of Online Behaviours* [217], was achieved by industry experts, Internet opinion leaders and representatives of network communities. The purpose of the Seven Bottom Lines is to serve as a prescriptive code of conduct for Internet users. It comprises of:

(1) *Legal bottom line*: *There are laws to follow; laws must be followed; execution of laws must be strict; law breakers must be prosecuted.*[4] Law breakers must be prosecuted, irrespective of whether the crime was committed online or offline.
(2) *Socialism bottom line*: Socialism and social regulations must be advocated so as to protect and maintain the social prosperity.
(3) *National interest bottom line*: Every citizen is obliged to safeguard the national interests as defined by the Constitution.

[4]Originally as '有法可依、有法必依、执法必严、违法必究',—the *Sixteen-Character Policy* version 1.0 devised by Chinese Government in 1978 for ruling the country by law [218].

(4) *Citizen statutory right bottom line*: Illegitimate or illegal approaches should be disallowed, which would break the law and violate the statutory rights of other users.
(5) *Social public order bottom line*: Although the Internet offers limitless space and new freedoms, it cannot operate as a public outlet without restriction. The Internet and reality are coexistent, therefore requiring collective effort from all users to formulate righteous public order.
(6) *Moral and ethical bottom line*: Moral pursuit has been a Chinese cultural virtue for thousands of years, the ideals of which should be carried over into the network space.
(7) *Information genuineness bottom line*: Users must seek truth from facts, and not spread rumours or disingenuous information.

6.2.2 National rumour-refuting platform

On 12 May 2016, the National Rumour-Refuting Platform was released, developed by Weibo in conjunction with the Ministry of Public Security, which is accessed via a hyperlink in the main Weibo page. The platform allows any user to report counterfeit information that is being disseminated on Weibo or any other online source. Cases are handled by China's Internet police and local security bureaus, with the ultimate purpose of identifying and removing fabricated stories and information on the Internet, as well as foster a positive ecology in the Chinese online community.

Whilst the Internet provides great convenience for information exchange, rumours or fabricated information can also be rapidly disseminated, violating the reputation of legitimate individuals and/or enterprises, weaken trust in the society and radicalise social positions. On this issue, Jinping Xi, the Chairman of the People's Republic of China, stated the need for… *clear weather in the Internet space and a positive ecology.* He further added: *We cannot allow lies to travel half of the world whilst the truth is still putting its shoes on* [219].

6.2.3 Real-name policies

Real-name policies (i.e. the requirement for users of a platform to disclose and register their real identities) have been a controversial topic in the social network domain. Its advantages include promoting positive online social behaviour and enhancing accountability, although it can also lead to undesirable consequences, for example, users may feel reluctant to give their genuine opinions on matters [220]. In China, strong attempts were made by a few Internet companies to enforce the real-name policy on the online community from around March 2012 [221, 222], although the policy is yet to be made a thorough and mandatory option across the major SNS platforms.

In practise, many QQ and Weibo users possess multiple identities (or accounts) on the two platforms. This tendency is promoted by QQ and Weibo as both allow for multiple accounts to be used simultaneously or alternatively. In QQ's mobile app, users can switch between accounts easily by simply tapping on another associate account in the settings page. In Weibo, users can switch between profiles via a one-step process.

By contrast, WeChat is the only notable platform that does not permit the use of multiple accounts. Each WeChat account must bind to a unique mobile number, and as explained in Section 2.2, one consequence of this is that WeChat is becoming a direct substitute for mobile phone services as well as negating the need for an explicit real-name user policy. This validity of this process is made possible since the majority of Chinese mobile SIM cards can only be purchased with proof of a Chinese citizen ID card. Thus, each WeChat user is, by default, already in possession of each user's identity.

Both QQ and Weibo have sought additional means to secure users' identities in order to promote public order within their respective communities. QQ's current registration process for a new account involves a verification procedure by sending a confirmation code to a specified mobile phone number. This therefore makes mandatory the link between a QQ account and a mobile phone number. As for Weibo, verified accounts (as described in Section 4.2.3) were initially designed for privileged or users with higher status, such as celebrities and opinion leaders. The system's current setting also allows any regular user to possess verified (or 'V') accounts so long as they also submit and register their real name and associated proof, such as in the form of a national citizen's ID card.

Future development 7

7.1 Global competitions

Fig. 7.1 shows a global mapping of the most popular messaging apps as of April 2016 [223]. It is clear from the figure that WeChat currently dominates the Chinese market, whilst Facebook Messenger and WhatsApp largely occupy the rest of the world.

In terms of the nature of current global competition and likely future development within the social network sector, two clear arguments can be made. The first is that it is extremely difficult for Chinese social network platforms to break into foreign territories. On this, WeChat has tried, but failed. Second, and similarly, it is difficult for foreign social network platforms to enter the Chinese territory. As in the case of WeChat for the west, Facebook has attempted but failed to enter the Chinese market.

- It is extremely difficult for Chinese social network platforms to break into foreign territories. On this, WeChat has tried, but failed so far.
- It is difficult for foreign social network platforms to enter the Chinese territory. As in the case of WeChat for the west, Facebook has attempted but failed to enter the Chinese market to date.

Not to rest on its laurels or succumb to apparent difficulties, Tencent has, since 2012, initiated a strategic plan to extend WeChat's reach to global markets. The initial stage of this process involved the selection of just a handful of countries as primary targets for marketing and promotion, Brazil and India being two [224]. Tencent has since invested substantial amounts on WeChat advertising on Facebook and traditional media in order to attract the attention of mobile Internet users. The company has also invested significant capital on promotional activities with celebrities in the hope of attracting their fans to WeChat.

Disappointingly, however, in spite of these efforts, WeChat remains a poor performer in both the Brazilian and Indian markets. In the ranking of free apps at Google Play Store, WeChat failed to enter into the top-100 position in either country, whilst WhatsApp, Facebook and Instagram all regularly appear in the top 10 [224]. The reasons for WeChat's inability to penetrate foreign markets can be summarised as follows.

Lack of first-to-market advantage. By the time Tencent coordinated and initiated their global expansion, competing IMs and the social network market had already reached a stage of relative maturity, with Facebook in particular having reached dominant status in many territories. WeChat simply arrived too late,

Social Networks in China. https://doi.org/10.1016/B978-0-08-101934-4.00007-8

Fig. 7.1 World map of most popular messaging app as in Apr. 2016 [223].

whilst the promotional strategy of using celebrities came with high costs and poor returns.

Chinese market is not representative of the global market. Prior to the existence of WeChat, Tencent's flagship product, QQ, had established a dominant position in the Chinese SNS market. As explained in Section 1.3.1.3, WeChat was subsequently created to address the then fast-growing IM market, especially in the knowledge that the migration of QQ users from traditional desktop platforms to the mobile domain would take time. This foresight gave Tencent extraordinary success with WeChat in China, where the platform has since become a necessity for mobile users across a range of functions such as online shopping and obtaining taxi services. However, on a global arena, such historic and context-specific phenomena cannot simply be repeated or reapplied in foreign markets.

Unsatisfactory localisation techniques. Tencent's experience and dominance in the Chinese SNS sector, including the Chinese mobile games market, means that the company has amassed a tremendous quantity of information on Chinese user behaviour since the inception of their first social networking platform. The success of WeChat serves as a direct reflection of Tencent's understanding of and ability to cater to Chinese user expectations with respect to a mobile social app. In foreign markets, however, Tencent falls notably short of local information and expertise, thus reflecting in the failure of its services in other cultural and regional contexts. One example of this can be found in the form of WeChat's Emoji Store which, as explained in Section 2.3.6.4, served as a major contributor to the platform's success in China. Despite the pertinent cultural relevance of WeChat's emojis, most are tailor-made for Chinese users such as in the case of Chinese New Year themes and festive occasions, and hence do not apply to users in other cultures and regions. Thus, in terms of the platform's desire global expansion, Tencent failed to provide sufficient emoji equivalents that could appeal to users from other cultures: for example, baseball, soccer and Independence Day themes for American audiences, and carnival themes for Brazilian users.

Tencent's inability to successfully penetrate foreign markets thus far is not a unique phenomenon. In similar vein, attempts have also been made by foreign companies to break into the Chinese SNS market, especially given the country's sizeable population and expanding Internet user base, though none have yet succeeded. Facebook is arguably the most significant example of a major western company who has sought to capture a sector of the Chinese market. Unlike Google, who was the leading search engine in China before it exited the Chinese market in 2010, Facebook has yet to step foot in China despite having tested the water on numerous occasions.

Notwithstanding such difficulties, Mark Zuckerberg, CEO of Facebook, remains dedicated in offering his goodwill and desire to expand in China. Numerous reports have documented his ongoing efforts to connect with China. According to an unofficial report in [225], several attempts have been made since 2009 to introduce Facebook to the Chinese market, comprising of varying proposals on how the platform can be adjusted to operate in accordance with Chinese regulations. Although such plans are still at a state of abeyance in terms of execution, Facebook's intention of entering the Chinese market remains alive and ongoing.

7.2 Social business

Fig. 7.2 shows a brief analysis of the overlap between user groups for three major service platforms: social, video and shopping, based on statistics from Ref. [66]. (Overlap in this instance refers to the case where a user possess an active account across two or three platforms.) Three typical examples for each category in the case of China are WeChat, iQiYi[1] and Taobao[2], respectively, whilst equivalent examples

[1]One of the leading video service providers in China (www.iqiyi.com).
[2]The dominant online shopping service in China (www.taobao.com).

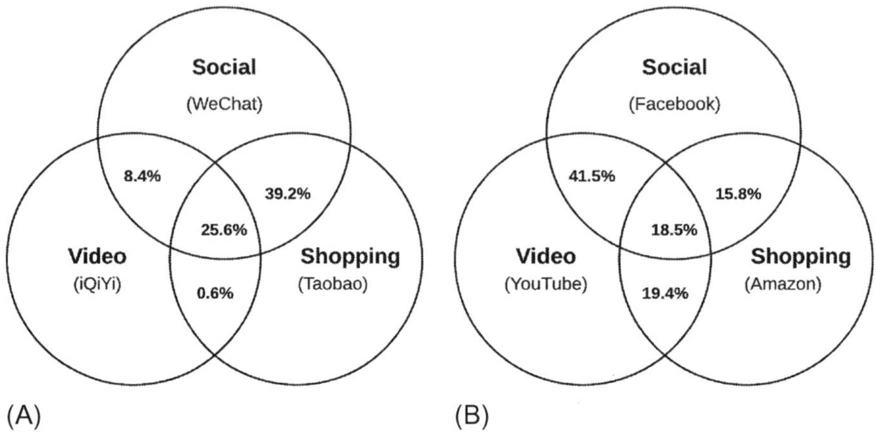

Fig. 7.2 An analysis of user overlap amongst different platforms. (A) China. (B) United States.

in the case of the United States are Facebook, YouTube and Amazon. From this analysis, Chinese users evidence the highest overlapping ratio (65%) between social and shopping platforms, whereas American users have the highest overlap (60%) between social and video platforms. Whilst social and shopping platforms have the least overlap in the United States, this combination records the highest figure in China.

Other recent articles such as [226] and [227] have also commented on the trend of social network development in China as one that will follow western trends in terms of the *medialisation* of social networks, meaning the gradual transformation of social networks into social media. However, in the case of China and as shown in Fig. 7.2, the substantial overlap between social networks and shopping reveals that the real opportunity for Chinese development resides in e-commerce. Whereas in the United States there exists substantial overlap between social and video platforms (i.e. Facebook and YouTube) and thus making for the logical trend where social platforms offer media-related services, the situation in China is such that the opposite is true (i.e. between WeChat and Taobao).

The adhesiveness and widespread uptake of online social activities (whether this be in the form of messaging, sharing of media, e-commerce and so forth) contribute to the development of both online and offline relationships between users, which in turn extends services that social networks can seek to further provide and/or augment. Wherever the number of end users becomes highly concentrated, as in the case of social network platforms, product and service providers will be naturally inclined to invest and increase their provisions to the target base—this is where the true value of social platforms resides. Indeed, all major social network platforms have, in one way or another, attempted to commercialise social networking in order to boost the online ecology and value of social chains. In doing so, however, increased quantities of information exchange can also lead to user fatigue (i.e. where users are bombarded by excessive content and the obligation of managing all aspects of usage), and thus the key challenge for the development of services is to ensure the delivery of valuable information to users whilst also increasing the frequency of user engagement. In terms of profit generation for SNS providers, there are currently three main channels in which this is achieved by the three leading Chinese platforms:

(1) *Placement of adverts*: Weibo, as with other media platforms, largely relies on advertising income for its revenue generation.
(2) *Importing e-commerce*: WeChat's Official Account feature has helped to create tremendous business opportunities for both account holders and the platform itself.
(3) *Add-on products*: All three leading Chinese social network platforms provide a wide range of add-on products to supplement their core services.

Beyond their individual nuances, all Chinese social network platforms can be considered as seeking to convert from purely social networks to multidimensional service platforms, encompassing strong connections to a multitude of third-party services. This phenomenon is not surprising in view of the trend that users no longer access social networks merely to exchange information with friends, but instead use platforms as the gateway to facilitate or enhance daily tasks and routines, such as from fitness to reading and from calling a taxi to booking cinema tickets. The explosive growth of social network payment facilities such as Red Packets has expanded in line with the national penetration rate of associated electronic payment systems such as WeChat Pay. The potential application of e-payment systems extends not only from online to offline scenarios, but will also likely impact on the operation and usage of financial and telecom services in the near future. As such, social network-based e-payment systems can potentially represent the key area of development for the future of monetary exchange in China's Internet infrastructure.

It is also worth noting here that WeChat's Enterprise Account provision has, in various ways, helped to enhance the internal operations within organisations (as discussed in Section 2.4.2), though there remains tremendous capacity for development and exploration in this area. Hence beyond everyday users and consumers, more substantial fusions between social network platforms and organisations can also be expected in the near future.

For foreign companies wishing to exploit the Chinese market via social network platforms, consideration needs to be made of three aspects:

Chinese Characteristics Chinese mainstream social network platforms are drastically different from those in the rest of the world, and even from those of neighbouring Asian countries. The traditional SNS model (with Facebook being representative of the western example) failed to take a foothold in China, having emerged during 2009 (see *SNS Models: Kaixin and RenRen* in Section 1.2.3), and was eventually eliminated from the market in 2011 (see *The Downfall of Traditional SNS: Kaixin and RenRen* in Section 1.3.1.1). The current leading social network giants[3] in China comprise of three stand-alone social network models—QQ, WeChat and Weibo—on which additional study and investigation on their potential future development will be worthwhile, especially on a more

[3]As described in *Three Current Social Network Giants* in Section 1.3.2.

international context. This book has used three independent chapters to research about these three social network platforms, respectively: Chapters 2–4.

One-to-One Socialising At the time of writing, WeChat remains as the leading platform in China amongst the three social network giants. One of the key elements contributing to its success is its minimalism design philosophy,[4] where users are offered distinct levels of privacy[5] and spam control.[6] Where Facebook or Twitter operate in the form of a public space where information is broadcast to audiences by default, Chinese users prefer a more personalised social space and engagement with one-to-one communication. As in the case of WeChat, users can customise the kind of commercial feeds they receive by subscribing to Official Accounts (see *Official Accounts* in Section 2.4). This subtle but vital process vastly enhances the appeal and quality of commercial content.

Social e-Commerce The Chinese Internet community has become versed and prevalent with online shopping, as witnessed by the fact that all Chinese social network platforms offer e-Commerce facilities, ranging from direct payment systems[7] to third-party services[8] in the form of cinema tickets, taxi services, food ordering, etc. The ability for external and/or foreign organisations to maximise opportunities in this area will depend on acquiring an in-depth understanding of Chinese SNS dynamics so as to deliver suitable and appealing value propositions to users.

[4]As described in *Minimalism Design* in Section 2.3.1.
[5]Explained in *Privacy Settings* in Section 2.3.5.2.
[6]Explained in *Spam Control* in Section 2.3.5.3.
[7]Described in *Payment System* in Section 5.2.1.
[8]Described in *Third-Party Services* in Section 5.3.2.

WeChat quick user guide

A

A.1 Download and installation

Supported mobile operating systems: iOS, Android and Windows Phone. There are two ways to obtain the download links for WeChat:

- Search 'WeChat' on the app store of your phone (such as Apple App Store or Google Play)
- Go to www.wechat.com

WeChat apps are available for MAC OS and Windows desktops, which can be found at www.wechat.com. However, these do not contain all the features and functions for the mobile version.

The following instructions apply to iOS version 6.5.5, as of 13 February 2017. Other versions may vary.

A.2 Registration and login

A.2.1 From mobile phone

The registration of a new WeChat account is performed by using your existing mobile number.

(1) Upon inputting your mobile number, you will receive a confirmation code via a standard SMS text message.
(2) Enter the confirmation code in WeChat and assign a password of your choice.

A.2.2 Log off

Once signed up, you will remain logged-in unless you manually log off. This differs from other products such as QQ where a certain duration of inactivity will result in an automatic log off.

To log off manually, go to *Me* → *Settings* → *Log Out*.

The only time WeChat will log off a user is when he/she changes their mobile device. Even in the case of iPhone that has performed a system restore from iTunes backup, WeChat will not perform an automatic login.

Should the password be forgotten, it can only be recovered by requesting a confirmation code to be sent via SMS to a designated mobile phone number.

A.2.3 Web-based WeChat

WeChat is mainly designed to be used on mobile phones, hence its sister web-based version (such as that for desktop PCs) does not contain the full features and functionalities of the mobile app. Web-based WeChat cannot be used without first registering for a WeChat account via the mobile app. This is performed as follows:

(1) Go to https://web.wechat.com/.
(2) The front page is simply a QR code with a message of *Scan to log in to WeChat.*
(3) Open the WeChat app on your mobile phone. Go to *Discover* → *Scan QR Code.*
(4) Place the front camera of your phone to focus on the QR code on the website. You will be logged in.
(5) Note that you may be logged off WeChat on your mobile phone whilst using the web-based version.

A.3 Chats

Upon login, the main Chat view will be presented by default.

There are four main tabs on the bottom of the screen: *Chats*, *Contacts*, *Discover* and *Me*.

A.3.1 Chat with friends

If the chat window is not already open with contact information, go to *Contact* → *your contact* → *Messages.*

A.3.2 Message types

There are a range of items that can be sent to a contact via the chat window, including Album, Camera, Video Call, Location, Red Packet, Transfer, Contact Card, Favorites, and Coupons.

A.3.3 Group chat

A.3.3.1 Establish a group

There are two ways to build a chat group:

- In the *Chats* page, go to the top right corner and click '+', then tap *New Chat.* Now you can select the contacts that you wish to join the group, and then click *OK.*
- Go to the chat window with a contact that you wish to add to the chat group, then click the person icon in the top right corner of the screen. This will show a new window where clicking the '+' button will allow users to select more contacts to be added to the group.

A.3.3.2 Add members to a group

Members can be added at any time using the second method explained in the previous section.

New members can be added by any existing member of a group.

Note that newly added members cannot view the chat history that took place prior to the join.

A.3.3.3 Delete members from a group

In the group chat window, click the top right group icon, which will open the group setup page.

Tap the '–' icon to select the members to be deleted from the group.

This operation can only be performed by the creator of the group.

A.3.3.4 Group options

Several options are available for customising group chat.

Note that most of these settings can only be applied as local changes, rather than as group settings. The group creator can configure the initial settings such as *Group Name*, whilst each group member can customise devise their own *Group Name* to appear in the chat list of their respective *Chat* window.

By default, WeChat will send notifications to all group members, whenever there is a new message received in the group chat. Notifications can be turned off by tapping the *Mute Notifications* option.

A.3.4 Red Packet

A.3.4.1 Send a Red Packet

Red Packet is an item listed in chat window. Tapping it will open a window to set up a new Red Packet.

- Send to individual: Specify the total amount followed by a greeting message, then tap *Prepare Red Packet.*
- Send to a group: There are two ways to prepare a Red Packet for a group.
  - Identical amount: Set the payment amount for each recipient, the quantity of Red Packets and a greeting.
  - Random amount: Set the total value of all Red Packets to be sent out, the quantity of recipients and a greeting message.

The greeting message can be left blank, in which case a default greeting message will be sent. A password may be required for verification if one has been set for the WeChat e-Wallet account.

A.3.4.2 Receive a Red Packet

To open a Red Packet, simply tap a Red Packet icon.

The sender of the packet(s) will also be shown a notification of who has opened the packet(s). The recipient can see only their own notification, that is *You have opened xxx's Red Packet.*

Once a Red Packet is received, the amount will be added to the user's account and can be viewed in *Me* → *Wallet* → *Balance*.

A.4 Contacts

A.4.1 Add contacts

Go to *Contacts* → *Add Contacts*.

Contacts can be added either via a known WeChat ID or by scanning a user's QR code.

A.4.2 Linking mobile phone contacts

Entering *Contacts* → *New Friends* will show the list of new friends. Any preexisting contacts from the host mobile phone address book who are also WeChat users will have his/her name listed here.

Another method of linking mobile phone contacts is by tapping *Mobile Contacts* in the page.

A.5 Moments

A.5.1 Browsing

To browse friends' updates, go to *Discover* → *Moments*. All posts are arranged in chronological order with each post appearing only once.

Only users with friends' status can see each other's entries in *Moments*, including original posts, and comments to posts.

A.5.2 Publishing posts

- Text only content: Tap and hold the camera icon in the top right corner of Moments to enter text-only mode.
- Mixture of texts and images: Tap the camera icon and select photos, from where the text entry mode will be presented.

A.6 Profile setting

Go to *Me* and then tap the user icon on the top. The following configurations can then be made to profile: photo, name to appear in *Moments*, WeChat ID (this is optional and can only be set once), gender, region and a status message.

A.7 Official accounts

A.7.1 Create an official account

Go to website mp.weixin.qq.com and register for an account.

Currently, no English version of this website is available.

A.7.2 Subscribe to an official account

There are two ways to follow an official account:

- In WeChat, scan the QR code of the Official Account. All Official Accounts have a QR code. Most organisations and businesses are displaying their QR codes in their official websites, office or branch outlets, and in promotional events.
- Go to *Contacts* → *Add Contacts* → *Official Accounts*, to search by the name.

Updates to Official Accounts are displayed in the Chat window, whilst for Subscription Accounts, these will appear under the *Subscriptions* folder in the Chat Window. Service Accounts will be displayed as an independent chat in the list of the main *Chats* page.

QQ quick user guide

B

B.1 Download and installation

QQ can be used on desktop computers, smartphones and mobile tablets.

Desktop QQ software apps are supported by MAC OS and Windows operating systems, and their download links can be found at https://im.qq.com/download/.

Mobile QQ is supported across a range of mobile operating systems including iOS, Android and Windows Phone, although not all features and functions from the desktop QQ are available on mobile QQ. There are two ways to find the download links for QQ's mobile apps:

- Search 'QQ' on the app store of your phone
- Go to https://im.qq.com/download/

An app called *QQ International* is also available in app stores, which provides an English language interface but does not possess the full features and functions in the native Chinese language versions. Chinese versions of QQ software or apps do not provide English language menus.

The following instructions are based on the QQ International iOS mobile app (version 4.8.3), as downloaded from the Apple App Store on 22 February 2017. Other versions may vary.

B.2 Login

B.2.1 Register a new QQ number

Signing-up in QQ currently requires the use of a mobile phone.

(1) Enter the mobile number and then a verification code will be sent to the host mobile phone.
(2) Enter the verification code, and then click *Next*.
(3) Set a password and a nickname, then click *OK*. The nickname can be changed later on.

B.2.2 Log off

If you remain inactive for 7 days, you will be automatically logged off.

To manually log off, go to *More* → your icon → *Account* → *Logout*.

B.2.3 Web-based QQ

Web-based QQ cannot be used without first registering a QQ account.

(1) Go to web.qq.com or w.qq.com.
(2) The front page is simply a QR code.
(3) Open the QQ app on your mobile phone. Go to *More → Scan QR Code*.
(4) Place the front camera of your phone to focus on the QR code on the website. You will be logged in.
(5) If you have already logged onto QQ elsewhere, there is a chance that you may be logged off in that location whilst using the web-based version. QQ's policy changes from time to time regarding simultaneous login across multiple locations.

B.3 Chats

B.3.1 Message types

A range of items can be sent to a contact via the chat window.

Message types are relatively limited in QQ International app. The native Chinese QQ app offers a wider collection of items that can be sent via the chat including Photos, Camera, Video Call, Voice Call, Files, Graffiti, and Location.

B.3.2 Group chat

B.3.2.1 Establish a group

To create a group, go to *Contacts* → + → *Create Group*. Enter a group name and group size, and click *Finish*.

A window will be displayed, from where group members can be selected and added by clicking *Invite*, or to do so later, click *Done*. A screenshot can be taken of the QR code as displayed on the screen, and shared with friends who wish to join the group.

B.3.2.2 Group management

In the group chat window, tap the persons icon on the top right corner.

- To add a member to a group, tap *Invite New Member*.
- To delete a member from a group, tap *Members → Edit → Remove Group Member*.

The *Membership* field has three options:

- Free to join: Anyone on QQ platform can see and join this group.
- Needs approval: Anyone on QQ platform can see this group. If they wish to join, a request needs to be sent which is subject to the approval from the group.
- Invite only: Only QQ users who have received an invitation can join this group. Requests to join cannot be made.

B.3.3 Red Packet

As of February 2017, the Red Packet function was not available on QQ International app.

B.4 Contacts

B.4.1 Add contacts

Go to *Contacts* → +, from where there are two ways to add a new friend to the contact list:

- The *Scan QR Code* facility can be used if available for a friend.
- Tapping *Add User* will allow a friend's QQ ID number to be entered.

B.5 Qzone

B.5.1 Browsing

To browse Qzone, simply go to *More* → *Qzone*. All posts are arranged in chronological order with each post appearing only once.

Qzone only permits the viewing of posts published by friends, although comments made by other users (irrespective of your friend status with them) on friends' posts are also visible.

B.5.2 Publish posts

- Text only content: Tap the + button on the top right and select *Say something*.
- Mixture of texts and images: Tap the + button on the top right and select *Upload photo*.

B.6 File manager

QQ allows file transfer between friends and even between unknown acquaintances.

Click *More* → *File Manager*.

B.6.1 My documents

In the list of *My Documents*, there are three categories of files:

- Recent Files: The files that have been recently opened or received.
- Cloud Files: The files currently saved on QQ's cloud storage.
- Local Files: The files saved on the device (e.g. mobile phone).

B.6.2 Transfer files from mobile phone to computer

Tap *My Computer* to open a new window.

Here, photos and videos can be chosen from the mobile phone gallery or new pictures and videos can be taken with the device's camera, and sent to a local computer. Tap the *Files* icon to choose a local file and send. Click the top right icon for further settings.

In native, Chinese QQ apps, files can also be transferred between mobile phones regardless the friend status of users. This feature is not available in QQ International.

B.7 Profile setting

Go to *More* and tap the user icon on the top to see a new window. Tapping on *My Profile* will enable options to edit profile photo, status, nickname, gender and birthday.

B.8 Account management

In the profile window tap *Account*.

QQ allows multiple accounts to be held by the same person. Another account can be easily added along with switching between accounts. An invisible status can also be selected whilst remaining logged-in to the platform.

Weibo quick user guide

C

C.1 Download and installation

Weibo can be used in a wide range of mobile operating systems including: iOS, Android, Windows Phone, Blackberry, Symbian, kjava and MTK.

There are two ways to access the official download links for Weibo app:

- Search "Weibo" on the app store of your phone
- Go to m.weibo.com/web/

On desktop computers, Weibo can be accessed via web browsers.

- www.weibo.com: Depending on your location, you may be redirected to overseas.weibo.com if you are not within the Chinese territory.
- www.weibo.cn: This will lead to the main Weibo page, regardless your current location.

The following instructions are based on the iOS version 7.1.0 as updated on 14 February 2017. Other versions may vary.

Note that although the interface of the demo app has been set to the English language, there still exists a large portion of menus in Weibo that is written solely in Chinese, such as Topics.

C.2 Register and login

C.2.1 Sign up

Signing up for a new account can be made on the main screen or a login can be made using existing credentials from another social network such as WeChat, QQ and Facebook. All options will require a mobile number to be provided so that a verification code can be sent to the target device.

C.2.2 Log off

To log off, go to *Me* → *Settings* → *Log out current account.*

C.3 Connections

C.3.1 Following someone

To search for another user, go to *Discover* page and search for his/her user name, though note that this needs to match the user name in the original Chinese language. For example, typing *Jackie Chan*, may not lead to the desired result in the results listing. Alternatively typing '成龙' (Jackie Chan's Chinese name) will give the results containing the profile for the famous actor.

Tap the Follow button next to the user's icon, and the system will make suggestions of groups to help the management of those followed. Choose a group and click Confirm.

C.3.2 View followers

A notification will be sent to you in the *Me* section if you are followed by another user. The list of followers can be viewed at *Me* → *Follower*.

C.4 Posts

C.4.1 Browsing

Opening the Weibo app will lead to the default browse page with a tab called *Weibo*. All posts are arranged in chronological order with each post appearing only once.

The browsing screen will typically present posts published by users that you are following, although this could also contain several posts from unknown users—Weibo frequently populates the page with paid advertisements or posts that receive additional promotion on the platform.

Posts and comments from anyone can be viewed in Weibo insofar as they can be searched and found.

C.4.2 Publishing posts

Tap the big '+' icon in the bottom middle of the Weibo app to see a wide range of items that can be posted.

You can view your own posts at *Me* → *Weibo*.

C.4.3 Interactions

Each individual post permits *repost*, *comment* or *like* actions.

If other users have responded to your posts, you will get notifications in the *Messages* section.

C.5 Messages

Go to the *Messages* section to start a private conversation with another Weibo user. Different types of items can be sent via the chat window including Albums, Camera, Location, Group, and Red Envelop.

Direct communication can be made with any Weibo user via the message function (regardless the follower/followee status). There are two ways of achieving this:

- Click the message icon on the top right corner of the *Messages* section, then tap *Chat* → *Search*. Type the user's name and then tap *Search online*.
- Find the person's Weibo page and click *Chat*.

C.5.1 Red Packet

Red Packet can be sent to another user via the chat window. There are two types of Red Packet: random value and fixed value.

Weibo does not have its own payment system, hence features involving payment (such as Red Packets) will require the Weibo account to be linked with a payment system such as that of Alipay.[1]

Also note that the Red Packet function does not have an English language interface.

C.6 Profile setting

To edit your profile, go to *Me* → your icon *Profile* → *More Basic Info* → *Edit Profile*.

C.7 Account management

Weibo allows multiple accounts to be held by the same person.

Go to *Me* → *Settings* → *Accounts*. You can add another account and switch between accounts.

[1] The equivalent of PayPal in China (www.alipay.com).

Bibliography

[1] N. Mook, ICQ celebrates five years, Available from: http://betanews.com/2001/11/15/icq-celebrates-five-years/, 2001 (Accessed September 2016).

[2] Winful, Review of Tencent's 15 years hard journey (回顾腾讯十五年艰辛路程), Available from: https://www.aliyun.com/zixun/content/2_6_14185.html, 2014 (Accessed October 2016).

[3] M. Dong (董美岐), The pros and cons of QQ (QQ的利与弊), in: Little Snowflakes: Happy Articles for Primary Schools (小雪花:小学快乐作文), vol. 10, 2015, p. 6.

[4] QQ, Available from: http://baike.baidu.com/item/QQ (Accessed July 2016).

[5] Tencent's worth: a Chinese Internet firm finds a better way to make money, Available from: http://www.economist.com/news/business/21586557-chinese-internet-firm-finds-better-way-make-money-tencents-worth, 2013 (Accessed June 2016).

[6] Special issue on all historical versions of Tencent's QQ (腾讯QQ全历史老版本专题介绍), Available from: http://www.rsdown.cn/s/qql/, 2014 (Accessed October 2016).

[7] Annoying adware: AOL/Mirabilis ICQ, Available from: http://cexx.org/icq.htm (Accessed July 2016).

[8] Self-regulation treaty for Chinese Internet industry (中国互联网行业自律公约), Available from: http://www.isc.org.cn/hyzl/hyzl/listinfo-15599.html, 2002 (Accessed August 2016).

[9] MSN(微软软件), Available from: http://baike.baidu.com/item/msn/111343 (Accessed July 2016).

[10] C. Ling, MSN, a latecomer to Asia, looks to draw users, ads, Available from: http://www.wsj.com/articles/SB1008970485605018 40, 2001 (Accessed July 2016).

[11] Microsoft prepares to launch MSN China, Available from: https://news.microsoft.com/2005/05/11/microsoft-prepares-to-launch-msn-china/, 2005 (Accessed July 2016).

[12] Interview with Weigang Lu on MSN's entering China and the competition situation (吕伟钢谈MSN进中国与门户竞争态势), Available from: http://tech.sina.com.cn/roll/2005-05-13/1259606981.shtml, 2005 (Accessed July 2016).

[13] L. Cao (曹丽芳), A calm reflection on the "studying-abroad heat wave" ("出国留学热"的冷思考), J. Hubei Univ. Econ. Soc. Sci. Ed. (湖北经济学院学报:哲学社会科学版) 24 (3) (2010) 102–103.

[14] The twenty-year-old NetEase online forum is closed—Internet waves goodbye to the traditional BBS era (20岁网易论坛关闭互联网告别传统的BBS时代), Available from: http://mt.sohu.com/20160920/n468807354.shtml, 2016 (Accessed October 2016).

[15] Tianya's sixteen-year journey of product operation (天涯十六年的产品运营之路), Available from: http://www.chinaz.com/manage/2016/0126/499672.shtml, 2016 (Accessed September 2016).

[16] S. Wei (魏寿华), The Tianya phenomena—how was BBS produced? ("天涯"现象-网络论坛是怎样炼成的?), News Battle Line (新闻战线) 4 (2010) 25–27.

[17] B. Yang (杨贝), Breakthrough and innovation of web portals' in-depth reporting (门户网站深度报道的突破与创新), 传媒4 (2016) 51–53.

[18] H. Han (韩华), Research on the Development Environment and Future Directions of Chinese Three Major Web Portals (Sina, NetEase, and Sohu) (中国三大门户网站发展环境与发展方向研究), Fudan University, 2001.

[19] J. Huo (贺骏), The Commercial Battle Between Baidu and Tencent has Begun (百度、腾讯商战硝烟渐起), vol. 7, Legal Person (法人), 2011, pp. 50–51.

[20] N. Xu (徐宁), Investigation of Subject Interactions Between BBS and Newspaper—Using "Furong Sister" as the Case Study (BBS与报纸之间的议题互动探讨-以"芙蓉姐姐"为个案), vol. 6, Press Circles (新闻界), 2005.

[21] N.B. Ellison, Social network sites: definition, history, and scholarship, J. Comput.-Mediat. Commun. 13 (1) (2007) 210–230.

[22] Special issue: building Chinese largest web portal–Sohu bought ChinaRen (专题报道: 建立中国最大的门户网站–搜狐收购ChinaRen), Available from: http://news.sohu.com/feature/merge/merge.htm, 2000 (Accessed July 2016).

[23] Life cycle of product: what happened to ChinaRen Alumni? (产品的生命周期: Chinaren校友录怎么了？), Available from: http://www.chinaz.com/web/2009/0807/85920_2.shtml, 2009 (Accessed September 2016).

[24] Kaixin Network (开心网), Available from: http://baike.baidu.com/view/1629630.htm (Accessed September 2016).

[25] S. Paquet, Personal knowledge publishing and its uses in research, Seb's Open Res., 2002.

[26] T. O'Reilly, What is web 2.0: design patterns and business models for the next generation of software, Commun. Strateg. 17 (2005). 200 (Kindle edition)

[27] G. Thevenot, Blogging as a social media, Tour. Hosp. Res. 7 (3) (2007) 287–289.

[28] J.H. Kietzmann, Social media? Get serious! Understanding the functional building blocks of social media, Bus. Horiz. 54 (3) (2011) 241–251.

[29] The strong collaboration of Sina and MSN China will construct multi-dimensional network platform (新浪与MSN中国强强携手打造多元化网络聚合平台), Available from: http://tech.sina.com.cn/i/2010-11-11/14304855052.shtml, 2011 (Accessed November 2016).

[30] Overview: MSN entering China will aggravate the IM market competition (综述: MSN挺进中国即时通讯市场竞争加剧), Available from: http://tech.sina.com.cn/i/2005-06-16/1446638000.shtml, 2006 (Accessed October 2016).

[31] Why did Microsoft shut down MSN messenger, Available from: http://www.speeli.com/articles/view/Why-did-Microsoft-shut-down-MSN-messenger (Accessed November 2016).

[32] Top 3 reasons behind the failure of MSN Messenger in China and the rise of QQ, Available from: http://www.allchinatech.com/top-3-reasons-behind-the-failure-of-msn-messenger-in-china-and-the-rise-and-rise-of-qq/, 2015 (Accessed December 2016).

[33] H. Liu (刘华), How much chance does QQ in the enterprise IM market? (企业IM市场腾讯的机会有多少), Available from: http://www.ctiforum.com/forum/2003/10/forum03_1007.htm, 2003 (Accessed November 2016).

[34] J. Zhang (张见悦), Tencent transformed to a comprehensive internet company—QQ.com website as a dark horse (腾讯转型综合性互联网公司QQ.com网站异军突起), Available from: http://news.qq.com/a/20040906/000047.htm, 2004 (Accessed November 2016).

[35] MSN, Available from: http://baike.baidu.com/item/msn (Accessed July 2016).

[36] The acceleration of overseas user growth for Xiaonei Network is increasing (校内网海外用户增长呈加速趋势), Available from: http://tech.sina.com.cn/i/2008-02-26/11012042683.shtml, 2008 (Accessed November 2016).

[37] RenRen Network: why cannot it become Chinese Facebook (人人网: 为什么成不了中国的Facebook), Available from: http://www.cyzone.cn/a/20120106/221415.html, 2012 (Accessed October 2016).
[38] The release of China Internet data (2009–2010年中国互联网数据发布), Available from: http://www.dcci.com.cn/list/2010/2.htm, 2010 (Accessed October 2016).
[39] Chinese Government Web Portal, People's Republic of China anti unfair-competition law (中华人民共和国反不正当竞争法), Available from: http://www.gov.cn/banshi/2005-08/31/content_68766.htm, 2005 (Accessed October 2016).
[40] 袁泓, 毕晓宇, 李诚, Prevention of youth criminals from Kaixin (QQ) farm veggie stealing game—in the perspective of social control theory based on criminology (开心(QQ)农场偷菜游戏与青少年犯罪预防-以犯罪学的社会控制理论为视角), 法制与社会13 (2010) 64–66.
[41] Have you stolen today? Veggie-stealing game makes people crazy (今天你偷了吗¿'偷菜"游戏让人疯狂), Available from: http://www.china.com.cn/culture/txt/2009-08/07/content_18294853.htm, 2009 (Accessed October 2016).
[42] Miss those vegetables we stole in the old days (怀念那些年我们偷过的菜), in: Inside and Outside the Classroom: High School Edition (课堂内外:高中版), 2013.
[43] X. Fan (范小青), Research on social interaction and social capitals of veggie-stealing games in social networks (社交网站偷菜游戏中的人际互动与社会资本研究), China Publishing (中国出版) 23 (2010) 66–70.
[44] M. Granovetter, The strength of weak ties, Am. J. Sociol. 78 (6) (1973) 1360–1380.
[45] S. Liu (刘少杰), The rationality of the existence of acquaintance society (熟人社会存在的合理性), 人民论坛) 10 (2006) 16–18.
[46] Three Chinese 3G licenses issued together—China has entered 3G era (中国3张3G牌照同时发放，中国进入3G时代), Available from: http://finance.ifeng.com/topic/3Gpz/ (Accessed June 2016).
[47] The second biggest event (among top 10) in mobile phone industry: iPhone entering China (2009手机行业十大事件之二iPhone进中国), Available from: http://tech.sina.com.cn/mobile/n/2009-12-28/17593718294.shtml, 2009 (Accessed May 2016).
[48] Z. Cao (曹之晨), Patent analysis report of mobile communication industry (移动通信行业专利分析报告), Available from: http://www.iptalent.com/yjgd_content.aspx?id=303, 2011 (Accessed October 2016).
[49] SJTU Centre for Public Opinion Research (上海交通大学舆情研究实验室), 2010 China Weibo annual report (2010中国微博年度报告), Available from: http://www.doc88.com/p-9942184763874.html, 2010 (Accessed October 2016).
[50] The 28th statistical report of Chinese Internet development (第28次中国互联网络发展状况统计报告), Available from: http://www.cnnic.net.cn/hlwfzyj/hlwxzbg/hlwtjbg/201206/t20120612_26719.htm, 2011 (Accessed July 2016).
[51] N. Henze, E. Rukzio, S. Boll, Observational and experimental investigation of typing behaviour using virtual keyboards for mobile devices, in: Proceedings of the SIGCHI Conference on Human Factors in Computing Systems, ACM, 2012.
[52] Countdown to iPhone entering China (iPhone进入中国倒计时), Available from: http://mobile.163.com/special/001127IJ/iPhone_china.html (Accessed May 2016).
[53] Mobile OICQ service enabled in seven regions of China (全国七个地区相继开通移动OICQ服务), Available from: http://news.sohu.com/38/47/news144374738.shtml, 2001 (Accessed May 2016).
[54] X. Su (苏小牧), Huateng Ma talks about WeChat and QQ: the best way to avoid being destroyed is a self-battle (马化腾谈微信和QQ: 防止被颠覆最好办法是自己打自己), Available from: http://www.caishimv.com/party/1433918062.html, 2015 (Accessed August 2016).

[55] The app analytics, Available from: https://www.appannie.com (Accessed July 2016).

[56] Site Rank Data—websites ranking stats, Available from: http://siterankdata.com/ (Accessed December 2016).

[57] Alexa Top 500 Global Sites, Available from: http://www.alexa.com/topsites (Accessed December 2016).

[58] RenRen goes to NYSE for IPO (人人赴纽交所上市), Available from: http://tech.163.com/special/renrenipo/ (Accessed November 2016).

[59] Sunwin intelligence plans to purchase the parent company of Kaixin Network—revenue and income of the social network are declining (赛为智能拟收购开心网母公司标的社交业务营收和毛利下滑), Available from: http://finance.sina.com.cn/stock/s/2016-10-31/doc-ifxxfuff7283061.shtml, 2016 (Accessed December 2016).

[60] Yizhou Chen: RenRen Network will become a social finance company (陈一舟: 人人网即将变成一家社交金融公司), Available from: http://tech.qq.com/a/20150513/041573.htm, 2015 (Accessed August 2016).

[61] J. Lei (雷建平), Binghao Chen's introspection: the root of Kaixin's downfall is not the emergence of Weibo (程炳皓反思: 微博兴起非开心网"降温"根源), Available from: http://tech.qq.com/a/20130904/002057.htm, 2013 (Accessed August 2016).

[62] X. He (何晓姿), The fatigue of social networks (社交网累了), Chin. Econ. Inform. (中国经济信息) 17 (2011) 56–56.

[63] J. Zhang (张京科), The battle between the real and the fake Kaixin Networks: the value of 34 million Internet users (真假开心网之争: 3400万互联网用户的价值), Available from: http://www.yicai.com/news/724966.html, 2011 (Accessed August 2016).

[64] H. Chen (陈慧颖), Users are turning to Weibo: who did not follow Facebook properly? (用户转向微博: 谁跟丢了Facebook?), Available from: http://news.qq.com/a/20110428/000474_1.htm, 2011 (Accessed October 2016).

[65] A commercial battle behind a Weibo domain name–"Weibo.com" worth millions (一个微博域名背后的商战"Weibo.com"价值百万元), Available from: http://www.china.com.cn/economic/txt/2011-04/18/content_22385009.htm, 2011 (Accessed November 2016).

[66] Kantar, Kantar social media impact report 2016, Available from: http://cn-en.kantar.com/media/1190989/kantar_social_media_impact_report_2016.pdf, 2016 (Cited June 2016).

[67] 2010 Sina Weibo's first micro novel competition (2010年新浪微博中国首届微小说大赛), Available from: http://Weibo.com/zt/2010weixiaoshuo/zt-hot.php (Accessed September 2016).

[68] Sina 11 Weibo's night—micro force leading the trend (新浪2011微博之夜微力量引领时代), Available from: http://ent.sina.com.cn/s/m/2012-01-04/23493525184.shtml, 2012 (Accessed September 2016).

[69] The first China Weibo developer conference (中国首届微博开发者大会), Available from: http://tech.sina.com.cn/z/Weibo_developer/ (Accessed September 2016).

[70] Sina Weibo successfully registered "Scarf" logo (新浪微博注册"围脖"商标成功), Available from: http://news.gbicom.cn/wz/14877.html, 2011 (Accessed October 2016).

[71] A. Shen (沈艾娥), Did you knit today? (今天你"织围脖"了吗?), Chin. Constr. (语文建设) 2 (2011) 36–36.

[72] Weibo lands in NASDAQ (微博登陆纳斯达克), Available from: http://tech.sina.com.cn/z/Weiboipo/index.shtml, 2014 (Accessed November 2016).

[73] Penetration rate among microblog users in China in 2012, Available from: https://www.statista.com/statistics/247988/penetration-rate-of-microblog-users-in-china-by-microblog-provider/, 2012 (Accessed August 2016).

[74] NetEase Weibo platform upgraded with users reaching 0.26 billion (网易微博平台升级用户数突破2.6亿), Available from: http://tech.163.com/12/1018/18/8E49Q121000915BF.html, 2012 (Accessed October 2016).
[75] M. Knoop, Application insights: how exactly is MAU calculated?, Available from: http://www.adweek.com/socialtimes/application-insights-how-exactly-is-mau-calculated/216387, 2009 (Accessed July 2016).
[76] Tencent performance report (腾讯业绩报告), Available from: http://www.tencent.com/zh-cn/ir/reports.shtml (Accessed October 2016).
[77] Why cannot Tencent Weibo win Sina Weibo (腾讯微博为何赢不了新浪微博), Available from: http://www.chinaz.com/news/2011/0922/211243.shtml, 2011 (Accessed November 2016).
[78] Why did Tencent Weibo lose to Sina (腾讯微博为何打不过新浪), Available from: http://www.williamlong.info/archives/3093.html, 2012 (Accessed November 2016).
[79] X. Dong (董晓常), Weibo business—whey did Tencent lose to Sina? (微博业务-腾讯为什么输给新浪？), Available from: http://www.yixieshi.com/13915.html, 2013 (Accessed November 2016).
[80] pchome, WeChat development journey: from birth to domination (微信发展历程: 从诞生到风靡), Available from: http://www.pintu360.com/article/54d7017414ec53c11660f022.html, 2014 (Accessed October 2016).
[81] H. Huang (黄何), The overview of the IM evolution from TalkBox—a reflection for the entrepreneurs after talkbox team being defeated by WeChat (从TalkBox看IM即时通信工具的演变- TalkBox团队被微信颠覆后的创业思考), 程序员) 10 (2014) 60–62.
[82] Talkbox: an IM product based on voice recording and real time transmission (Talkbox: 基于语音录制和传输的即时通讯产品), Available from: http://www.showeb20.com/?p=3090, 2011 (Accessed November 2016).
[83] J. Constine, Facebook is forcing all users to download messenger by ripping chat out of its main apps, Available from: https://techcrunch.com/2014/04/09/facebook-messenger-or-the-highway/, 2014 (Accessed October 2016).
[84] Fetion user over 0.1 billion, entering top 3 IMs (飞信用户数破亿已进入IM前三甲), Available from: http://cq.qq.com/a/20080829/000204.htm, 2008 (Accessed October 2016).
[85] Ex-employee criticising fetion—Fetion can never replace WeChat: too much politics (飞信前员工痛斥飞信永远无法取代微信: 后宫水太深), Available from: http://www.tmtpost.com/25317.html, 2013 (Accessed September 2016).
[86] J. Hao (浩钧), Huidi Li from China Mobile: Fetion's active users reached 82.7 millions (中移动李慧镝: 飞信活跃用户数已接近8270万), Available from: http://tech.qq.com/a/20110823/000206.htm, 2011 (Accessed September 2016).
[87] X. Guo (郭晓峰), Over 80% users stopped playing—China Mobile prepared to give up Fetion completely (超八成用户不玩了中国移动准备彻底抛弃飞信), Available from: http://gd.qq.com/a/20150428/020316.htm, 2015 (Accessed September 2016).
[88] Three major issues for Fetion's return to China Mobile company (飞信归来中移动企业IM的三大难题), Available from: http://www.bbtnews.com.cn/2016/1121/169971.shtml, 2016 (Accessed September 2016).
[89] S. Guha, N. Daswani, An experimental study of the Skype peer-to-peer VoIP system, in: Proceeding of the 5th International Workshop on Peer-to-Peer Systems, 2006.
[90] M. Ricknäs, Microsoft goes on the defensive with Skype, Available from: http://www.pcworld.com/article/227497/article.html, 2011 (Accessed October 2016).

[91] BerryReview Team, RIM pulled kik messenger over "number of issues and customer concerns", Available from: http://www.berryreview.com/2010/11/16/rim-pulled-kik-messenger-over-number-of-issues-and-customer-concerns/, 2010 (Accessed December 2016).

[92] X. Wang (汪轩然), Why did Jun Lei fail with Miliao: Miliao users are only one tenth of WeChat users (雷军为何兵败米聊: 米聊用户仅为微信的十分之一), Available from: http://finance.sina.com.cn/leadership/mroll/20120815/211012859903.shtml, 2012 (Accessed October 2016).

[93] Ruskin, Miliao: simultaneous online users reached 1 million (米聊: 同时在线用户突破100万), Available from: http://news.mydrivers.com/1/237/237220.htm, 2012 (Accessed October 2016).

[94] Leading social networks worldwide as of September 2016, ranked by number of active users (in millions), Available from: https://www.statista.com/statistics/272014/global-social-networks-ranked-by-number-of-users/, 2016 (Accessed November 2016).

[95] WhatsApp messenger free for limited time, Available from: http://www.touchmyapps.com/2011/06/01/whatsapp-messenger-free-for-limited-time/, 2011 (Accessed November 2016).

[96] Horizontal comparison and testing between WeChat 4.0, Miliao, and Momo (微信4.0、米聊、陌陌横向对比评测), Available from: http://www.3lian.com/edu/2012/04-21/25937.html, 2012 (Accessed August 2016).

[97] M. Moon, WhatsApp voice messaging updated with one-press record-and-send feature, Available from: https://www.engadget.com/2013/08/07/whatsapp-one-press-voice-message/, 2013 (Accessed August 2016).

[98] Chinese 4G licenses issued (中国4G牌照正式发布), Available from: http://mobile.163.com/special/4g_china/ (Accessed November 2016).

[99] Y. Hu (胡杨), Overview of the O2O layout from internet three giants BAT (互联网三巨头BAT的O2O布局大观), Market Modernisation (商场现代化) 3 (2014) 57.

[100] Alibaba group: becoming the world's largest retail entity (阿里巴巴集团: 已正式成为全球最大零售体), Available from: http://kuaixun.stcn.com/2016/0406/12656105.shtml, 2016 (Accessed November 2016).

[101] GWI Insight, Social media engagement summary, Available from: http://insight.globalwebindex.net/hs-fs/hub/304927/file-2615393475, 2015 (Accessed December 2016).

[102] CNNIC, Chinese social app user behaviour research report 2015 (2015年中国社交应用用户行为研究报告), Available from: http://www.cnnic.net.cn/hlwfzyj/hlwxzbg/sqbg/201604/P020160408334860042447.pdf, 2016 (Cited June 2016).

[103] F. Gong (龚飞纯), 2016 WeChat usage investigation report (2016微信使用情况调查报告), Available from: http://bbs.yjbys.com/660578.html, 2016 (Accessed October 2016).

[104] CNNIC, Statistical report of Chinese Internet work development status (中国互联网络发展状况统计报告), Available from: http://www.cnnic.net.cn/hlwfzyj/hlwxzbghlwtjbg/201608/P020160803367337470363.pdf, 2016 (Cited August 2016).

[105] Tecent-Technology, WeChat impact report ("微信"影响力报告), Available from: http://tech.qq.com/a/20160321/007049.htm, 2016 (Cited June 2016).

[106] Y. Zhou (周勇), Sotoo statistical report: Chinese Weibo user reached 75 millions (易观智库数据显示报告: 我国微博用户达7500万), Available from: http://www.sootoo.com/content/75009.shtml, 2010 (Accessed August 2016).

[107] B. Zhang (张宝), Discussion of Tencent WeChat's impact on text messages (浅谈腾讯微信对短信的冲击), Youth Literator (青年文学家) 8 (2014) 145.

[108] H. Zhu (朱红梅), WeChat: the terminator of text messaging (微信:短信的终结者?), Mob. Commun. (移动通信) 37 (5) (2013) 44.

[109] MIIT, Provincial distribution of telecommunication levels in the first quarter of 2016, Available from: http://www.miit.gov.cn/n1146312/n1146904/n1648372/c4802518/content.html, 2016 (Cited 10 Jul 2016).

[110] J. Liu (刘京改), Investigation of mobile text message length (关于手机短信长度的探讨), China New Commun. (中国新通信) 14 (2012) 28–29.

[111] China Mobile, Available from: http://www.10086.cn/ (Accessed January 2017).

[112] Olivier, Top 10 mobile apps in China, Available from: http://marketingtochina.com/lets-see-top-10-mobile-app-china/, 2016 (Accessed December 2016).

[113] Why Chinese prefer WeChat over Whatsapp—Chinese appreciate some WeChat's advantages and innovations, Available from: http://tech.blorge.com/2015/04/19/chinese-prefer-wechat-whatsapp-chinese-wechats-advantages-innovations/138316, 2015 (Accessed November 2016).

[114] J. Meyer, Minimalism: Art and Polemics in the Sixties, Yale University Press, 2004.

[115] W. Isaacson, How Steve Jobs' love of simplicity fueled a design revolution, Available from: http://www.smithsonianmag.com/arts-culture/how-steve-jobs-love-of-simplicity-fueled-a-design-revolution-23868877/, 2012 (Accessed November 2016).

[116] Mel, Steve Jobs and minimalism, Available from: http://www.applegazette.com/ipod/steve-jobs-and-minimalism/, 2011 (Accessed July 2016).

[117] H. Mei (梅花园), WeChat, Xiaolong Zhang, and their minimalism (微信、张小龙与他们的极简主义), Available from: https://www.huxiu.com/article/33313/1.html, 2014 (Accessed August 2016).

[118] Inuey, WeChat and QR code triggering new wave of WeChat promotion (微信、二维码,或引发新一轮"微"营销风), China KB (中国厨卫) 6 (2013) 36–37.

[119] S. Zhang (张守信), Upgrade and recreation: WeChat shake opening new pathway for TV interaction (升级与再造: 微信摇一摇开启电视互动新路径), Voice Screen World (声屏世界) 7 (2015) 62–64.

[120] I. Androutsopoulos, J. Koutsias, K.V. Chandrinos, G. Paliouras, C.D. Spyropoulos, An evaluation of naive Bayesian anti-spam filtering, in: Proceedings of the Workshop on Machine Learning in the New Information Age, 2000, pp. 9–17.

[121] V. Luckerson, 9 Super simple ways to make Facebook less annoying, Available from: http://time.com/3576169/facebook-tips-how-to-unfollow/, 2014 (Accessed November 2016).

[122] Facebook ads, Available from: https://www.facebook.com/notes/facebook/facebook-ads/6972252130/, 2007 (Accessed November 2016).

[123] How to buy instant messages ads, Available from: http://www.mediapost.com/publications/article/9267/how-to-buy-instant-message-ads.html, 2001 (Accessed January 2017).

[124] Ads placed for hundreds of yuan in moments—is the initial intention of WeChat social network gone? (朋友圈广告数百元可投微信社交初衷已死?), Available from: http://cq.cqnews.net/html/2016-09/27/content_38730824.htm, 2016 (Accessed October 2016).

[125] E. Hamburger, Mark Zuckerberg finally explains why he forced you to download the Standalone messenger app, Available from: http://www.theverge.com/2014/11/6/7170791/mark-zuckerberg-finally-explains-why-he-forced-you-to-download-the, 2014 (Accessed November 2016).

[126] J. Martin, 5 Reasons Facebook messenger is terrible, and 5 reasons it's great, Available from: http://www.pcadvisor.co.uk/opinion/social-networks/5-reasons-facebook-messenger-is-terrible-5-reasons-its-great-3600646/, 2015 (Accessed October 2016).

[127] J. Constine, Facebook adds voice messaging to messenger for iOS and Android, tests open source VoIP in Canada, Available from: https://techcrunch.com/2013/01/03/facebook-voice-messaging/, 2013 (Accessed November 2016).
[128] WhatsApp Blog, Introducing voice messages, Available from: https://blog.whatsapp.com/378/Introducing-Voice-Messages, 2013 (Accessed November 2016).
[129] Top 3 problems that the Facebook Messenger users have, Available from: https://www.iskysoft.com/data-recovery-tips/facebook-messenger-troubleshooting.html (Accessed October 2016).
[130] G. Hammond, 6 Common WhatsApp voice message problems on iPhone and solutions, Available from: https://www.imyfone.com/ios-data-recovery/whatsapp-voice-message-problems-on-iphone/, 2016 (Accessed October 2016).
[131] E. Crouch, Facebook's WeChat-ification, Available from: https://www.techinasia.com/facebook-messenger-wechat-fintech-features, 2016 (Accessed October 2016).
[132] Facebook is suspiciously copying WeChat, Available from: http://www.xiaomiinsider.com/facebook-is-suspiciously-copying-wechat/, 2016 (Accessed October 2016).
[133] C. Deamicis, K. Wagner, Facebook's David Marcus: the Asian paradigm has shown messaging is the next frontier, Available from: http://www.recode.net/2015/10/8/11619402/facebooks-david-marcus-the-asian-paradigm-has-shown-messaging-is-the, 2015 (Accessed October 2016).
[134] Why was voice mail service not favoured in China (语音信箱为何在中国受冷遇), China Bus. Update (中国经贸) 2 (2006) 51.
[135] K. Tang (唐魁玉), D. Liu (刘冬), Research of the behaviour comparison between young and old WeChat users (年轻人与老年人微信使用行为的对比研究), J. Party Sch. CPC Hangzhou (中共杭州市委党校学报) 6 (2015) 74.
[136] R. Kelly, L. Watts, Characterising the inventive appropriation of emoji as relationally meaningful in mediated close personal relationships, in: Experiences of Technology Appropriation: Unanticipated Users, Usage, Circumstances, and Design, 2015.
[137] WeChat launched emoji development platform (微信推表情开发平台), Available from: http://www.chinaz.com/news/2015/0803/429805.shtml, 2015 (Accessed October 2016).
[138] Y. Wu (吴勇毅), The wide and longlasting innovation in mobile office brought by WeChat enterprise accounts (微信企业号将给移动办公带来广泛而持久的变革), IT Time Weekly (IT时代周刊), vol. 12, 2015.
[139] Tencent announced 2016 Q3 performance report (腾讯公布2016 年第三季度业绩), Available from: https://www.tencent.com/zh-cn/articles/8003251479983154.pdf, 2016 (Accessed February 2017).
[140] X. Chen (陈昕), QQ's Social Link Propagation and Impact Study (QQ的人际传播及其影响研究), Liaoning University (辽宁大学), 2011.
[141] The 12th China's 500 Most Valuable Brands (2015第十二届世界品牌大会), Available from: http://www.worldbrandlab.com/brandmeeting/2015china500/, 2015 (Accessed July 2016).
[142] L. Shi (施恋林), The beginning and end of 3Q battle (3Q之争始末), China Telecommun. Trade (中国电信业) 12 (2010) 33–33.
[143] C. Li (李春生), Tencent's buffet (腾讯的自助餐), Voice Screen World: Advertiser (声屏世界:广告人) 7 (2012) 141–142.
[144] Huateng Ma: WeChat is free, only to get a ticket for mobile internet (马化腾:微信不收费只拿到移动互联网"站票"), Available from: http://www.ccidnet.com/2013/0508/4919327.shtml, 2013 (Accessed October 2016).

[145] Y. Wozi (我自悠悠), Three issues with QQ (QQ使用三点注意), Electron. Comput. (电子与电脑) 8 (7) (2001) 62.

[146] F. Yuan (袁飞), Booster for the growing journey (成长路上"助推器"), Head Teacher (班主任), vol. 11, 2015.

[147] H. Yao (耀华), From lucky numbers (从吉祥数字谈起), Shanxi Elerly (山西老年) 2 (2000) 26.

[148] X. Liang (梁小庆), Digits in life (生活中的数字), Creative Articles Inside and Outside Classrooms: Middle School Edition (课堂内外创新作文:初中版) 3 (2012) 40.

[149] X. Chen (陈雪莲), What happens to QQ number after you die? (死了之后,QQ号怎么办?), Vision (视野) 12 (2009) 67.

[150] Y. Li (李怡), M. Tong (仝明丽), Study on the legal inheritance issue of QQ numbers (QQ号的继承法律问题研究), Legal System Expo (法制博览), vol. 22, 2015.

[151] Z. Yu (于志刚), Discussion on legal nature and protection of QQ numbers (论QQ号的法律性质及其刑法保护), Legist (法学家) 3 (2007) 49–58.

[152] N. Wang (王纳), B. Liu (刘斌), L. Tong (童蕾), Shenzhen theft case of highly valued QQ number 98888 with principal offender jailed for one year (深圳"天价QQ号98888被盗案"主犯被判入狱1年), Legal System and Economy Quarterly (法制与经济旬刊) 9 (2010) 1.

[153] Y. Luo (罗勇), Tricks for batch managing QQ contacts (批量管理QQ好友出妙招), Comput. Knowl. Technol. Exp. Tech. (电脑知识与技术:经验技巧) 3 (2010) 21–22.

[154] Y. Ye (叶勇), Batch management of QQ contact management (管理QQ好友也用批处理), Computer Fan (电脑爱好者) 18 (2011) 32.

[155] Large image template for QQ space (QQ空间超长大图模块), Available from: http://www.poluoluo.com/qq/200807/25290.html, 2008.

[156] Pink template for QQ space (QQ空间粉色大图模块), Available from: http://www.111cn.net/fw/127/ee5f07c550ee3a269dc7a17dd9524dd1.htm, 2008.

[157] S. Zhang (张思), QQ membership, how is a 15-year-old business still keep growing quickly (QQ会员，一个成立了15年的业务为何依然保持快速增长), Available from: http://www.tmtpost.com/1500040.html, 2016 (Accessed December 2016).

[158] M. Mu (木木), Differences between QQ official accounts and WeChat official accounts (QQ公众号到底和微信公众号有什么区别), Available from: http://mt.sohu.com/20150917/n421350675.shtml, 2015 (Accessed December 2016).

[159] Usage regulation and management process for using QQ at work (工作QQ使用规定与管理流程), Available from: http://www.docin.com/p-543874824.html, 2012 (Accessed November 2016).

[160] J. Zhou (周人), D. Huo (贺大为), Q. Ye (叶前), Simplifying complex matters (把复杂的事情做简单), Enterp. Cult. Q (企业文化旬刊) 3 (2014) 34–36.

[161] Z. Yang (杨正瑭), Comparative analysis of QQ and WeChat regarding functionalities and user experience (QQ与微信的功能及用户体验比较分析), China New Telecom (中国新通信) 18 (4) (2016) 10–11.

[162] N. Xu (许诺), Evolution history of virtual currency (虚拟货币进化史), Qi Lu Weekly (齐鲁周刊), vol. 46, 2015.

[163] X. Wang (王馨语), Viewing the different routes taken by Twitter and Weibo from their contents (大路朝天,各走一边-从内容看Twitter和新浪微博的不同路线), Brainpower (新知客) 10 (2010) 24–27.

[164] Industrial statistics: 2011 Q4 Chinese Weibo market active users reached 249 millions (行业数据: 2011年第4季度中国微博市场活跃用户规模达2.49亿), Available from: http://www.kland.com.cn/2012/0309/661.html, 2012 (Accessed September 2016).

[165] New breakthrough of Weibo 2015 users, activity, and revenue generation (微博2015年用户、活跃度、收入增速创新高), Available from: http://tech.sina.com.cn/i/2016-03-03/doc-ifxqafha0314064.shtml, 2016 (Accessed October 2016).

[166] Perfect! Weibo officially announced the cancellation of 140 character limit (完美！微博正式向普通用户取消140字限制), Available from: http://www.techweb.com.cn/internet/2016-03-03/2288829.shtml, 2016 (Accessed September 2016).

[167] Weibo shining up Sina (微博照耀新浪), Available from: http://tech.sina.com.cn/i/2010-12-09/17414964554.shtml, 2010 (Accessed November 2016).

[168] WeChat games contribute 60 million to WeChat's MAU figure, Available from: http://huxiu.me/post/80239320865/wechat-games-contribute-60-million-to-wechats-mau, 2014 (Accessed August 2016).

[169] S. Millward, WeChat still unstoppable, grows to 697m active users, Available from: https://www.techinasia.com/wechat-697-million-monthly-active-users, 2016 (Accessed October 2016).

[170] 孙辉筱, Discussion of privacy violation on Weibo (浅析微博对隐私权的侵犯), Legal System and Society (法制与社会) 9 (2011) 58–59.

[171] Twitter developer documentation, Available from: https://dev.twitter.com/basics/counting-characters (Accessed November 2016).

[172] V.V. Bochkarev, A.V. Shevlyakova, V.D. Solovyev, Average word length dynamics as indicator of cultural changes in society, CoRR abs/1208.6109, 2012.

[173] H.F. Zhu, D.Y. Hu, Z.G. Wang, T.C. Kao, W.C.H. Chang, Chinese character encoding for internet messages 1996, request for Comments: 1922.

[174] J. Zhou (周荐), Double character combinations and dictionary entries (双字组合与词典收条), in: Chinese Dictionary and Linguistics Collection (中国辞书学文集), 1998, pp. 304–309.

[175] C. Newton, Twitter #Music is officially dead, Available from: http://www.theverge.com/2014/3/21/5534814/twitter-music-is-officially-dead, 2014 (Accessed February 2017).

[176] B. He (何冰洁), Comparison study of Twitter and Sina Weibo (Twitter与新浪微博的比较研究), Youth Journalist (青年记者) 24 (2014) 94–95.

[177] D. Gauntlett, Web Studies: Rewiring Media Studies for the Digital Age, Arnold, 2000.

[178] Dedicated zone for disclosing counterfeit information on Sina Weibo (新浪微博不实信息曝光专区), Available from: http://hi.news.sina.com.cn/news/Weibopiyao/index_iframe.php?dpc=1 (Accessed January 2017).

[179] D. Li (李丹丹), Governmental Weibo accounts reaching 280k and governmental WeChat accounts reaching 100k (我国政务微博账号近28万政务微信号已逾10万), Available from: http://tech.ifeng.com/a/20151030/41498808_0.shtml, 2015 (Accessed December 2016).

[180] S. Liu (刘苏芬), The phenomena of "Celebrity Blog" in the perspective of communication studies (传播学视野下的"名人博客"现象), Youth Journalists (青年记者) 10 (2007) 95–97.

[181] E.J. Yuan, M. Feng, J.A. Danowski, "Privacy" in semantic networks on Chinese social media: the case of Sina Weibo, J. Commun. 63 (6) (2013) 1011–1031.

[182] J. Dong (董杰), Impact analysis of the three rationals of Beijing Olympic Game on national fitness (北京奥运会三大理念作用于全民健身运动意义探析), Sports Sci. (体育与科学) 28 (5) (2007) 40–43.

[183] S. Zhang (章书勤), Discussion on freedom of speech on Weibo (浅论微博言论自由), News Study (新闻研究导刊) 7 (10) (2016) 311–312.

[184] J. Wang (王娟娟), Freedom and regulation of speech on Weibo (微博言论的自由与规制), Law Mag. (法学杂志) 33 (12) (2012) 73–77.

[185] Y. Zheng (郑燕), Freedom and boundaries of internet users—a reflection on freedom of speech in public area of Weibo (网民的自由与边界-关于微博公共领域中言论自由的反思), 社会科学研究) 1 (2012) 187–191.

[186] G. Lu (陆谷孙), The English-Chinese Dictionary (英汉大词典), 2nd Edition, (2007) 816.

[187] Z. Zhang (张治中), Speech right guarantee for grass root users in Weibo era (微博时代的草根话语权保障), News Knowl. (新闻知识) 6 (2011) 6–8.

[188] Linfeng Yang Pichayut (Petch) Jirapinyo, Six degrees of separation, Available from: http://isites.harvard.edu/fs/docs/icb.topic707165.files/pdfs/Jirapinyo_Yang.pdf (Accessed January 2017).

[189] Weibo anti-corruption (微博反腐), Available from: http://baike.baidu.com/item/微博反腐 (Accessed December 2016).

[190] Y. Li (李妍), Overview of Weibo anti-corruption events: many officials dare not to wear watches (盘点微博反腐"门事件": 很多官员不敢再戴表), Available from: http://news.qq.com/a/20121211/000818_all.htm, 2012 (Accessed January 2017).

[191] Y. Liu (刘洋), Lady assaulted in Heshuo Hotel, the rectification Rujia promised not entirely implemented (女子在和颐酒店遇袭如家承诺的整改未完全落实), Available from: http://Weibo.com/ttarticle/p/show?id=2309351000654038389245556160, 2016 (Accessed December 2016).

[192] Why did some internet users claim Weibo more effective than calling police? "Hotel assault" (为什么网友感慨"发微博比报警还管用"? #酒店遇袭#), Available from: http://finance.sina.com.cn/roll/2016-04-07/doc-ifxrcizu3734848.shtml, 2016 (Accessed December 2016).

[193] C. Bei (贝晓超), New mode of disaster relief on social media line—Sina Weibo becoming the most convenient channel for seeking missing persons and donations (社交媒体线上救灾新模式-新浪微博成为寻人、捐助最便利通道), News Frontline (新闻战线) 5 (2013) 24–26.

[194] iiMedia, 2013 Q3 China Mobile game research report, Available from: http://www.iimedia.cn/37026.html, 2013 (Accessed September 2015).

[195] iiMedia, China Mobile game market semi-annual research report of 2014, Available from: http://www.iimedia.cn/1410321392965n95n6.pdf, 2014 (Accessed September 2015).

[196] iiMedia, 2015 H1 China Mobile game market research report, Available from: http://www.iimedia.cn/39566.html, 2015 (Accessed September 2015).

[197] CNNIC, China Mobile game users research report, Available from: https://www.cnnic.net.cn, 2013 (Cited 1 Jul 2015).

[198] X. Che, B. Ip, Packet-level traffic analysis of online games from the genre characteristics perspective, J. Netw. Comput. Appl. 35 (1) (2012) 240–252.

[199] Global-Mobile-Game-Confederation, 2015 Global mobile games whitebook, Available from: http://2015.gmgc.info, 2015 (Accessed September 2015).

[200] Tencent-Games, WeChat reaches 40 million registered users 10 days after release, with 25 million active users per day, Available from: http://games.qq.com/a/20130815/006511.htm, 2013 (Accessed July 2015).

[201] L. Von Ahn, L. Dabbish, Designing games with a purpose, ACM Commun. Mag. 51 (8) (2008) 58–67.

[202] S. Yuan, Conspicuous Consumption of Chinese: Antecedents and Consequences, Economic Press, China, 2013.

[203] Tencent, Annual performance report, Available from: http://www.tencent.com, 2014 (Accessed July 2015).

[204] How Madbid.com leveraged a great business model, Available from: http://mission0ps.com/why-madbid-rocks/, 2013 (Accessed December 2016).

[205] H. Wang, It's time for Facebook to copy WeChat, Available from: https://www.forbes.com/sites/helenwang/2016/08/11/its-time-for-facebook-to-copy-wechat, 2016 (Accessed October 2016).

[206] L. Feng (冯琳), Investigation of reasons for WeChat packet's popularity (微信红包走红情况探究), Journalism & Communication (新媒新论) 18 (2015) 74.

[207] Over 5 million users participated in Red Packets during Chinese New Year Eve and New Year Day (除夕、初一两天参与"抢红包"的用户超过500万), Available from: http://news.163.com/14/0207/07/9KFDPI6G00014JB6.html, 2014 (Accessed October 2016).

[208] J. Lan (蓝鲸), 2016 WeChat statistical report: elderly surprisingly like sending Red Packets with average 25 times monthly (2016微信数据报告: 老年人竟爱发红包每月平均发25次), Available from: http://www.cfi.net.cn/p20161229000234.html, 2016 (Accessed February).

[209] Investigation report of Red Packet socialising on WeChat and QQ (微信、QQ2016春节红包社交广告洞察报告), Available from: http://www.planpr.cn/html/baogaoshu/2016/0226/733.html, 2016 (Accessed November 2016).

[210] The most complete statistics: viewing Chinese rooster spring festival in the perspective of WeChat Red Packet (最全数据: 从微信红包看中国人的鸡年春节), Available from: http://mt.sohu.com/20170131/n479729327.shtml, 2017 (Accessed October 2016).

[211] H. Huang (黄河), Spring of WeChat taxi (微信打车的春天), Chin. Econ. Inform. (中国经济和信息化) 6 (2013) 86–86.

[212] C. Ji (际川), What do Internet police do? (网警要做什么?), Exploration of Countryside Youth Science (农村青少年科学探究), 2016.

[213] Central Government Website (中央政府门户网站), The notice from Ministry of Culture regarding improving and strengthening the content management of online games (文化部关于改进和加强网络游戏内容管理工作的通知), Available from: http://www.gov.cn/gzdt/2009-11/21/content_1470116.htm, 2009 (Accessed January 2017).

[214] Criminal Law of People's Republic of China, Revised Edition (9) (中华人民共和国刑法修正案(九)), Available from: http://www.gov.cn/gzdt/2009-11/21/content_1470116.htm, 2015 (Accessed January 2017).

[215] Measurements for filing management of non-profit Internet information services (非经营性互联网信息服务备案管理办法), Available from: http://www.miit.gov.cn/n11293472/n11293877/n11301753/n11496139/11537734.html, 2007 (Accessed January 2017).

[216] The resolution for network information protection from the national people's congress standing committee of the People's Republic of China (全国人民代表大会常务委员会关于加强网络信息保护的决定), Available from: http://www.npc.gov.cn/npc/xinwen/2012-12/29/content_1749526.htm, 2012 (Accessed January 2017).

[217] Seven bottom lines for Internet (网络七条底线), Available from: http://www.hnr.cn/news/xwzt/web/ (Accessed January 2017).

[218] Governing country by law—remarks on the legal system of socialism country (依法治国铸伟业-记建设社会主义法治国家), Available from: http://dangshi.people.com.cn/GB/220777/14953538.html, 2011 (Accessed February 2017).

[219] National Rumour-Refuting Platform only functions with the bravery to disclose truth (敢亮真相, "全国辟谣平台"才有作用), Available from: http://cpc.people.com.cn/pinglun/n1/2016/0512/c78779-28346090.html, 2016 (Accessed November 2016).

[220] L. Edwards, D. McAuley, What's in a name? Real name policies and social networks, in: Proceedings of 1st International Workshop on Internet Science and Web Science Synergies, vol. 1, 2013.

[221] X. Liu (刘星), Discussion on the measurement of network real name policy in our country (论网络实名制在我国的实施), Legal System and Society: Quarterly (法制与社会:旬刊) 3 (2012) 161–162.

[222] J. Liu (刘建明), Network real name policy: being reliable for individual's words and deeds (网络实名制:为个人言行负责), News Frontline (新闻战线) 2 (2012) 81–82.

[223] J. Schwartz, The most popular messaging app in every country, Available from: https://www.similarweb.com/blog/worldwide-messaging-apps, 2016 (Accessed November 2016).

[224] C. Custer, WeChat's globalisation is a disaster, why is the internationalisation of WeChat (and other Chinese apps) not easy? (微信的全球化扩张简直是一场灾难，为什么微信(和大多数中国App)国际化之路不顺畅), Available from: http://www.cyzone.cn/a/20160601/297376.html, 2016 (Accessed January 2017).

[225] Some useful facts about Mark Zuckerberg, FB and China (关于扎克伯格、FB和中国，一些有用的事实), Available from: http://tech.163.com/14/1027/11/A9ID7AEB000915BF.html, 2014 (Accessed January 2017).

[226] Which social networks do not serve as media? (社交软件那么多，不做媒体的有几个？), Available from: http://www.donews.com/idonews/article/6657.shtm, 2015 (Accessed February 2017).

[227] The social medialisation of live broadcast, Internet celebrities, and social networks (直播、网红和社交网络的Social Media化), Available from: http://tech.sina.com.cn/i/2016-05-18/doc-ifxsenvm0562423.shtml, 2016 (Accessed February 2017).

Index

Note: Page numbers followed by *f* indicate figures, *t* indicate tables and *b* indicate boxes.

Made in the USA
Monee, IL
13 September 2026

62977016R00090